WHEN THE HANGMAN
CAME TO GALWAY

Dean Ruxton is a writer and journalist from Dublin. He worked with *Hot Press* magazine before joining *The Irish Times* as a digital journalist in 2014. Since then, his byline has appeared in nearly every section of the site, but his name is mostly associated with the Lost Leads archive series – a retelling of some of the lesser-known stories that have appeared in the paper since 1859.

WHEN THE HANGMAN CAME TO GALWAY

A gruesome true story of murder
in Victorian Ireland

Dean Ruxton

Gill Books

Gill Books

Hume Avenue

Park West

Dublin 12

www.gillbooks.ie

Gill Books is an imprint of M.H. Gill and Co.

© Dean Ruxton 2018

978 07171 8085 1

Print origination by O'K Graphic Design, Dublin

Edited by Neil Burkey

Proofread by Esther Ní Dhonnacha

Printed by T.J International, Cornwall

This book is typeset in 11/15 pt Adobe Garamond Pro with headings in Modesto Condensed.

The paper used in this book comes from the wood pulp of managed forests. For every tree felled, at least one tree is planted, thereby renewing natural resources.

5 4 3 2 1

For permission to reproduce photographs, the author and publisher gratefully acknowledge the following:

© The British Library Board. All rights reserved. With thanks to The British Newspaper Archive (www.britishnewspaperarchive.co.uk): 127; Courtesy of Ian Waugh (www.ianwaugh.com): 187; Images from *My Experiences as an Executioner* by James Berry, London, P. Lund, 1892: 2, 8, 18, 30, 39; Courtesy of Tom Kenny, Kennys Bookshop, (www.kennys.ie): 91, 103: © Topical Press Agency / Stringer / Getty Images: 220; © Wikimedia Commons: 37.

ACKNOWLEDGEMENTS

I would like to sincerely thank the many people who helped this book get to print, in ways perhaps they haven't realised: my family, particularly Pat and Nicky; my friends and loved ones, ever-fortifying; the excellent and patient staff at the National Archives in Dublin, the Galway County Council archives and the James Hardiman Library at the National University of Ireland, Galway; my colleagues at *The Irish Times*, particularly David Labanyi and Paddy Logue, who took a chance on an idea for a new archive series in 2016; the staff at Gill Books, particularly Sarah Liddy, who first reached out about telling these stories.

Above all, I would like to acknowledge the work of the writers gone before me who ensured the past was not forgotten. Grisly detail rarely escaped crime reports in the late 19th century; the bloody frankness of description may now have the ability to shock, but it's in that vivid detail, defended by generations of meticulous journalists, where the true value of long-forgotten stories lies.

I tried my very best to preserve that value.

For Kieron, Paula and Adam

CONTENTS

'One of the questions which is most frequently put to me is, whether I consider capital punishment is a right and proper thing. To this I can truly answer that I do. For my own part I attach much weight to the Scripture injunction, "Whoso sheddeth man's blood, by man shall his blood be shed…" and I think that the abolition of capital punishment would be a defiance of the divine command.'

JAMES BERRY

STRANGERS ON A JOURNEY

J ames Berry sat alone, collar raised and head lowered, chin on his chest. His stocky frame made it hard to become small, but he always tried his best. Travelling was a necessity of the job, not a pleasure. Particularly bad were journeys on the Irish Sea.

The job had its pitfalls, you could say, one being an air of grim celebrity that he didn't much care for. It all attracted a special breed of shameless onlooker, the pointer and starer, the penny-dreadful addict with a bloodlust, falling over himself to spot the gnarled castaway with an axe on his shoulder. Thankfully, his journey that day had been a peaceful one. No attention had come his way – all eyes aboard his ferry were turned elsewhere. As the vessel chugged slowly over the waves – he could be thankful, at least, that he was homebound this time – the hum of the engine was pierced only by the bothersome wails of a man sitting a short distance away. His complaints had begun in Dublin and slowly; now, he was openly remonstrating with the helpless stewards.

Passengers, annoyed in the face of a nice journey spoiled, looked on as the man alternated between filling a bucket with vomit and pawing the side of his face. Berry himself was irritated at this point, however grateful that, for once, he was as good as invisible. The stewards could do little but try to quieten the gentleman, who was apparently suffering through a cocktail of seasickness and a nasty toothache.

As the man flailed and agitations steadily rose, from the corner of his eye Berry noticed an exasperated steward bark a few sentences at the patient and point over the heads of the other travellers, in his own direction. The sick man turned, wide-eyed, followed the young man's finger and ran to Berry's side.

'They said you could help,' he said quickly through winces of pain. 'Can you do anything? What can I do?'

'Well,' Berry began. His cover, now, was as good as blown. But he wasn't beyond having fun when the opportunity presented itself.

'I'm in the habit of giving drops that could instantly cure you of both the toothache and sea sickness,' he told the man, who hung on his every word, 'but I don't think you'll be willing to take my remedy.'

The new client pleaded. Anything.

'Very well,' said Berry, reaching deep into his coat and plucking out his business card. The man took it eagerly from his pinched fingers.

It was an ornate little briefing – gold borders surrounded a delicate green fern – underneath, his details: 'James Berry, Executioner – 8 Bilton Place, Bradford, Yorkshire'.

'As he was a sensitive man,' Berry later wrote, 'it gave his nerves a shock that was quite sufficient to relieve him of the toothache, and me of his presence for the rest of the voyage.'

DECEMBER 1883

In Wexford, a sister scrambles desperately to restrain her brother. Their mother cowers in the corner of the small house. Newly engaged Thomas Parry is in a rage. He strains and pulls, promising to put a bullet in the old woman's head for her transgression; how dare she tell him how to conduct his business? Her crime was to berate him for carrying messages for his employer, Major Braddell. Surely, she says, that was a job for a lesser servant. The act of even considering it was demeaning. Thomas, through gritted teeth, is calmed by Catherine, his sister. He sits down for a moment as the place falls to silence, then gets up and calmly leaves the house. Outside, on the road, his father spots him, but keeps his distance – Thomas looks wild, stomping around like an animal. He hasn't been the same since the sunstroke.

In Galway, a farmer named John Moylan leaves his father-in-law's house with his wife, Mary. Visits to the old man's home have become a weekly tradition for the couple since John's return to Ireland from America a couple months previously. It's about 9 pm when the visit winds up; the night is cold and sharp, and a mist hangs low over the fields. Rain has turned the ground of the main road into slush, and the pair veer off into a narrow boreen, known to locals and sure to cut their minutes-long walk even shorter. John reaches a stile, steps up and offers a hand back to Mary. Just feet away, hidden in the shadows, a pair of eyes watches closely.

In Scotland, two poachers, Robert Vickers and William Innes, trespass on land near Gorebridge, Midlothian. The plan goes awry. They end up murdering two men: a gamekeeper named John Fortune and John McDiarmaid, a rabbit-trapper. Two hundred miles away, James Berry, a young Bradford shoemaker and fledgling hangman, doesn't know it yet, but they're going to be his first.

A SCOTTISH DEBUT

The first proved difficult. On the last night of his stay at Calton Gaol in Edinburgh, James Berry's appetite abandoned him.

His mind played only on Robert Flockhart Vickers and William Innes; the men were being held some feet away, awaiting death. The two were miners – family men, described as 'harmless' and 'inoffensive' – but in the early hours of Saturday, 15 December 1883, they set out on a frosty, clear night to poach on the lands of Lord Rosebery in Gorebridge. The pair almost got away with their bounty of pheasants, but for the intervention of experienced head gamekeeper James Grosset, his assistant John Fortune, and a rabbit trapper named John McDiarmaid. Poaching was rife in the dark winter months, and the men had been patrolling in anticipation. Having heard the clap of a gunshot about a mile from their position, the trio set out for the noise armed only with sticks. It was Grosset who first recognised one of the men – Innes – through the darkness. He told him as much, insisting there was no use in running. Thoroughly cornered, Vickers and Innes – armed with a great deal more than sticks – fired on the men, inflicting what would be fatal wounds on Fortune and McDiarmid. Grosset, too, was winged with a spray of shotgun pellets.

But the shot failed to stop him; he successfully fled through woods and terrain he knew like the back of his hand. The head gamekeeper raised the alarm, and Vickers and Innes were hunted down and arrested. When the trial opened, opinion was split on the supposed evil in the men's actions, with some commentators positing they meant only to injure or scare their apprehenders. Fortune only died a few days later on 18 December, while McDiarmid lingered for three painful weeks before succumbing on 8 January.

Could it therefore be said with any certainty that Vickers and Innes were shooting to kill? In the end, it didn't matter. Both were sentenced to hang, and the job of carrying out the honours became available. A young shoe salesman named James Berry stepped up.

It was Sunday when his stomach turned. Since his arrival to the Edinburgh prison on Thursday, Berry had spent his time reading, smoking and pacing the prison grounds. Berry was clear in one aspect – justice had to be served the following morning – but as he sat in his room listening to the rhythm of the mail trains departing south, his thoughts were crushed by how those men must have felt, knowing a blooming flower would never adorn their graves. The resulting unease made him physically ill, and despite the good food laid on for him by his hosts, it all felt like sand in his mouth. A deep regret set in.

The first day of his stay had been easier, or at least busier. It was a cold spring morning when Berry left his terraced Bradford home, bolstered by a word of encouragement from his wife – a parting gift he would need on more than one occasion. Dressed smartly and carrying a signature black gladstone bag, he marched promptly to Midland Station. Berry seemed, as he strode confidently to make his train, like a businessman – partly because until that point, he had made and sold shoes for a living. Aiming for a better life for his young family, Berry was trying a new career. He was about 5' 9" and of medium build; his open face and warm brown eyes did not give his fellow Englishmen a clue as to the appointment he had to make. Like most men of his time, he wore a moustache, accompanied by a light, sandy beard. The only thing betraying his harmless visage was a distinctive scar, running from the outer corner of his right eye, over his cheekbone, to his earlobe. A souvenir from a former life.

Berry had already had six days to prepare his equipment and steady his nerve before he bought a third-class ticket to Edinburgh on the morning of 27 March 1884. While he had agreed a second-class fare as part of his expenses, as well as 21 sovereigns and lodgings and board, his aim in his new venture had been to make money. Third-class would be quite sufficient.

Berry wasn't alone, though he may as well have been. His assistant, Richard Chester, was the quiet type. Berry had hired him as an extra pair of hands on the scaffold. Not unlike Berry, Chester was a man of average appearance, about the same age, height and breadth as his employer. He had light brown hair, a cropped moustache and high cheekbones. He wore a tweed overcoat and a distinctive jerry hat, with a portion of a peacock's feather sticking out the side. Edinburgh was to be their first collaboration of many; though he was being paid per job at this stage, he would prove to be reliable, and Berry would eventually pay him a weekly wage for his services. The name 'Chester' was made up, such was the value he placed on his privacy.

The train snailed to a halt in Waverley Station at about 4.20 pm. The pair alighted and hailed a cab to the prison gates, where a warder was waiting to greet them. A stray comment, or look, or even a fleeting air of disgust from prison workers was something Berry grew to detect as the years went on, and while most were perfectly courteous and often his only conduit for conversation, some treated him like a criminal. Berry signed his name in the log book and the warder pulled a rope to ring a bell, summoning J.E. Christie, the governor of the prison. Christie was a formidable character – military in his appearance, with a strong handshake. To Berry's surprise, Christie's opening gambit was all small talk. The interrogation and inspection, he was yet to realise, would come later. The magistrates had put in place a long delay between Berry's arrival and the execution hour, for just such a purpose.

The governor's chat idly turned to weather. They chewed the fat about the long journey from Bradford. The travellers must be hungry, the governor decided. They were sent to a room to gather themselves, and when they had freshened up, food was served; 'the tea was there, everything that could be desired', as Berry wrote. The spread was excellent, and thoroughly enjoyed by hungry stomachs not yet turned by coming events. Berry spent the evening reading and smoking, until the head warder showed him to his room at about 10 pm. Opening the door for the Bradford man, the warder remarked that the last man to stay there was William Marwood. Berry's heart lifted at the mention of an old friend's name. He flew into a flurry of questions, and the warder responded by uncomfortably freezing up. Small talk it was, then. Before he left, he turned to Berry with an intense look of grief. In a tone of confession, the warder said he really did hope the two men earmarked for death would be reprieved. This was understandable – Berry was human, too, and both men had large families; both men were married: Vickers had eight children and Innes nine. One of the women had been admitted to an asylum amid the episode.

Berry thanked the warder and locked the door after he left. He turned to his bed, knelt and prayed.

After breakfast the next morning he met with the magistrates, who were very keen to make his acquaintance at the platform. A handful of noisy construction men were still hammering about near the structure, building a shed to shield the execution from the public. This was necessary, as the townspeople who were bothered to climb would be afforded a fine view from Calton Hill, opposite the prison site. In the familiar swagger of the salesman, he proudly produced his black bag and took from it the coiled, Italian silk ropes he had specially designed for the task. Berry insisted on using ropes with a diameter of ⅝ of an inch, though the diameter did often contract to a half-inch once a man was hanged. Rather than use a slipknot, a brass eye was woven into the tip of the ropes. This was partly for precision; the slipknot, Berry believed, was less specific and more likely to result in strangulation. Precision was essential. 'When an unfortunate human being is to be put out of existence it is only right to do it in the most scientific manner and with the least possible pain,' he later said.

Using cement bags to represent the men, he satisfied the magistrates of the integrity of the ropes and confirmed the length of the drop each man needed. He announced the lengths to the magistrates, who seemed happy with their brief run-through. Daubing the trapdoors with chalk, he scribbled the men's names where they would stand. It was only after this meeting, seeing the dangling masses which stood for the lives he had to take, that his fondness of the good food wavered. 'I regretted for a while,' he wrote, 'and then I thought the public would only think I had not the pluck, and I would not allow my feelings to overthrow me, so I never gave way to such thoughts again.'

A meal of pudding, beef, vegetables and broth was washed down with ginger ale by 1 pm. A stiffer drink was offered, but as a proud teetotaler, he declined. On a full stomach, Berry's humour returned to him, and he struck up light conversation with the warders coming off their duty. The weather again passed for adequate conversation; he learned from his first encounter with the warder not to stray into talking shop. As he separated from the men and they passed by, he heard one remark to another, at a volume not meant to reach Berry's ears: 'He looks a nice fellow for a job like that,' to which a colleague replied: 'But he has a wicked eye, I'm sure he could do it.'

At a loose end, Berry was left smoking in the lodge with the gatekeeper, and a single remaining warder. The latter said very little, but listened very closely to any conversation, eyes darting to the Bradford man and back again to the false object of his attention. 'I looked him over, and could see by the look of his face that I was not to say much in his presence,' Berry later wrote of the curious warder. Eventually, owing to Berry enforcing boring conversation, the eavesdropper left. The gatekeeper followed the warder with his gaze, then turned to Berry: 'I am glad you never began to say anything in the presence of that man, as he would stop until morning.' Feeling, at last, that he was in appropriate company, Berry relaxed a little. The men sat smoking in silence.

Calton Goal

Saturday rolled in. The rhythmic clap of Berry's shoes hitting the stone floors as he paced began to play on his mind. Far more irritating was having to endure the second round of testing at the hands of the magistrates. Besides a brief and welcome city jaunt in an open carriage on Saturday, Berry's sanity was saved by the conversations with the gatekeeper. It was during one of those easy, smoke-filled evening chats that the final word came through: there was to be no reprieve for Vickers and Innes. Berry played off the news like it was part of the plan (which, of course, it was), and forced the cold reality out of his head. He spent a pleasant evening chatting to his new friend and one of the less sneaky warders. Before fully simmering down, however, he sent for the next available paper – the thick, black capitals bluntly spelled the men's fate, and his own: 'GOREBRIDGE MURDERS: NO REPRIEVE'. A restless night lay ahead for Berry, who spent his sleeping hours thinking of how Vickers and Innes, two young, familied men in 'full bloom', were wasting their last, precious minutes in slumber just yards away.

As he attempted to dine on Sunday, he found out the two condemned men were spending the day in the chapel. The plate of food, as plentiful as the others, was only ever looked at.

On Sunday night, he retired to his bedroom at about 10 pm, but sleep didn't come to him. He tossed and turned. His mind played tricks. Idly, it visited the far corners of his imagination, conjuring the worst possible scenarios he could encounter the following morning. Most, he knew, were impossible; others, he would have to deal with in a very real sense by the time his career came to an end. By 5 am on Monday, Vickers and Innes were on their knees in the prison chapel, in fervent prayer. Berry rose at the same hour, 'more dead than alive'. The day's task was too much to bear. His role was too great. What if the rope broke? What if his hands trembled on the scaffold? What if he was sick at the very point of pulling the lever? The rattle and clang of the prison doors at 6 am startled him from his frenzy – breakfast was being served earlier than usual. By 7 am, the crowds predicted by the prison authorities began to assemble on the hill overlooking the prison yard. One estimate for the gathering was about six or seven thousand – believable, considering there hadn't been an execution there for six years.

Berry made his way to the scaffold, making sure everything was in order and clearing the execution shed. The head warder locked the door. Shortly after, the deputy city clerk arrived to the gates of Calton, followed by the magistrates Roberts and Clark. A group formed, consisting of those men, the governor, five press representatives and the prison chaplain. The last scene of the drama, according to Berry, came in the doctor's room at 7.45, when Vickers and Innes saw each other for the first time since being convicted. It was a sight that didn't help Berry's resolve.

'The prisoners were brought face to face,' Berry recalled. 'They kissed each other; and the scene was a very painful one, to see mates going to meet their end on the gallows.' The two men resumed prayer in a room adjoining the doctor's room until the time came to approach the scaffold. Led by the High Bailiff, and with the chaplain holding tall, white wands at a slow, walking sway, the procession reached the platform just before 8 am. The chaplain read the litany for the dead and the two condemned men needed no restraint or help as they walked. They were placed under the beam and handed over to Berry and his assistant, Chester.

On that day, 31 March 1884, Berry and Chester took a man each, according to one report, though Berry would later assign Chester to just the leg pinions. Vickers, Berry said, had been cool and collected in the lead-up, spending his days praying with Innes and regularly asking if 'the reprieve' had come in. Even as Berry shook his hand that morning, he seemed calm – cheerful even.

All was quiet, until the rope touched Vicker's neck. Perhaps letting go of some fleeting hope of a messenger boy in a mad dash across the yard with a crumpled letter of reprieve in hand, he lost his cool. 'Lord be merciful, God bless my wife and family, remember me!' he shouted, before passing out. Innes, for his part, repeated the words, though his utterance was just barely audible to the reporters. He hadn't seen his companion faint – or being supported by a man on either side – as both already had the white caps over their faces.

Any worry Berry had of his nerves disrupting his performance was unfounded. He was a natural. A report in the *Cork Examiner* and the *Nenagh Guardian* described how he 'pinioned the prisoners with great coolness and marked precision'. The chaplain stood in front of the culprits reading scripture. As he delivered the line 'the hour of my departure come', Berry pulled the lever and the two men dropped. The bodies were cut down at 10 am and buried on the prison grounds, but not before an inquest and post-mortem. The necks of the convicts were broken – this was an ideal result, so to speak, as the ugly alternative was strangulation. The medical officers had seen broken necks, but this was perfect. One report said 'the surgeons stated that immediately after the execution, there was a more feeble pulsation discernible than in any previous case they had known'.

Berry had a cool resolve, but his nerves were rattled. What certainly helped were the overwhelmingly positive remarks from the officials. In a game that wasn't salaried or pensionable, you were only as good as your endorsements, so Berry made sure to get these in writing. J.E. Christie's letter, dated 31 March, was the most flattering: 'the whole of his arrangements were gone about in a most satisfactory and skilful manner; and, further, that the conduct of Messrs Berry and Chester, during the four days that they resided here, has been all that could be desired'.

Despite the success, Berry was far from able to enjoy it by the time he was served his own breakfast at 9 am. The wafting smell of the usual hearty spread of eggs and bacon was wasted on him. A cup of coffee was quite enough. Solid food could wait.

3

MAKING A HANGMAN

In the late 19th century, selling shoes didn't attract the same casual vitriol from the public as hanging condemned men. Nor did it pay as well.

The latter was the main motivation James Berry had each time he pinioned a prisoner's arms and legs, draping the white cap, and pulled the lever releasing the trapdoor on which they stood. The rope would go taut and – hopefully, though not always – remain still.

Historically, the position of executioner was, in the public eye, reserved for the disfigured, lecherous margins of Britain – the hooded non-humans who veered from civilised society. A biographer of Berry's, Justin Atholl, illustrates the contempt towards the hangman's character using the case of a man named Derrick, who was spared the gallows by the Earl of Essex following a rape conviction, on the condition that he carry out subsequent hangings. That begs the question: what drives a 31-year-old, middle-class shoe salesman and former policeman to embark on a career that would see him hang more than 130 men? Thanks to Berry's meticulous note-taking, guessing isn't necessary.

Berry was the son of a woolstapler and carpet bag manufacturer. He was born on 8 February 1852, at Heckmondwike in England, the 13th of 18 children – not many of whom reached adulthood. His father's prominent position afforded him what he later described as a 'fair education' at the Wrea Green School, near Lytham – though it was possibly cut a little short. After leaving school, he worked in his father's warehouse, before being apprenticed to his uncle, a printer at Heckmondwike. After three years of printing, he joined the Bradford West Riding Police and later the Nottingham police force, retiring in 1883. It was then that he took up shoemaking and selling, at Bradford. In the interim, in 1874, he married 21-year-old Sarah Ann Ackroyd at the Richmond Terrace Chapel. The couple had six children; of these, two boys and a girl died while young, and two boys and a girl lived.

Berry was a practical man, precise and communicative. He kept detailed diaries and logs of each execution he performed, the meat of which was published in an 1892 book – *My Experiences as an Executioner* – part ghost-written and edited by H. Snowden Ward. Berry distanced himself, at any opportunity, from any innate desire to be an executioner: 'When a policeman I strove to do my duty as well as any man could, and often wished that I could make some better provision for my wife and family, but I never so much as dreamed of becoming an executioner, or took any interest in the subject of hanging,' he wrote. He came to it, instead, by chance.

Berry's true starting point was a fluke meeting with William Marwood – the cobbler and famed executioner. Marwood was the pioneer of the long-drop method – a statistical, proportional system of execution that used mathematics to determine the exact length a drop must be to sever the spinal cord, ideally producing a humane, instant death. Prior to this method, strangulation was also seen as a desirable end product; executioners like the more brutish Calcraft were known to simply throw a rope over a beam and walk a few paces until a prisoner was left dangling, sometimes for minutes.

How exactly Berry met Marwood differs depending on the source. In at least one account given by Berry, the two met on a Bradford-bound train from London, then arranged to meet at Marwood's office and cottage in Horncastle: 'We fell into chat, and after a while I discovered who my fellow traveller was. As I had always taken a deep interest in executions – I never missed an opportunity of reading the fullest details concerning them – I need hardly tell you I became greatly interested in my strange acquaintance,' Berry told the *Freeman's Journal*. Elsewhere, Berry said that back when he was a policeman he had called into a friend's house while on his beat, and Marwood happened to be there.

Marwood had come to the profession later in life, and was the first of the breed not to be known by sight – only through newspaper reports. This was due to the abolishment of public executions three years before he entered the game. He proudly displayed his tools of death alongside those of his cobbling trade. Berry described him as a quiet, unassuming man, kindly and almost benevolent in his manner, who was in no way ashamed of his calling, though very reticent about speaking of it, excepting to those whom he knew well. He keenly felt the odium with which his office was regarded by the public, and aimed, by performing his duties in a satisfactory manner, and by conducting his private life respectably, at removing the stigma which he felt was undeserved.

Marwood faced stigma – the same stigma Berry encountered again and again throughout the seven-or-so years he performed executions. Between the self-snookering effect of being the executioner (it was hard to get any other work when your name was associated with breaking necks) and the unwavering encouragement of his wife, he trudged on – though that would prove difficult after a number of unfortunate episodes at the scaffold. 'My position is not a pleasant one,' Marwood had truthfully told Berry during an evening rendezvous in Bradford, without realising he was counselling his successor. His words, Berry later said, seemed to come from the depths of a full heart. Berry insisted Marwood never promoted his line of work to him, despite the fact that he described, with detail, the physical particulars of the job.

Though Marwood's advice wasn't solely about lengths of rope. The skill of calming a man at the scaffold was just as essential. Whispering to them, saying they wouldn't be hurt. He explained to Berry that condemned men hung to the hope of reprieve until the bitter end and warned against the torture of false hope. Once, in Glasgow, Marwood had spotted a letter being handed to the governor of the gaol as he pinioned a prisoner; he didn't move, or interrupt his process, and hanged him as though he had seen nothing. As it turned out, the letter had nothing to do with the man on the scaffold. Marwood had saved him 30 seconds of agonising suspense.

When Marwood died in September 1883, aged 63, Berry applied for the position of executioner to the city of London and County of Middlesex. By his own admission, he wasn't a man of any extraordinary ability, though he reckoned the salary would be better. 'I was simply driven to it by the poverty-stricken condition of my family,' he wrote, explaining that a shoemaker's salary left him unable to keep up reasonable comforts.

Berry's book, which the *Irish Examiner* decided was pervaded with a 'gruesomeness' people would enjoy (although the gorier details were removed), details his personal struggles with applying for the position. He found it difficult to weigh his family's needs against his wants; hanging people, he says, wasn't his cup of tea. That said, his final decision was swayed by his deteriorating financial situation and a resolution that he would probably be good at the job, and would likely improve the craft.

The decision to apply wasn't an easy one, and he spent two or three days in contemplation before sending the letter. He made his application to the sheriffs of London and Middlesex and was promptly called for an interview at the Old Bailey on Monday 24 September. Berry kept the appointment, and was told the successful candidate would hear back. From the hundreds of applications, the sheriffs whittled the field down to two: James Berry and Bartholomew Binns.

The Bradford man had other forces to contend with, however, as his relatives did everything they could to keep him from getting appointed. Friends and neighbours went as far as writing to the sheriffs, and members of his family lobbied the Home Secretary in a bid to get his application thrown out 'on the ground that if the appointment was given to me, a hitherto respectable family would be disgraced', as Berry later wrote.

In the end, Bartholomew Binns was appointed. Berry's application was a failure. One deal-breaker had been physical stature; Binns, a tall, strong-looking man, seemed as though he could handle the task. He also came with glowing references as to his demeanour and sobriety, something they were particularly concerned about. As a former navvy on the railway, he seemed more than fit for the job. But Berry's pursuit didn't end. The experience gave him new ambition. He used his spare time to consult doctors on how best to improve an already solid scientific framework left to him by Marwood. While a systemic approach gave him a legitimacy not usually associated with executioners, he knew that medical professionals held the necessary education around the physiology and circulatory nature of the neck – essential knowledge for a budding hangman.

Berry's suspicion that his family had something to do with him not being chosen over Binns was, by and large, correct. 'I objected to all applicants who had large families,' said Colonel Phineas Cowan, sheriff of London from 1883 to 1884, along with Alderman Savory. 'I said that they had no right in my opinion, to take that position, where the consequences might be very injurious to the children.' Later, Berry discovered his parents had engaged some solicitors at Heckmondwike to withdraw his application. He vowed to be ready for the next time the position would be available, which, as luck would have it, was six months later, when Vickers and Innes were sentenced to hang.

Bartholomew Binns, to put it simply, had not worked out. Tales of his drinking reached the ears of the sheriffs in London. So much for his famed sobriety. Mr Leonard Ward, chief warder at Newgate, later recalled his sole execution at that prison, revealing that Binns 'gave the man an 8-foot drop, and managed to tie the rope in such a way that it slipped 15 inches, so that by the time the man had been hanging an hour, his feet were within three inches of the floor of the pit'. An innate clumsiness pervaded stories of Binns' exploits. Ward said of his brief encounter with him that 'he did not seem as if he could grasp the subject, in fact, when pinioning a man he had the pinioning straps' back part in front, and I had to take them off and put them on right'.

And so, Berry got his second chance. Bolstered by a recommendation from the city, he sent a letter to the magistrates of Edinburgh on 13 March 1884:

Dear Sirs,

I beg most respectfully to apply to you, to ask if you will permit me to conduct the execution of the two convicts now lying under sentence of death at Edinburgh. I was very intimate with the late Mr Marwood, and he made me thoroughly acquainted with his system of carrying out his work, and also the information which he learnt from the doctors of different Prisons which he had to visit to carry out the last sentence of the law. I have now one rope of his which I bought from him at Horncastle, and have had two made from it. I have also two Pinioning straps made from his, also two leg straps. I have seen Mr Calcraft execute three convicts at Manchester 13 years ago, and should you think fit to give me the appointment I would endeavour to merit your patronage. I have served

8 years in Bradford & West Riding Police Force, and resigned without a stain on my character, and could satisfy you as to my abilities and fitness for the appointment. You can apply to Mr Jas Withers, Chief Constable, Bradford, also to the High Sheriff for the City of London, Mr. Clarence Smith, Mansion House Buildings, 4, Queen Victoria Street, London, E.C., who will testify as to my character and fitness to carry out the Law. Should you require me I could be at your command at 24 hours' notice. Hoping these few lines will meet with your approval. I remain, Sirs,

Your Most Obedient Servant,

JAMES BERRY

P.S. An answer would greatly oblige as I should take it as a favour.

Berry was accepted. And so it began.

'He hanged them,' William Marwood would often say to Berry, speaking about his predecessor, Calcraft, 'I execute them.'

Berry took to Marwood; he was an older gentleman and he was kind, talkative and to the point, much like himself. Over the door of his single-storey cottage in Church Lane in Horncastle, Marwood erected a little notice, reading 'Crown Office'. Inside, he displayed his own, slender ropes beside the brutish, thick ones of his predecessor, Calcraft. Before and after executions, he would discuss his methods openly – which he did with Berry during a friendship which lasted until his death. Marwood's opinions of Berry aren't known, but Berry had a healthy and honest curiosity about the hangman's methods – one the elder man was happy to oblige.

The apprentice inherited a lot from Marwood – one was christening his residence at No 1 Bilton Place with an official title. He was more on the nose: 'Executioner's office'. This appeared on the business cards he had made up and gave out freely. A green fern with gold detail originally adorned the card – not a cheap option at about four pence a pop, though he bought in bulk. Eventually, he removed the decoration.

James Berry (1852–1913)

Biographers, journalists, officials or anyone else who had cause to describe Berry's character routinely repeated their shock at his good humour, 'which he cannot entirely shake off even when talking on serious subjects'. He enjoyed the countryside, was observant and had a reputation for being able to talk at length about most things. A soft spot for animals meant he kept a large number of pets, tending to his pigeons and rabbits during his downtime. He was a fan of sports, and enjoyed hunting and fishing. When he was allowed out of the prison on his 'business trips', he often could be seen striding through the gates with his basket and rod in hand, on his way to discover what the local rivers held for him. He usually didn't get a nibble, but that didn't stop him from spending half a day fishing, before or after executions – whichever suited. A natural curiosity made him the perfect overnight tourist. Once, on a job in Cork, he found time to slip out among the public and visit Blarney Castle.

According to Justin Atholl, author of a book on Berry named *The Reluctant Hangman*, the executioner's home was a typical Victorian, terraced house in Bradford. Atholl – said by some researchers to be a pseudonym of British journalist Thomas Sidney Denham – describes an ordinary dwelling which visitors found somewhat unremarkable. 'In fact, there is no indication of the business of the occupant,' wrote one observer, as though disappointed not to find nooses hanging from the chandeliers. Closer inspection of framed photograph collections in the sitting room would, to the trained eye, reveal visages of Berry's more famous hanged criminals. (He kept them without captions.) In a glass-fronted sideboard, goblets, cruet stands and other sparkling trinkets sat with prominence, as per any display of finery; all were gifts given to Berry while he was executioner, from admirers of his work.

Beyond the plain-sight relics Berry displayed, he owned a number of curiosities not befitting a spot on the mantle. Berry was a believer in hanging as the best execution method. After witnessing an electrocution in the US in 1911, he labelled the technique a 'bungling' affair. 'Hanging is far superior,' he told the *Evening Telegraph*, 'for the corpses have a beautiful appearance after hanging. The faces are smiling and not contorted, and it is a peaceful death.'

Although he didn't care for America's way, he had some time for China's. Those executioners had perfected beheading down to a science, and were 'probably the most skilful headsmen in the world'. It was out of respect more than anything that he traded a 13-foot rope he had used in a number of hangings for a huge knife, used by a Chinese executioner to behead nine pirates, with nine successive blows. This was a feat in itself, as many beheadings took more than one swipe – part of the reason he didn't much care for the guillotine, either. In the right company, he would fetch the sword from the cupboard.

But for his own technique Berry looked to Marwood more than anyone else. Marwood marked a number of 'firsts' in the execution game. He was a new breed, citing progressive ideas like 'humanity' and 'service to society' as reasons for taking up the job. The odium attached was never something he tried to hide – on the contrary, he made efforts to combat it. Perhaps his open door policy was another demystifying agent for the common man; he himself had never performed a public execution – they were banned in 1868 in Britain, three years before Marwood's first assignment.

In any case, Marwood believed the 'long-drop method', which he pioneered, was certainly a far cry better than Calcraft's approach – the latter would only usually allow a drop of about two or three feet. That might kill a particularly heavy man quickly, but for the majority, it meant a slow death; he didn't much care for tinkering with the formula.

In contrast, the long-drop method used a prisoner's weight to calculate the length of rope needed to dislocate the neck and produce – hopefully – instant death. For this, the ropes had to be thin. Marwood was also the first to do completely away with slip-knots, using a metal ring worked into the ropes, which sat underneath a convict's left ear before the lever was pulled.

Berry paid close attention to Marwood's counsel, and with the backing of the sheriffs, was as trained as he could be. All that was left was to put it into practice.

4

TOOLS OF THE TRADE

A s Berry's career progressed, he perfected his routine. Step 1: Make sure the chaplain gives them this, ahead of time:

Lines for one sentenced under death

My brother – Sit and think,

While yet some hours on earth are left to thee;

Kneel to thy God, who does not from thee shrink,

And lay thy sins on Christ, who died for thee.

He rests His wounded hand

With loving kindness, on thy sin-stained brow,

And says – Here at thy side I ready stand,

To make thy scarlet sins as white as snow.

I did not shed My blood

For sinless angels, good and pure and true;

For hopeless sinners flowed that crimson flood,

My heart's blood ran for you, my son, for you.

Though thou hast grieved me sore,

My arms of mercy still are open wide,

I still hold open Heaven's shining door,

Come then – take refuge in My wounded side.

Men shun thee – but not I,

Come close to me – I love my erring sheep.

My blood can cleanse thy sins of blackest dye,

I understand, if thou canst only weep.

Words fail thee – never mind,

Thy Saviour can read e'en a sigh, or tear;

I came, sin-stricken heart, to heal and bind,

And died to save thee – to My heart thou'rt dear.

Come now – the time is short,

Longing to pardon and to bless, I wait;

Look up to Me, My sheep so dearly bought,

And say, 'forgive me, e'er it is too late.'

The rest of the equipment was important, but for Berry, those foreboding lines, scrawled on a piece of paper, were the foot in the door. In the early years that poem came to the prisoner days before the Bradford hangman darkened the door of the condemned's cell. It was a warning shot, in a way. A chance for the condemned to begin the process of acceptance.

The envelope always arrived addressed to the prisoner, care of the chaplain. For a long time, this was one of Berry's calling cards. The practice continued until one particularly irked governor refused to pass on the lines on Berry's behalf; the body was the hangman's business, but the soul was God's. It wouldn't be the first time Berry stepped on someone's toes, but after the rebuttal, he decided to leave spirituality to the chaplain and mind his own business. And in the 1880s, business was booming.

The equipment was simple, but hangmen had specific tastes; the first item in James Berry's gladstone bag was the white cap. Reports of murders were followed closely by executioners and the public alike in the 19th and early 20th centuries. Those familiar with newspaper coverage of crime in Victorian Ireland and Britain will recognise the mention of the 'caps' at various stages of the narrative. The first was the black cap. Sentencing hearings demanded a high word count in newspaper reports at the time; they were the climax of a trial, which may have lasted for days or weeks, but the last report was usually the longest. Recorded in minute detail to captivate an audience closer to death and disease, reporters ended up paying particular attention to a prisoner's physical reaction when they learned their miserable fate. Thus, a prisoner's pallor might be 'ghostly' or his appearance 'distressed'. Part of that essential crescendo detail included the judge's assumption of the 'black cap' worn when passing a death sentence. It wasn't really a cap; rather it was a black square of material, arranged to sit with one corner pointing forward atop a judge's wig – a throwback, based on court dress in Tudor times. Although capital punishment, and with it the official need for the black cap, was scrapped in the UK in 1969, the black cap can still be seen on some occasions, when full ceremonial dress is required.

While the black cap was the starting gun for the executioner's process, the white cap concluded it. Of all the grisly accoutrements carried by an executioner, it was probably the simplest. Though called a 'cap', it was more of a hood, resembling a cloth bag, which was placed on the head and lowered over a prisoner's face in the moments before execution. The assumption at the time, Berry said, was that the white cap was a device of mercy for the benefit of the condemned man – and in one way, that was correct. Even the Galway Gaol doctor at the time Berry made his visits, Richard Kinkead, said the cap 'pulls down over the eyes of the criminal to prevent his seeing the final preparations'.

The location of a scaffold wasn't regulated: sometimes it was tucked away in the corner of the grounds; other times a condemned prisoner might have to walk a hundred yards, meaning that his or her mechanism of death was in view for longer than was necessary. Therefore the cap may have proved useful to ensure that a skittish prisoner being transported didn't catch site of the gallows and panic. But the true benefit was, perhaps, for the executioner.

Like the blindfold on a man facing a firing squad, the white cap served a dual purpose, protecting the humanity of the person charged with taking a life in the name of the law. It meant that Berry didn't have to look a prisoner in the eye in the seconds before he pulled the lever. Also (and especially in the days of public executions, when an audience could contain any member of the public, of any age), it saved any spectators the distressing view of a hanged man's contorted face. There were occasions where the eyes would stare, 'livid'. The tongue might darken and protrude. Sometimes, it was a bloody affair. The hood saved onlookers this graphic displeasure, and in later years, it saved the executioner the same sight when they descended into a death pit to cut down their latest assignment.

The next item was the rope – the *pièce de rèsistance*. Berry bought his first length from his accidental mentor, Marwood, who understood the potential for selling them on after high-profile hangings. To that end, he would often make them twice as long as they needed to be, and distribute segments to collectors, as souvenirs, at a hefty price. Berry, for his own executions, used a 13-foot rope made from Italian silk – another departure from Marwood, who used manila hemp.

'For successful working the rope must, of course, be strong, and it must also be pliable in order to tighten freely,' Berry advised. 'It should be as thin as possible, consistent with strength, in order that the noose may be free running, but of course, it must not be so thin as to be liable to outwardly rupture the blood vessels of the neck.'

Madame Tussauds in London still has the cache of material sold to it by Berry, which occupied a proud space in its 'Chamber of Horrors', until the attraction's closure in 2016. Tastes, it seems, haven't evolved much. Berry was serious about his ropes, and took exception to a notion raised by the papers at the time, which said he used a rope with a wire through the centre. The accusation annoyed him, mostly because it was false, but particularly because 'A rope with a wire strand, would possess no possible advantage that I can see, and it would have so many practical disadvantages that I do not think anyone who had studied the matter would dream of using such a thing.'

Berry preferred his own ropes, but as the 1880s wore on, some sheriffs insisted he use ones approved by the Home Office (though evidence suggests he didn't always comply). Government-issued ropes were produced to the specifications of an agreed pattern, made by contractors Edgington & Co. Each was made of white Italian hemp, four-stranded and about 2.5 inches in circumference. They were robust; one warder estimated you would need a man of 34 stone falling through a 10-foot drop to risk a breakage. 'Government' ropes were ordered ahead of an execution and, in James Berry's time, stored at Clerkenwell Prison for collection. It was all a bit of a fuss, when Berry could just reach for one of the ropes he kept dangling and stretched with weights at his home in Bradford.

Next were the pinion straps, designed to keep a prisoner's arms by their sides. This was partly with flighty-fighty prisoners in mind, but, generally speaking, prisoners didn't struggle all that much. Strapping the arms to the body primarily prevented them from moving too much amid possible convulsions after hanging (in the case of accidental strangulation). Bodies were easier to manage, after the deed, in a tighter package.

The pinion itself was a broad leather-body belt, clasped around the middle. To that, arm straps were fastened. Those leather pieces, an inch and a half wide with steel buckles, pinned the convict's arms together at the elbows. Another leather strap of the same strength went around the wrists and was fastened to the broad belt at the front. Finally, a two-inch leather strap was tightened below the knees. Berry, in a rambling interview in 1885, also described a set of ankle straps of similar design, which he himself devised. All told, the process left a convict well-contained, with shivering hands barely able to clasp fingers at the front and the elbows slightly protruding at the back, while the legs were bound tightly, their mobility reduced to barely a squirm.

Pinion straps were not always used. In 1856, a convict named Bousfield managed to get his feet to the edges of the platform and delay the inevitable. In that case, 'the inevitable' meant William Calcraft positioning himself below Bousfield's feet, grabbing them, and holding them still.

The scaffold was equally important. Evidence suggests that in earlier years, a prisoner with a noose fastened around the neck would be pushed from a height, usually a ladder. Next they stood the condemned man or woman on top of a cart, which would be driven from underneath them at the executioner's signal. A platform was then developed, which was collapsed by the executioner, to leave a prisoner dangling. This led, then, to the scaffold as Berry knew it, with a trapdoor and 'bolt' that could be drawn to leave a prisoner suspended, feet through the hole.

When Berry started hanging, there was no real formula for the scaffolds, leading to a huge disparity in quality and form. Exeter, for example, was so flimsily constructed that Berry actually gave the governor (unheeded) tips to improve it. Galway Gaol, by comparison, had a marvellous construction, which Berry could not praise highly enough. In most prisons, the scaffold was taken down and stored after use, kept out of sight. A handful retained permanent fixtures.

In 1885, Lt Col Alten Beamish drew up a design for the Home Office in an attempt to create a uniform template. It was submitted to Berry, quite to his satisfaction, before being distributed to gaols. For a man who regularly baulked at government attempts to railroad and homogenise the nuanced practicalities of execution, Berry's reaction was a surprising one; he thought it was nearly perfect. The only alteration he made was to swap Beamish's staircase for a gradual slope. Dragging, in some cases, a prisoner to his death on a scaffold was difficult enough, but forcing a person to climb stairs was just a needless hurdle, Berry thought. 'It was a simple improvement,' Berry said of his own work, 'but it has turned out to be a most useful one.'

The basic construction consisted of a cross beam, with strong hooks embedded to hold the rope. The beam was either fed into the scaffold house walls or secured onto two upright posts. The drop, or trapdoor, was the most important aspect, and the one to which Berry paid most attention at his inspections. Two large oak doors were fitted into a level oak floor, sitting over a deep, brick-sided pit. The doors had to be large and heavy, to ensure that when the lever was pulled and the bolt drawn they fell as suddenly as possible, even without the weight of a man on top. Spring catches were ideally fit to prevent them from rebounding and colliding with the criminal on his way down.

Beyond the tools listed above there were a handful of other things Berry thought appropriate to bring. The first, sometimes, was his family. Once, on a trip to Ireland, he brought his son Luther in an effort to blend in. A revolver (and sometimes a second revolver) could also be a hangman's best friend. Berry kept his loaded and close to hand when travelling, especially to Ireland.

A single piece of thread played a key role in keeping the process a clean one. An unfortunate incident at Marwood's hands had inspired Berry to tie the slack of the rope to the cross beam during his preparations. Marwood used to let the slack of the rope dangle behind the condemned, but on one occasion in Galway, the man's elbow became caught in the rope as he disappeared through the platform. The prison doctor recorded that the resulting interruption was enough to ensure death by strangulation, instead of the clean separation of the vertebrae sought by purveyors of the long drop.

But perhaps the most important tool wasn't a tool at all. Rather, it was a mathematical equation. Berry dug deep in his preparations to become an executioner, listening closely to Marwood's explanations of weights and rope lengths, even before Berry knew he would apply for the job. The end product of this highly technical approach was a table of drops – compiled from an equation that calculated the precise length of rope to be used according to a person's weight. Berry was at pains to explain to the public that no two men were alike, and it was no longer a case of simply stringing them up. He said: 'If all murderers who have to be hanged were of precisely the same weight and build it would be very easy to find out the most suitable length of drop, and always to give the same, but as a matter of fact they vary enormously.'

The abolishment of public hangings in 1868 had changed the practice. Calcraft was still in business at that time, and well set in his ways, having embarked on his career in 1829. He was unlikely to change, and was certainly uninterested in experimentation on the basis of improving a murderer's experience. The long drop became popular, partly, out of the realisation that hanging need no longer be a spectacle. The sight of a man wriggling for life was hardly a deterrent once the scaffold was brought within the prison walls, and a crowd couldn't look on in the flurry of gasps which newspapers at the time relished in reporting. Calcraft, for his part, disliked the long drop for technical reasons; he used a slipknot, and the downward force could have tested their strength and resulted in a slip-through. Without an exact knowledge of the force required to kill a man, he was afraid a heavy prisoner could even break a rope. He played it safe: the short drop would kill a man and satisfy the public, but certainly wouldn't ensure a quick death. He was happy enough with that.

Change, for that reason, came slowly. Even the primitive wording of a judge's sentence, that 'the prisoner be hanged from the neck until he was dead', was not very prescriptive, and endured into the 20th century. To that end, in the execution game the table of drops was akin to the discovery of fire. It distanced those who used it from the old-school brutes who threw a rope over a beam and hoisted a man to strangulation. Men who could deftly mentally detach from the gruelling abuse they got. Men who were also called upon to perform beheadings and quarterings at times, and quite a lot of whipping. Those notions were repugnant to Berry and the long drop enthusiasts, who simply wanted a foolproof way to humanely and accurately perform the job as quickly as possible. Dislocation, not suffocation, was the aim. And if dislocation didn't get them, rupturing the jugular would do the trick, just as quickly.

While the long drop had its opponents and critics, medical evidence heard at a government committee at the end of the 1880s (more on which later) indicated that it was better than suffocation:

> The evidence adduced makes it too certain that this form of death [suffocation] involves at least one to three minutes of extreme agony, and also the appearance of intense suffering, lasting for a much longer period, which, even if only an 'appearance', and even if we could be assured it was accompanied by absolute insensibility, is nevertheless very distressing to all whose duty may oblige them to be present.

The confirmation of prolonged discomfort, to put it mildly, may be obvious to an observer. But this was an important acknowledgement, as common thought for decades had been that the lack of oxygen, in all cases, produced an anaesthetic effect.

In the first days of the long drop, the length of the rope given to prisoners was no more than three feet. Such lingering deaths were a pet hate of Berry's. For a hangman, he was particularly sensitive to the needs of the condemned; he once referred to a 60-yard walk from the prison door to the scaffold as a form of 'torture' for the prisoners who had to lay eyes on the apparatus as they approached.

In review of Marwood's stagnant predecessors, Berry wasn't flattering. To be fair to the subjects of his critique, even in its rudimentary form, hanging had gone through some evolution since the days of beheading. Marwood's input advanced the long drop, but did not invent it. The dislocation of spinal cords had happened accidentally for years, usually when prisoners flung themselves from the height to avoid a painful death. Marwood, though, was the first to at least attempt a system whereby information about the prisoner could help streamline his or her death. In Marwood, Berry saw the first executioner to take the job seriously. Like a craft. Certainly a huge advance from the days when sailors were commonly hired for the job because they could tie the best knots.

In his diaries, Berry spoke about Marwood's advances with some affection, and he was clearly personally fond of him: 'He, as a humane man, carefully considered the subject, and came to the conclusion that the then existing method, though certain, was not so rapid or painless as it ought to be. In consequence he introduced his long-drop system with a fall of from seven to ten feet, which caused instantaneous death by severance of the spinal cord.' As part of the long, winding conversations they would have in Marwood's cottage/workshop/executioner's office, Berry inherited his calculations, which he used in his first execution to the letter. The first, Vickers, was 10 stone 4 pounds, and got a drop of 8 foot 6 inches; the second, Innes, was 9 stone 6, and got 10 feet. The executions were flawless.

Still, Marwood's guideline was just that – a guideline – and executions still benefited from an experienced eye. In an effort to remove any doubt, Berry drew up his own table of drops, which he entered into the inside cover of his notebook, where he also kept a record of every person he hanged, with red lines denoting reprieved prisoners. The ones who got away.

Berry considered, first, a man of 14 stone, and figured he'd need a drop of 8 feet. He then calculated that every half stone would need about two more inches in rope length. Thus, he created his first proper formula:

14 stone	8 ft 0 in.
13½ '	8 ' 2 '
13 '	8 ' 4 '
12½ '	8 ' 6 '
12 '	8 ' 8 '
11½ '	8 ' 10 '
11 '	9 ' 0 '
10½ '	9 ' 2 '
10 '	9 ' 4 '
9½ '	9 ' 6 '
9 '	9 ' 8 '
8½ '	9 ' 10 '
8 '	10 ' 0 '

Berry used these numbers for what he called a man of 'average' build and neck strength, but still couldn't land on an absolute ratio. On more than one occasion, for instance, a prisoner in Berry's charge had attempted suicide by cutting their own throat. Reducing unnecessary gore was high on any humanitarian executioner's to-do list, so in cases of these types of wounds, the drop was sometimes reduced by as much as half. The same was the case with prisoners with glandular diseases, or really any physical issue that compromised the integrity of the neck. In his writings, Berry aligns himself further with the medical professionals, praising the 'useful hints' he received from gaol doctors. In cases where he was unsure, he would reduce the drop in relation to the table, but the threat always remained that if the rope was too long, the head would come off.

One shocking incident (see Chapter 19) led Berry to reconsider his system after some time using Marwood's table. After a couple of years he recognised that very short lengths were the difference between success and catastrophic failure. Even the ropes themselves could not be trusted to record a drop accurately, as a moving knot or stretch in the rope could also play a pivotal role. During a drop his ropes had stretched up to a foot on occasion, usually returning to their original length in about a day.

SCALE SHOWING THE STRIKING FORCE OF FALLING BODIES AT DIFFERENT DISTANCES.

Distance Falling in Feet Zero	8 Stone	9 Stone	10 Stone	11 Stone	12 Stone	13 Stone	14 Stone	15 Stone	16 Stone	17 Stone	18 Stone	19 Stone
	Cw. Qr. lb.	Cw. Qr. lb.	Cw. Qr. lb.	Cw. Qr. lb.	Cw. Qr. lb.	Cw. Qr. lb.	Cw. Qr. lb.	Cw. Qr. lb.	Cw. Qr. lb.	Cw. Qr. lb.	Cw. Qr. lb.	Cw. Qr. lb.
1 Ft.	8 0 0	9 0 0	10 0 0	11 0 0	12 0 0	13 0 0	14 0 0	15 0 0	16 0 0	17 0 0	18 0 0	19 0 0
2 ,,	11 1 15	12 2 23	14 0 14	15 2 4	16 3 22	18 1 12	19 3 2	21 0 21	22 2 11	24 0 1	25 1 19	26 3 9
3 ,,	13 3 16	15 2 15	17 1 14	19 0 12	20 3 11	22 2 9	24 1 8	26 0 7	27 3 5	29 2 4	31 1 2	33 0 1
4 ,,	16 0 0	18 0 0	20 0 0	22 0 0	24 0 0	26 0 0	28 0 0	30 0 0	32 0 0	34 0 0	36 0 0	40 0 0
5 ,,	17 2 11	19 3 5	22 0 0	24 0 22	26 1 16	28 2 11	30 3 5	33 0 0	35 0 22	37 0 16	39 2 11	41 3 15
6 ,,	19 2 11	22 0 5	24 2 0	26 3 22	29 1 16	31 3 11	34 1 5	36 3 0	39 0 22	41 2 16	44 0 11	46 2 5
7 ,,	21 0 22	23 3 11	26 2 0	29 0 16	31 3 5	34 1 22	37 0 11	39 3 0	42 1 16	45 0 5	47 2 22	50 1 11
8 ,,	22 2 22	25 2 4	28 1 14	31 0 23	34 0 5	36 3 15	39 2 25	42 2 7	45 1 16	48 0 26	51 0 8	53 3 18
9 ,,	24 0 11	27 0 12	30 0 14	33 0 23	36 0 16	39 0 18	42 0 19	45 0 21	48 0 22	51 0 23	54 0 25	57 0 26
10 ,,	25 1 5	28 1 23	31 2 14	34 3 4	37 3 22	41 0 12	44 1 2	47 1 21	50 2 11	53 3 1	56 3 19	60 0 9

Berry next focused on calculating the 'striking force', enlisting the help of an engineer from Newgate prison to ensure precision. He did this for a wide range of weights from 8 to 19 stone after falling all distances from 1 to 10 feet, and calculated that the force needed was 24 cwt (cwt being short for 'centrum weight', commonly known as 'hundredweight'; one hundredweight is equal to 8 stone).

His new equation gave much shorter drops than Marwood's rule of thumb. It still certainly required a keen eye; these calculations were applicable to the averagely built prisoner. If, for example, an old or frail-looking person didn't seem to need 24 cwt, Berry might have reduced the drop by a sixth. For Vickers and Innes, his debutants, the drops would have reduced by 3 feet each. These disparities are huge, considering that in theory, the difference between strangulation and decapitation was as little as 6 inches.

5

THE PLAY

Berry kept the play as formulaic as possible. As simple and as quick as it could be. Some tension existed amongst the figures involved in the care of a condemned prisoner; Berry considered himself the expert in the field, and felt he should be trusted to use his expertise. Prison doctors similarly often felt that they, as medical professionals, knew the best practice, and intervened on points such as rope length. Chaplains too would often chime in, as shown in the case when Berry was asked to stop sending poetry about death to prisoners before his arrival. Nevertheless, each had a part to play in the drama.

Nearly all executions in Britain and Ireland were set for 8 am. On the morning of the execution, Berry would rise early, sometimes taking breakfast, other times waiting until after the execution. At about 7.30 he would ascend the scaffold or step onto the platform and arrange the ropes. By then, the length of the drop was already decided.

If more than one prisoner was to be hanged, Berry brought along an assistant. Richard Chester was his primary man for this job, though he used other people in the course of his career. In some cases, Chester would come along for a single execution – to strap the legs while Berry strapped the arms. From the time he entered the cell to the time the trapdoor opened, Berry allowed three minutes.

The Bradford man would check his watch closely in the minutes leading up to the execution hour, aiming to enter the condemned's cell at exactly 7.57 am. In order for the hanging to go ahead, the hangman needed to receive from the sheriff a signed document known as an 'authority to hang'. Some of these were overly wordy, which Berry didn't care for. It should rather be a simple expression of permission – simple, but vital, as it made the hanging a legal act. Technically, the charge of hanging fell to the sheriff of the gaol, and it was up to him to hire a man for the job. This was the basic structure that gave rise to the 'freelance' nature of the position throughout the 19th century. If no death practitioner could be found, the duty fell to the sub-sheriff. If, for whatever reason, they could not do it, the sheriff himself had to step up. It was also the sheriff's job to ensure that the gallows was built and fit for purpose.

The sheriff was issued a death warrant, which was presented to the governor of the prison on the morning of the execution, and the prisoner was then handed to the sub-sheriff; in this way, the convict passed entirely out of the remit of the gaol, technically. The person was then passed over, via the authorisation above, to James Berry. With all the paperwork in place, the prisoner's arms were pinioned in the cell. A group of people would be waiting in the room ahead of the hangman, including the chaplain and two attendants who would have been with the prisoner during his last nights. When Berry appeared in the doorway, the attendants would hand the prisoner over.

If a convict had not confessed already, Berry would need to know. As a former policeman, he respected the law and the process, but a shred of doubt seemed to linger in some cases; a string of 'humanity' in an otherwise orderly, pragmatic operator. He openly admits the reason in his diaries; it was important to him that he felt he wasn't hanging an innocent person. If he was going to ask the question, this was the time. In the majority of cases, he got what he needed. 'Of course,' Berry explained, 'the confidences reposed in me at such moments I have never divulged, and it would be most improper to do so; but I am at liberty to state, that of all the people I have executed, only two or three have died without fully and freely confessing their guilt.'

The procession could then begin. It was typically led by the chief warder, followed by the chaplain and the convict, flanked by warders. Then came Berry, more warders and the prison officials. His assistant (if he needed one) and wand bearers would accompany the convict as well. For the bog-standard murderer who turned to religion in the weeks before the execution, this part was usually painless. Others went kicking and screaming, quite literally. It was usually during this walk, to the sounds of the chaplain's service being chanted ahead of the prisoner, that Berry would reach forward and place the white cap on top of the prisoner's head. If he thought the convict couldn't handle the occasion he would pull it down prematurely, to save hassle. Otherwise, the cap would usually be pulled down just as they stepped onto the scaffold.

In a matter of seconds, the convict was placed under the beam and the leg pinions strapped. The prepared noose was draped over the head and tightened, with Berry placing the knot behind the left ear. He wasn't too dogmatic on this point though; if there was a wound on that side of the neck, for instance, the ring could be placed behind the head or, as Dr Kinkead of Galway would have preferred, under the chin. Berry said he preferred behind the ear because it gave three possible causes of death: a broken neck; failing that, strangulation; failing that, 'if a third factor were necessary', the ring could rupture the jugular vein, 'which, in itself, is sufficient to cause practically instantaneous death'.

The gaol doctor and Berry then examined the body, either by walking under the scaffold or, in later years, descending into the death pit. The body was left hanging, unless some accident had occurred, for an hour, before being lowered into a coffin, constructed in the days ahead by the prison warders. (On more than one occasion in British history, prisoners had actually recovered after over-eager hangmen had cut them loose, convinced they had expired.) Somewhere on the prison grounds a hole would already be dug, usually with bags of quicklime at the ready. An inquest was usually held in the mortuary by noon, after which the prisoner was buried.

Once the execution was completed, usually a few minutes after the appointed hour, a notice was pinned to the door of the gaol; this part of the process was taken up after the barring of members of the public from viewing hangings following the Capital Punishment Amendment Act, 1868. A black flag was hoisted high above the prison walls to indicate the carrying out of the law, for the benefit of crowds which often gathered outside or climbed nearby ascents to catch a glimpse of the grim parade.

When all was said and done, Berry collected his fee and, in most cases, left shortly thereafter, though not before getting the appropriate commendations from the officials.

Berry was a businessman, at pains to highlight the financial needs of his family as the main reason he went for the job. As part of his effort to eradicate the foul taste surrounding the practice, he wanted to distance himself from any connotations of a morbid fascination with death. When he started, he was required in most districts to send a letter of application outlining his qualifications and price – each possible execution would receive many applicants, and the motivations were not all as above board as his. As he became better known, it wasn't necessary to apply each time to be the executioner, as he was usually called upon. This was true except for Ireland, where he had to send to the magistrates a contact card bearing his name and address for the duration of his career.

His customers, technically, were the sheriffs. They decided who to charge with the responsibility of hanging convicts. And like any customer, they bargain-hunted, and so to remove confusion Berry drew up a type of quote template. At a basic rate, Berry charged £10 a head (so to speak), or £5 if a prisoner was reprieved. With an average of about one execution every two weeks, his annual salary was around £250 – though by 1887, he never earned less than £270 per annum. This doesn't include any extras he made from expenses, such as the cash saved by skimping on train fare. Berry wasn't thrilled with the pay, but in all it wasn't bad, and it came with some perks. Berry knew from his first early meetings with Marwood that the executioner could benefit from other 'investments'. Souvenirs – such as prisoners' possessions and lengths of rope – did a big trade.

But though Berry's time at the gallows saw him hang many notorious gunmen, poachers, poisoners and cut-throats, he simply hadn't garnered the kind of big names Marwood boasted – Charlie Peace chief among them. Peace, whom Marwood hanged in 1879, was a burglar and murderer, convicted after killing a police officer and later the husband of the woman he regularly harassed. The crime captured media and public attention, and the execution was remarkable enough to earn a reconstruction at Madame Tussauds chamber of horrors (though Marwood would have tutted at the slipknot used in the model).

It was for this reason perhaps no coincidence that Marwood made his ropes extra long. Once, Berry purchased a single rope from Marwood, which had been made so long that Berry was able to cut it in two and each still allowed a 10-foot drop. A rule was brought in before Berry's time that put a spanner in the works of this lucrative side-business (which he, in any case, said he never took part in). 'In [Marwood's] time, also, there were considerable perquisites, for instance, the clothing and personal property possessed by the criminal at the time of his execution became the property of the executioner,' Berry wrote, in a tone that seems positive, yet somehow bitter. He continued:

> These relics were often sold for really fancy prices and formed no mean item in the annual takings. But the sale and exhibition of such curiosities were only pandering to a morbid taste on the part of some sections of the public, and it was ordered by the Government – very rightly, from a public point of view, but very unfortunately for the executioner – that personal property left by the criminals should be burned.

It's worth noting that Berry wrote the above passage about a year after selling a sizeable chunk of his various collectables to Madame Tussauds in London, though not only for financial gain. It's hard to know how much money Berry made from souvenirs, if anything. One estimate had the potential supplement for an executioner at anything up to £100 extra, depending on the year.

In 1882, to firm up the employment of a single executioner, Sir William Harcourt suggested to the Corporation of London that one be hired, full-time, for London and Middlesex. Although sheriffs in other counties would often end up employing this man, they were not bound to the person selected. Even his position with London and Middlesex, though technically thought of as an 'appointment', was quite spurious. This individual was paid a £20 annual sum, but as Col Phineas Cowan, sheriff of London 1883–4, told the Home Office in 1886: 'There is no appointment whatever, and the sheriffs have no obligation upon them to take the service of this man', adding that the money owed was 'a sort of retaining fee'.

The position was one of private enterprise – anyone could apply to hang a condemned prisoner outside the City of London. However it was often easier to simply hire the man being employed by London. Col Cowan saw that as a flaw, and asked why sheriffs would resign themselves to the London executioner when they didn't have to. What if they hired an incompetent man?

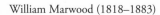
William Marwood (1818–1883)

Execution of Charles Peace
by William Marwood.
An 1879 wax sculpture at
Madame Tussauds, London.

One upshot of the zero-hour contract approach, which Berry found most repugnant, was having to pore over papers for the 'good news' of someone's conviction. Berry regretted that he 'should have to regard as evil days and hard times those periods when there seem to be lulls in the annals of crime, and when one might reasonably hope that a better state of things was dawning in the land'. It wasn't as though he could supplement his income. Berry was let go as a boot salesman; he was good at his job, and his boss had no problem with him personally, but the business would suffer for his presence. Security, too, was an issue. The contempt people had, and at the very least the unpredictable attitude, meant he was subjected to ridicule at the low end and permanent injury on the other. He had a bucking prisoner named Sowrey to thank for one such dent.

When business picked up, Berry was asked to leave the Bradford home he had shared with his wife and family. This happened two or three times throughout his career. It became quickly apparent to landlords that neighbours-to-be weren't thrilled about living next door to the hangman, despite his famed normality out of office hours. He found this hard to navigate, and discovered most landlords had the same outlook. As a result he ended up purchasing a number of houses in a different area in Bradford – if he was the landlord, he figured, he couldn't be evicted. It was unlikely his tenants would complain. What he couldn't control was abuse received by his family.

In 1887, after a meeting with a local MP, Berry had the opportunity to write to the president of the committee on capital punishment, Lord Aberdare, in which he addressed his gripes, and asked for a salary. He aimed high, asking for £350 per annum. Drawing attention to his peculiar social position, he wrote:

> I am to a great extent alone in the world, as a certain social ostracism is attendant upon such office, and extends, not to myself alone, but also includes the members of my family. It therefore becomes extremely desirable that my children should, for their own sakes, be sent to a school away from this town. To do this of course would entail serious expenditure, only to be incurred in the event of my being able to rely on a fixed source of income, less liable to variation than the present remuneration by

QUOTE
No. ....

Bradford, ... 189

YORKS.

Sir,

I beg leave to state in reply to your letter

of the .... that I

am prepared to undertake the execution you name of

_____

at .... on the................................

I also beg leave to state that my terms are as

follows : £10 for the execution, £5 if the condemned

is reprieved, together with all travelling expenses.

Awaiting your reply,

I am, Sir,

Your obedient Servant,

James Berry.

The High Sheriff,

for the County of.................................

Berry's application form

commission alone. I am also unable for obvious reasons to obtain any other employment.

As a lowball offer, in a postscript he suggested that a 'nominal' sum of £100 could be granted, as a retainer.

It was only fair, as Berry saw it, to give him a regular salary. Calcraft, who retired in 1874 on a 25 shilling per week pension for life, was on a retainer worth £1 1s 0d from the Sheriffs of the City of London and a second from Horsemonger Lane Gaol in south London. Calcraft also had fees and expenses, undertaking the same countrywide £10-a-go payment Berry pursued, on top of the retainers. Even Marwood had the £20 per year from the London sheriffs, though he didn't enjoy the more sturdy status of Calcraft. What he did have was an absolute inheritance on prisoners' belongings after their death – which is no doubt why he developed a hard skin for souvenir-trading.

Berry thought executioners in many other places, despite their barbaric methods, had better conditions. In France at the time it was a family business; the Deiblers had occupied the position for many years. Even Malta, a British territory, offered a £30 salary.

Despite his impassioned reasoning, it did not become a salaried position. The Home Office took greater notice in who they hired as years went on, but executioners grew to be less well known, less prolific and, as they became more anonymous, less hated. Therefore, many took extra jobs. In that sense, Berry has been called the 'last professional hangman'.

6

SHADOWS ON A BOREEN

As midnight struck, a mist settled over the streets. A calm darkness filled the alleys. The watchmen pulled their overcoats tighter against the cold. Drinking on the job wasn't uncommon. On the contrary, it had been part of the reason for a small spike in staff turnover in recent weeks. Of course, not all of Galway's watchmen were drunkards, but on a dozy, mid-December night, a bottle passed around did just as good a job as the Irish frost on their shoulders.

It was Wednesday. Businesses were shut for the night and the town was quiet, save for the noise of the Corrib, whose waters rushed fast through the city. A woman's screams pierced the air. Shaken from their stupor, the men stood and looked north through the fog towards the noise, and the source of the anguish became clear. A group of people materialised, and a woman stumbled into view from the Headford Road, tired, filthy and gasping – 'in a state of frenzy', according to an *Irish Times* account. Blood and mud covered her sleeves, and she was making little sense, but they gathered the basics. The woman, 35-year-old Mary Moylan, had reportedly come to the city from Clonboo, a tiny townland in the parish of Annaghdown, miles north. The journey would have taken hours, but she needed help. Her husband, John, had been killed.

It was the middle of the night when District Inspector Stephens got the telegram from Galway city. The county inspector was on the move to Clonboo. Another farmer dead. Nothing new there, he thought; Stephens, like anyone else in law enforcement in the west of Ireland at the time, was no stranger to violence. He thought little of boarding a small boat on the west banks of Lough Corrib and setting out for the remote parish on the other side of the water. By the time he arrived, a little after 2 am on 20 December 1883, Mary had calmed down, and police were given a fair idea of events. She was still shaking from the ordeal when she gave her account.

Annaghdown is a low-lying parish on the banks of Lough Corrib, north of Galway city. Its green lands are divided by short, aged rock walls, and most transport at the time was through networks of winding, narrow country lanes. The area was poor, save for a few dominating landowners, with fields subject to floods during heavy rains. After the Famine its population had fallen sharply, and had just about levelled out by the 1881 census, to 876 people.

Nestled in the eastern reaches of the parish was Clonboo (spelled Cloonboo in some documents), one of Annaghdown's many townlands – a tiny area of flat land, boreens and about six or seven houses. Described as barren in reports at the time, the only prominent property was Cregg Castle, a country house at the southernmost reach of the townland. The lands and their houses belonged to Francis Blake, whose family controlled more than 5,000 acres in Galway at the end of the 19th century. Among his tenants by the time of the Griffith Valuation in the mid-1800s were the Moylan family, who occupied a patch of farmland.

John Moylan had lived on the farm all his life, and inherited the land by the beginning of the 1880s. Born in 1844, just before the Famine, John had seen first-hand the decimation of the region, by starvation at first, then disease, and then an unstoppable wave of emigration. The population of the county would fall by more than 50 per cent in the 50 years following John's birth, and Clonboo was no different.

At the time John died, he had five children – all boys – from an infant to a 15-year-old. The farm had a modest output, but he had done his best to provide for his family, even getting a significant reduction in his annual rent – from more than £30 to a little more than £7. Nearly three years before the night his wife alerted authorities to his death, John faced the hardship so many in Annaghdown had faced before him. And in 1880, he did something that was common among men at the time – he left his wife and young family for America.

The absence had been a long one, but Mary continued to keep the farm ticking over. 'He from time to time sent money to his wife and children to help support them and it is understood that on his return … he brought with him a considerable sum of money,' reads a report in the *Freeman's Journal* in the days following John's death.

John was a short time back in Ireland – about three months – when his wife was forced to recount the details of his brutal death. On his return, she admitted, their first marital interaction had been a tense one, as John discovered his rent unpaid and monies due to rate collectors. John had diligently sent money back each month from America, and to find it squandered was, to put it lightly, a disappointment. As one report said, he was 'dissatisfied that the place was not more comfortable, and appeared to be at a loss to know what had been done with all the money he had sent'. It wasn't exactly clear how much he had sent back, but by calculations at the time, it was at least £103.

It had been a shock, certainly, but life between the couple had returned to something approaching normal. Part of their routine involved evening visits to the house where Mary's father and brother lived, in the nearby townland of Cregduff – only about 600 yards south-east, as the crow flies.

On Wednesday evening at about 5 pm, Mary set out for her father's house, but John didn't join her immediately, promising instead to meet her there a couple of hours later, at about 7 pm. John kept his appointment, and the couple stayed with Mary's father, chatting beside the fire. The conversation lingered a little longer than usual, and it wasn't until just before 9 pm when the pair finally decided to walk the short distance home. John rose from his chair when his pipe extinguished, carefully tapping the clay bowl in his hands and letting its ashen contents drift into the hearth. He returned the pipe to his coat pocket – the walk was short, about five minutes. There was hardly enough time to light up again.

After saying their goodbyes at the door, the pair made off into the darkness. The roads were unlit at the time. The only sign of life was a newly erected police hut. A mist was coming in, and the night was cold.

In the darkness, a shadow stalked them, just silhouettes at the old man's door. When the light distinguished the couple, the shadow retreated back into the shelter of the shrub, hands covered in a thick dust from rubbing feverishly at the steel barrel in his pocket.

Mary's father's house was reached by a narrow, overgrown country road, which ran from the back door, between the new police hut and the main cluster of houses that made up Clonboo. The couple left by the boreen – one of many remote lanes that webbed through the parish – and walked in silence. The path was well-trodden and the mud was likely to be high and thick; in the pitch darkness, they decided to play it safe, taking a shortcut through an adjacent field, a diversion known well by the locals.

'Portion of the boreen leading from the brother in law's is usually very dirty and for this reason, Moylan and his wife on this occasion as on many others took a path through the field, leaving the boreen at a distance of only forty yards or so from the house they had just left,' wrote one reporter who visited the area.

The couple veered through a gap in the tall hedge and traipsed through the grass. They were about 50 yards into the field, marching in single file, John a couple of paces in front of Mary, when a shout came from the hedge nearby. 'Is that you, Tom Browne?' – or was it 'Burke?', Mary wondered aloud to police – it was all a blur, and she wasn't sure which.

The shape of a man materialised to the couple's side, just against the hedge. John, startled, wheeled around to face it, but made no reply.

The voice demanded again: 'Is that you, Tom Browne?' Then the first shot came, casting a shock of light over the grass. John collapsed backwards into Mary's arms, and the two fell into the shrubs. She grabbed at his torso and turned him over to speak to him, but he stayed silent. She let go of her husband's coat and turned her palms upward to find them pooled with blood. The shooter took a step towards the couple piled on the ground and presented the gun again, taking an executioner's stance. By Mary's account, she 'threw herself over the prostrate body' of John in an attempt to save him. A strong hand clasped the back of Mary's dress; the man made easy work of dragging Mary – all 5 foot 2 of her – from her guarded position on top of John's body. She turned back in time to see the long barrel of the gun again come to point into John's face, and a second shot rang out, throwing another flash of light against the darkness.

As her ears rang, she saw the attacker approach her husband, grab him by the scruff and lift him halfway off the ground. He shook John stiffly, enough to satisfy himself the deed was done. As quickly as he appeared he darted off, fleeing across the fields, but not before dropping a note onto John's lifeless body. Mary made a feeble attempt at grabbing the assailant, whose long coat was stiff and hard to grasp. Her eyes followed the man as he fled, but took little notice of any details about him, save for a cursory sketch; it wasn't too dark, she would later say, but her eyes were clouded with tears and dirt.

She turned her attention back to John. He was unrecognisable. Both shots had been point-blank. Reports at the time indicate the destruction to his face: 'Both [shots] appear to have taken effect in the forehead, above the left eye,' reads one. 'The ball struck the unfortunate man in the face, shattering the jaw and destroying his whole face.'

Mary let go of her husband, his body collapsing into a wet mound, without resistance. She rushed to raise the alarm at her father's house and a crowd gathered by lamplight at the scene. Her brother went for the priest, and she for the authorities.

The body was carried back to the house – that of Mary's father, Patrick Small – from where the couple had set out, a little over 140 yards from the spot where John Moylan was shot. Mary was in an exhausted and understandably skittish state. Nevertheless, she was the sole witness to the murder. The coroner for Dunmore, James McDonagh, presided over the inquest; also present were Messrs Reed and Lyster, resident magistrates, Galway; County Inspector Murphy; District Inspectors Lennon and Cary; and Dr Duggan, the medical officer of Turloughmore, where the murder took place. The jury were sworn in, and the body of John Moylan was revealed to them.

John's face, for a large part, was skinless; the doctors commented that they found skin 'wanting'. The scant coverage that remained was badly charred by gunpowder. A doctor named Turner, with Dr Duggan's assistance, had conducted a post-mortem of John's body, though the cause of death would have been hard to miss. The skull and facial bones were a spiderweb of fractures, with all the bones of the nose simply missing. On opening the brain, they discovered grains of shot and one slug – specifically, a clump of lead, which had been heated and crudely rolled into a ball. A piece of paper – presumably wadding from the shot – was lodged where the nose bones should have been.

Both doctors concurred, and the jury agreed, that John Moylan died as the results of a gunshot wound to the face. That he was shot was indisputable, but the question as to who pulled the trigger remained.

The most important witness, the only person present in the boreen, was called first. Mary Moylan's testimony, detailed in a *Freeman's Journal* report, revealed specifics about the encounter that the press were not yet privy to, serving to demuddle some of the finer points. At the same time, it raised much larger questions.

Mary had done her best to till the land and work the farm while her husband was in America. But she was unable to do all of the farm work herself and lacked the money to pay a servant, and so she relied heavily on help from locals, namely her brother and a smattering of young men in the district.

'Why was he obliged to go to America?' the Coroner asked Mary, looking for specifics beyond the general poverty, which would not have been uncommon for any family of that size in Moylan's class. 'A sister of his own, Bridget Moylan, was living in the house,' the widow explained. 'He was obliged to give her a fortune out of the house. We used not to have a bit to eat, and it was to help to give her a fortune that he went to America. We were badly off when he went – no provision or food at all.'

A bleak picture indeed. But, as it happened, it seemed Moylan's yield was good in America – the money back was consistent. As good as they'd ever had it; so much so, Mary said, that she wrote to John some months after his departure, asking whether she and the boys should follow over – what did they have left to lose? She could sell the land to pay for their passage.

'No' was the response from the States. An emphatic 'No'. The land had to be kept – he'd gone this far. He did, however, send back £12 to pay for the passage of Bridget to the US.

The only reason John had returned when he did was because he was badly injured in America, and was afraid that it could happen again. Mary didn't go into the specifics of the injury when she addressed the inquest, but it was bad enough that he spent a good amount of his savings on doctors, which made him well enough for the journey back. Bridget, who had made it to America by the time of John's injury the previous Christmas, was the one who advised him to go back. John returned, in that case, with quite short notice.

Mary also spoke on the issue of money. Though the feeling in the neighbourhood had been that John was angry with Mary for squandering the money he sent back, she said he was 'quite satisfied' with how she spent it.

On the day before John's murder, his sister, Mary Casey, showed up to the house at Clonboo. 'She was about paying her rent,' Mary said, 'and she was a pound short. He had not it that night, but he said he would have it in the morning and would go back with it to her house.' Evidently, John still had a reputation for having some financial means, despite the depletion by the medical men in America. The following morning, Wednesday, he went to Barna, where Mary lived, to deliver the pound. He asked his wife to go to Cregduff, where he would meet her later. This wasn't odd; since he came back, Mary said they'd been to her father's house about ten times, often in the evening, but rarely at the same times. Sometimes John went with her, other times he met her there, but he always walked her home.

She didn't see him that morning, but made the dinner early and left it for one of her sons to give to John. She had spent the day washing clothes, and went straight to her father's at about 2 or 3 o'clock. John followed at about 6 pm and they left just before 9 pm. She saw no one, talked to no one and nobody came to the house.

'Nine o'clock, is that usually the hour you leave?' the coroner asked. Mary was vague in her answer. 'I could not say,' she said, 'it would sometimes be 10 o'clock, sometimes eight.'

The next part, however, she remembered very well:

When we were going home there was no one with me but my husband. We went together. He was in front and up a little road leading from my father's house. I am not sure how far we went down the little road. We went as far as the stile on the left hand side of the road. We went into the field there. My husband was first through the gap. We crossed the field to another stile. My husband was still before me. I was not half a yard behind him at the second stile. There are two steps that you have to rise on to get through that stile.

He went up on the first step, and left his other foot on the second step. He was going out then. He did not stir his foot at all, and I heard a man

on the other side of the wall say, 'Is that Tom Brown, is that Tom Brown?'
The last words were not out of his mouth when he shot him. He fired
twice into John's face. John made no answer. I am in doubt whether he
had time to answer. I saw no weapon at that time. I did see two flashes. I
did not see the figure of the man at that time. The flashes were very quick
together. I saw two distinct flashes and smoke too. They were very close to
my husband's face. It was at the second flash my husband fell.

At first, when his head hit the ground, she didn't think he had been hit.

I took up his head with my right hand and I placed my left hand under
his head, and the place was full of blood on the minute. The man then
jumped over the wall to the right hand side of the stile. He then caught
me by the right shoulder and he pushed me back from my own husband.
He then put his right hand into a pocket and drew a white paper out of it,
as I thought, but it was a letter. He left it on my husband's bosom loosely.
I was screeching then, and I thought to catch the man.

The murderer turned and went back over the stile – she couldn't recall if he
used the step or leapt over in a single bound. She didn't speak to him, and he
didn't speak any words after the shots, she said.

His coat was very large, she remembered. *Was it long enough to reach his
heels?* She couldn't say. It was trailing on the ground as he went over the wall.
It was black. *Did you see his face?* Yes, though not fully. She couldn't remember
the colour of his hair, but he had a 'great long', black beard, with no side
whiskers and the skin on his face was red. His nose shape was a mystery to her,
too, but it was red. *And his boots?* She didn't get a good look. She remembered
her husband was carrying a little whip, however, which he had set on the wall.
He definitely put his pipe into his pocket before they left her father's – she'd
seen him do it. He had no bottle in his hand, but she had a little tin in her
hand at the time of the shooting. After the man jumped the wall, she didn't
see him again.

The coroner seemed to sense Mary's testimony veering from the description
of the criminal. *Do you swear on your oath that you do not know who that man*

is? 'I do. I think if I saw him again I would know him. I never saw him before; he was a very big man. When I tried to catch him, he was very high and very heavy.' He hadn't hurt her when he grabbed her, she said, adding that he 'spoke very smart; it was not like the voice of the neighbours'.

Mary said she had been screaming when the man fled. She tried to pick John up, but couldn't move him; she ran, 'screeching' all the while, back to her father's house, and 'bruised the door in' with her fists. Tom Small, Mary's brother, answered the door, and she told him John was dead; he accompanied her, with his daughter, Mary Small. Guided by a lantern, they found the body, and between Mrs Moylan and Tom, they could not lift him. Tom sent Mary Small to round up some neighbours to help carry John back to the house. John, she said, was still somehow alive when they lifted him, despite the blood loss and devastating damage to his face.

From the time they left the house to the time they brought John back was about 15 minutes, and he died another 15 minutes after that. 'The last words I spoke to him,' the widow recalled, 'was to ask him what time he came home from Barna. At the last stile he said: "Stop and I will bring you over."'

The story then turned to the letter. Mary had told Tom of the piece of paper as they hurried to the second stile. 'It is not a piece of paper, but a letter,' he said when they found it again, holding the lantern nearer Mary's hand as she plucked it from her husband's breast. 'Mind that now.' She handed the letter to Catherine Small, Tom's wife. Mary, Mrs Moylan's niece, read the outside of the letter, seeing it was addressed to 'Tom Brown, Cregduff'. The letter – saturated in blood, as was seen when it was produced at the inquest – was later given to the priest, who didn't open it, but gave it to the sergeant, who was the first person to read its contents.

The note was written in 'fair' handwriting, which the reporter said did not look to be disguised: 'Notice to you, Thomas Browne – I heard about your work at Creggduff, so don't put me to any trouble any more. I don't like to disgrace your friends. Don't put me to any more trouble for you ought to give up before I give you the double-barrel gun.' At the top of the letter, which was scrawled in pencil on a half sheet of notepaper, was a little drawing of a gun.

You had no quarrel with your husband? No, she said, of course not. *Do you know of anyone who did?* She knew no reason he should have been murdered. There were no strangers around that night and her husband never found fault with her regarding the management of the farm. John wasn't angry that she suggested selling up and moving the family to America, either.

Next up to address the inquest was Thomas Small, Mary Moylan's brother. His sister, he said, had arrived at the Cregduff house between half three and four o'clock on Wednesday – a bit later than Mary's recollection. John followed between five and six, and they all had tea at about eight that evening. John Moylan's pipe, he said, was passed around, and used by Mary and Mary's father, before being returned to Moylan's waistcoat pocket. The pair then shortly left.

It was about 10 or 12 minutes later that he heard his sister's screams. The sound came before Mary did – as she laid her hand on the latch, she wailed: 'Oh, oh, oh – Oh Tom, my John is killed. Come with me!' She ran back down the lane, and Tom followed.

John was still breathing when they reached him. Long, heavy breaths, his life rattling in his throat, his body covered in blood. The first time he saw the threatening letter, it was in Mary Moylan's hands. She hadn't mentioned it on the way, by his own recollection.

'What is that you have there?' Tom said he asked Mary, who replied that 'It was a paper or letter [he couldn't remember which she said] that I got near him there.'

And what did Mary do with the paper then? Tom had no idea, it was the last he saw of it. Thomas Murphy had heard the ruckus and ran to the scene in the boreen. Between the two of them, they managed to carry in the injured man; Martin Cassidy ran for the priest, but by the time he arrived, John was expired.

'The priest, after looking at the dead body in the kitchen, went into the room, and Mary Moylan followed him with the letter in her hand. She laid it down on the table as there was blood on it, and then she turned up the other side, where the address was and the priest said it was for Tom Browne of Cregduff.'

The priest told Tom to go for the sergeant, and he did so, bringing the letter with him. And that was that; he was as shocked as his sister – there was no reason on earth why Moylan should be shot.

'I don't believe you,' the coroner said, plainly.

On that rebuke, Tom conceded that he was certainly aware that John complained about the rent not being paid, despite him sending £103 back. But it wasn't that bad; he didn't complain about anything else, Tom insisted, softening a moment later. Perhaps he had heard of one thing. John had recently ejected his neighbour Michael Downey's only sister, Bridget, out of the house. He had given no reason for throwing her out, as far as he knew. Tom finished his evidence by saying he hadn't seen anything that night or heard the shot – the scene was 140 yards away, and the night was dark. Mary Moylan had never mentioned what the man looked like to him.

The coroner, dissatisfied now with Mary's omissions, called her back. She didn't change her story – she absolutely told Tom about the letter on the way to the scene of her husband's murder. *And about your husband putting Bridget Downey out of the house?* She flatly denied it as rumour. Then, shortly after, she admitted it was true.

'He took her [Bridget] by the arm and walked her out and told her not to come back again. I asked him what he did it for and he would not tell me,' Mary told the inquest. She pressed him on it several times, and after about a week, he told her: 'Never mind that. If I told it to you maybe you would stir yourself with her.' The incident had occurred about a week previous, but Michael Downey had continued to call to the house after that, every day, and sometimes twice a day.

One last time, Mary refuted reports, echoed in her brother's statement to the coroner, of ill feeling with her husband over the rent allegedly not being paid. John never complained about it; she had paid £9 10s while he was away.

The jury were then given the post-mortem analysis, and came to the appropriate conclusion, the entire inquest having taken about six hours, according to one report. What weren't settled, however, were any strong motives for the murder; instead, more confusion arose over the testimony of the widow. Why was she being reticent about the story concerning the girl, Bridget Downey? If she screeched the whole way home, why didn't anyone from the neighbouring houses hear her? Why had she insisted she told her brother of the note, when he didn't recall seeing it until she held it in her hand at her husband's dying body? And why, if all accounts were to be believed, did it take her 10 or 12 minutes to get back to her father's house and raise the alarm, when the entire round trip should take less than two minutes?

7

A BLOODY PUZZLE

In 1883, the constabulary office was busy, though not quite as inundated as it had been. A patch of relative prosperity in the agricultural economy, followed by successive poor harvests in the late 1870s, saw tillage farmers and labourers impoverished and in severe debt, both to landlords and shopkeepers. Evictions and counter-movements followed. The Land War of 1879–82 saw a spike in agrarian violence in rural communities; in a province gripped by unrest, John Moylan's murder, though shocking to its close community, was only one piece of a bloody puzzle.

The constabulary office recorded each 'outrage' for the region for each year. At that time, violent crimes often had to do with squabbles over land or, in many cases, drink. Each branch of the constabulary would send a short summary of any outrage, along with a line of motive, to the head office. At the end of the year, an overall report was produced, with a brief run-through of each incident. Its pages are a tapestry of reckless, often vengeful, violence.

The short description of John's murder – an eight-line, one-paragraph entry in the 1883 report – is nestled between two other deaths that happened in the county around that time. The first involved a card game gone wrong in a Gort pub, during which a man named Joseph Geraghty received a knee to the abdomen that killed him three days later. The second was the result of another pub brawl, in which Michael Mulvey, a 50-year-old publican, died from 'softening of the brain' after trying to stop a man named Charles Tully from beating his female companion. For his troubles Mulvey had a large stone thrown at his head with such force as to lacerate it deeply and eventually cause his death, on Christmas Eve.

Drink-fuelled outrages were a common sight in that year's report, as they were most years. But these grim bulletins make it clear that death was common and life was cheaper than land. In Leitrim in January, for instance, a man named John Sheridan was struck on the side of his head with a heavy stick as he walked a dark road with two other men, on the way home from the Ballinamore fair. A man named Thomas McCartan had swung the object, and the motive was a common one. 'The deceased was suspected of having written notices with the intention of boycotting McCartan, for having taken the grazing of a farm from which the former tenant was evicted.' McCartan and his brother-in-law, who was also present, pleaded guilty, and got just three months with hard labour.

In Westmeath in October, a landowner and RIC sergeant named Patrick Crowley was murdered on the day of his wedding as he walked with his bride in front of the house they were staying in. A man named John Eighan had approached the pair and thrust a knife into the man's abdomen; Sgt Crowley had recently evicted Eighan from a residence at Rochfort Bridge.

In the same month, a little over eight weeks before the night Mary Moylan reported her husband's death, a gang of 60 men and boys converged on a 62-year-old farmer named James Spence and beat him to death, the fatal blow apparently coming from the strike of a large stick, which fractured his skull. Spence's crime had been to graze cattle on a field he had rented in Co. Cork from a woman named Kate Murphy. Kate's brother John, who owned the farm the field was contained in, evidently disapproved of Spence's cattle, and had impounded them when he found out. The next day, Spence had discovered a mob driving the cattle off the land – when they spotted Spence, they attacked, causing 'injuries which caused almost immediate death'.

The agrarian 'outrages' weren't all crimes of vengeance, built upon broken deals and tenant disagreements. To qualify as agrarian, an outrage had to concern land. In Mayo in April, a 45-year-old farmer named John Prendergast was attacked by two farmers, and killed, simply for walking through their field.

The crimes listed didn't always result in death. In Cork, in February, a postmaster at Ballydehob was clearing the letterbox when he found an oddly shaped parcel. When he opened it, he found a stick of dynamite, a detonator and a length of fuse, arranged in such a way that his stamping of the package would have set it off. 'A man named Richard Hodnett, senior, was committed to gaol on the day before the parcel of dynamite was found in the letter box, for having made an inflammatory speech against landlordism at a meeting of the Irish National League. It is believed the outrage was committed by his son, Richard Hodnett, junior, in retaliation for the imprisonment of his father.'

'Firing into dwellings,' the 19th-century, rural version of a drive-by, had also become popular towards the end of the 19th century, especially for crimes of retaliation. Though it wasn't an agrarian crime, just nine days before John's murder in Co. Clare, a younger farmer named Patrick Kelly had been shot through the nostril as he sat by the fire with his mother and a servant boy. Three bullets came through the window, with another hitting a wall and the third entering Kelly's heart. Police couldn't completely narrow down the suspect list, but it emerged Kelly had embarked on a two-year campaign of love affairs with quite a number of married and single women in the district, including the seduction and impregnation of two young girls. The families, the police surmised, weren't happy with him.

The list goes on. At that time in the records, the constabulary office went to the trouble of including a special category for agrarian crimes. Not all were murder; they ranged from homicide and firing at a person at the top end, to

Agrarian outrages, total, by year

Year	Agrarian outrages (total)
1874	213
1875	136
1876	212
1877	236
1878	301
1879	863
1880	2,585
1881	4,439
1882	3,433
1883	870

appearing armed, illegal shearing of sheep and perjury at the other. In 1883, there were more than 35 crime categories listed.

Overall, 870 agrarian outrages were reported to the constabulary offices, which was actually a remarkable drop off from 1882's 3,433 and a peak of 4,439 in 1881. One each of murder and manslaughter was reported, down from 26 and 1, respectively, in 1882.

Mary's account of events was the version that first reached the public and started the police investigation. With a tight turnaround and no solid motive to go by, it isn't surprising which angle newspapers in the following days decided to go with when reporting the Clonboo murder. The pro-forma agrarian tragedy stories began to roll out, filled with 'shocked' and 'stirred' quiet communities, and speculation based on the holdings of the deceased.

'AGRARIAN MURDER NEAR GALWAY' was the capped-up headline in the *Irish Times*, which reported that

> The citizens of Galway were startled this morning when the news came that a farmer was shot within five miles of the borough late last night. At first, the meagre tidings came that a man was shot at Clonboo, and it was not till the wife of the unfortunate man ran into Galway in a state of frenzy that the few simple facts connected with the crime were learned.

Information was thin on the ground, with different reports naming John Moylan as 'Pat' and 'Thomas'. The exact mechanism of how he was shot, how many shots were fired and even how exactly the perpetrator escaped were points of contention; some said the man 'walked leisurely away' while others said he jumped over a hedge.

And while 'agrarian' was the first port of call for the papers, the first report in the *Belfast Newsletter* best signifies the bet-hedging that went on in those early days. It begins by saying the crime was said to be agrarian, committed in consequence of Moylan taking a vacant farm. It goes on to say that the shooting at Annaghdown, according to another correspondent, was a case of mistaken identity. It finishes by returning to a quote from its Dublin correspondent: 'The crime is agrarian, as the unfortunate man had recently taken a farm from which another had been evicted.' Other papers pondered on a possible nationalist motive, while others took a punt on a non-specified feud. At least one thing was unanimous: 'On every hand in the city of Galway, horror is expressed at the shocking assassination.'

8

HUNTING A GALWAY MURDERER

Police arriving to the scene on the night of the murder and early the next morning were none the wiser. The main men involved in the case, besides Stephens and local sergeant Dalton, were District Inspector Lennon, District Inspector Cary and County Inspector Murphy. Philip T. Lyster, Resident Magistrate, was also heavily involved.

Cary and Stephens were the first to reach Clonboo. The area was dark, and the community tightly knit; little was to be gleaned from a quick look. However, a couple of things stood out.

People had gathered at the scene once the alarm was raised and many still lingered when the police arrived. Despite early reports, the official facts of the case detailed said it was Mary who alerted the people in her father's house to the tragedy – although the scene of the crime was in shouting distance. Minutes after the murder, the body had been carried to Mary's father's house, where the inquest was held.

John's injuries were devastating. Bloodier reports gleefully detailed a mishmash of wounds – including a shot discharged in the forehead and another in the chest. One shot and slug had entered his face and lodged in his lower jaw – his nose, which seemed to take the impact of the gun, was missing. This didn't tally with Mary's account, who insisted there had been two barrels and two shots, but perhaps the attacker missed. More likely, her mind blurred the details amid her 'frenzied state'.

Stephens and Cary scoured the scene with the help of a group of constables. The ground was bloodied and damp, and the darkness didn't help.

The assailant, it appeared, had actually been lying in wait behind a stile when John and Mary approached. He emerged when John stepped up to climb over it, hence how he fell backwards towards Mary. The ground was still disturbed where John collapsed, and a clay pipe lay shattered, near where his head fell.

A couple of hundred yards from the crime scene was a newly built police hut. Interviews with the constables stationed there revealed they hadn't heard any shots, or a commotion afterwards. Mary, on this point, said she had been terrified of the gunman, and in fact he had spoken some words to her. 'He told me he'd blow my brains out if I let the peelers hear me shouting,' she explained. It tallied with her story in one way; she seemed terrified and shaken, and openly worried about what she and her five children would now do to get by. But surely the voice of her husband's attacker gave her a clue as to whom it may have been? Despite the extra detail, she still couldn't say she recognised any aspect of the man.

In the wake of the shots being fired, locals had assembled around the body before Mary made off for Galway. When they gathered to lift John, Mary had spotted the letter, dropped by the assailant onto the man's breast. She held it aloft, and handed it to Catherine Small, one of the neighbours in the crowd; she asked her to keep it safe. It was folded a number of times, and covered with dirt and some blood. For police, this was as good a lead as they could have asked for.

The remoteness of the scene struck investigators. It was, in one way, an ideal place for an ambush, with plenty of nearby hedgerows and little hideaways. Reporters on the scene branded the entire area 'a barren patch of mountainside', which probably didn't do justice to the effort needed to search the scene. But the boreen which led between Cregduff and Clonboo was off the beaten track. Its existence and the minutiae of its terrain – namely the stile behind which the murderer knew to hide, despite the pitch darkness – was known only to a handful of locals. It narrowed the search, but lips in the area seemed tightly sealed; as police would find out, Clonboo had an engine that ran on rumours.

The night was getting on, and they needed to arrest some people for questioning. The first arrests were made within a short time of the murder, early enough to be reported in the first dispatches. Police, throughout the entire investigation, were reticent with the press, but early details of the detainees can be garnered from patchy reports in the following days. It was a Sergeant Horan who pulled up the first two: a man named Gannon and a man named Scott. Little is recorded about these arrests; neither made it as far as being lodged into the prison records. Their main red flag seemed to have been a suspicion based on their movements; the first was from the area of Clonboo and had been recently in England, while the second was an Englishman himself. The two were collared on their way from Headford, travelling to Liverpool.

Annaghdown, like many rural parishes, had its own Fenian presence. Armed gangs, in those years, targeted landlords, and in other cases farmers and tenants. Consequently, shootings and intimidation, followed by a small exodus of certain young men to England for a period, were not unheard of. Certainly, two men travelling by night to Liverpool in the hours following the murder of a farmer was enough to raise suspicions of police. Both said they knew nothing of the killing.

Police then quickly set about finding Moylan's enemies. To that end, two other arrests were made. One was a built-in lead: Thomas Browne, of Cregduff, who had been identified in the note. Inquiries quickly revealed that Tom Browne had indeed been caught up in a row of sorts with men in the area in recent times, over land. He was quickly picked up by Cary's men. Another character police became keen to speak to was Michael Downey, a young man of about twenty-four who, it was known to the locals – and even some of the more embedded sergeants – was not on the best of terms with John Moylan. He lived close to the boreen, too, and his own property was immediately adjacent to the Moylans'. It was shortly after 2 am when they arrested Downey, who was woken from his sleep and taken away. In his bedroom, steeping in a bucket of water, police discovered a pair of corduroy trousers, which they took.

The above four men were arrested, each pleading their ignorance of the deed and offering alibis. It was early days and nobody was charged, but all were brought before a magistrate and remanded. The first two were quickly set free, and many others were unofficially questioned in those first hours, including John Browne, one of the main characters with whom Tom had apparently been disputing. There were many Browne families strewn across

Annaghdown, as will become clear. In the case of the land dispute which police had the complicated task of unravelling, John Browne had not been on speaking terms with Tom Browne; the two appear to have been of no direct relation – or at least not close enough to merit mention in official reports. The word in the townland was Tom Browne had been seeking to acquire James Browne's land, and James's son, William, had not taken kindly to Tom's greed. Willie was a good friend, though no apparent close relation, of John Browne, who joined him in collective ire towards farmer Tom. John, in turn, was fast pals with Michael Downey.

Many were quizzed in the first hours of the investigation, but it was Tom Browne and Michael Downey who were conveyed to Galway Gaol. Despite being arrested on the Thursday morning, they technically weren't lodged into the gaol until early on Friday morning, delaying the beginning of their week remand period by one day.

On 21 December 1883, prisoners 932 and 933 were booked into the city jail. The men had similar features; Downey was 25, as listed on the prison registers, though his age at the time of arrest was actually 24, according to later documents. He was about 5 foot 4 with dark hair, a fresh complexion and grey eyes. Browne, about ten years Downey's senior, was 5 foot 6 with black hair and blue eyes. Both men were Catholic; Downey was an uneducated labourer, while Browne was listed as a farmer, who could read and write. That night, they had one important thing in common on the register books; they were remanded, due to 'being concerned in murder'.

Police soon discovered how tight-lipped a small community could be. As teams of men searched the fields for a weapon, police had to admit the arrests they had made, to which they 'attached great importance', had stemmed from rumour.

In Clonboo and nearby Cregduff, Fenianism, or rather a whisper of it, and the possibility of getting embroiled in an unnecessary feud, meant young men in the vicinity were reluctant to come forward. Speaking to the 'peelers', even the well-known ones, became a no-go after a day or so of questioning.

Doors were shut, farmers away in Galway for the day. Even the priests would eventually warn parishioners about cooperating, when no murderer had been definitively located.

To that end, in the first days of the investigation, police had already apparently resorted to oiling palms. William Reed, another figure closely attached to the case, wrote to Assistant Under Secretary Jenkinson in Dublin Castle on 23 December, seeking a cash float for County Inspector Murphy and his men as the well ran dry:

I entirely recommend that £100 be sent to County Inspector H.C. Murphy to aid with the constabulary in procuring information with ease of the murder of John Moylan. I believe a good deal of information will be obtained by the expenditure of a little money. I trust this amount will be paid as soon as possible as it is now needed.

A draft from Bank of Ireland was received, with thanks, from County Inspector Murphy some days later.

Fortunately, gossip is where the local sergeants thrived – they seemed to have great knowledge of the locals themselves, before a door was ever knocked. In the case files, County Inspector Murphy once noted that he wasn't sure where all the information he received was coming from, informants, or the local constables themselves.

Tom Browne, a 35-year-old farmer in Cregduff, was a neighbour of Mary's father. He would have known the family well, and was known to have been seeking extra land to buy. This, according to the neighbours, brought with it predictable animosity among local farmers. The obvious question about Tom Browne's guilt was that he was named in the letter, which did lead to the possibility of a case of mistaken identity. It was dark, after all, and misty on the night Moylan was shot. The assassin, according to Mary, had tried to ensure that it was Tom Browne – twice – before firing a bullet.

But police had to consider the fact that the note's contents might not be genuine. After all, if Tom Browne was seeking more land, surely he stood to gain from the nearby Moylan's farm becoming vacant. That, and Tom Browne was one of the few men brought in who could read and write.

On the other hand, Downey's supposed motive wasn't strictly agrarian.

Mary Moylan, in her husband's absence, was unable to tend to the farm. Downey was well-known to the family, and hadn't been in trouble before. On the contrary, he insisted he had known John well his entire life and wouldn't dream of doing anything to hurt the family. A labourer by trade, Downey had been employed by Mrs Moylan in John's absence, helping her to keep the small farm ticking over. Certainly, those in Downey's position traditionally had ill will against farmers following an uptick in prosperity in the late 1870s, during which not all boats rose, and the prospect that he himself eyed the land adjoining his was reasonable. But if the neighbours' whispers had any truth to them, Downey may have been providing more than manual labour to Mrs Moylan.

Nothing could be proven from hearsay, though the odd relationship between Mary Moylan and Michael Downey was the worst-kept secret in Clonboo. One spanner remained in the works, however; as evidenced by the crooked 'X' with which he signed any surviving documents, Downey could not write. This ruled him out as the scribe of the threatening letter, but either way, with little to go on and a new motive – not to mention the recently washed trousers – he was brought in.

Events moved quickly on the Saturday and Sunday. After intense questioning, Tom Browne's involvement appeared less and less likely. Despite his clear involvement in a land dispute, the police had a number of doubts. Browne had no history of animosity with the dead man, as far as police could tell. Mistaken identity seemed unlikely; the two men were quite different physically, with the inspector noting their divergent dress habits in particular. Increasingly, it began to seem his only crime on the night was to be named in the letter; such notices were a common sight for police as one of the few non-physical forms of intimidation used in land disputes. With no evidence to keep him and nothing further to be learned, Tom Browne was released without charge a day after being lodged in Galway Gaol.

Neighbours were reticent when it came to the crime and disputes in the area, but seemingly willing to impart information on the supposed infidelities of Mary Moylan; police were told that on at least two occasions during John's absence in America, Downey was known to have spent the night in Mary's house. A labourer staying in his employer's residence – though usually in an out-building – was not shocking on its own, but when the labourer in question lived literally yards away, it was enough to raise eyebrows in a townland of six or seven houses.

It was enough, too, to thoroughly annoy John Moylan. Understandably. Already having to deal with the fact that the huge amount of money he'd sent back from America was squandered and misspent by his wife, he also had unwelcome gossip to attend to. On his return from America, he was greeted by words of welcome from his family and neighbours, but also of stories of young Downey spending more time than was necessary at their farm. Whispers of carryings-on at the Moylan house seemed to follow him throughout the townland, to the point where he and Mary fought constantly. Police received evidence from one of Moylan's sons that this came to a head about one week before John Moylan was killed, when he came home to discover Downey in the house. Loudly, and in front of his children, he banned the young labourer from the house forcefully, telling him in no uncertain terms that he didn't want to see 'his kind' around his house again.

Downey himself hadn't said much in custody, other than that the trousers discovered in the bucket of water were being washed by his sister, Bridget, ahead of the Christmas period, and that he was at a neighbour's house on the night of the murder – though that only accounted for his time from about 10 pm. More importantly to police, some questions hung darkly over Mary's recollection of the murder.

The widow's statement, on closer scrutiny, was shaky in parts. She had insisted the gun produced by the man in the shadows was double-barrelled, and that two shots were fired, but all official documentation of the injuries said John Moylan died by a single shot. She also stood firm on her position that she couldn't possibly have known the shooter, despite him having talked to her a number of times throughout the assassination. There wasn't a huge pool of possible suspects – surely she had an idea. It was Mary, too, who had alerted those gathered around her dying husband to the presence of the letter, as though she wanted it to be found.

Then there was the clay pipe – a detail quite small in the grand scheme of things, but yet another inconsistency with the truth. Mary had insisted her husband's pipe was not lit when the murderer approached the couple in the dark, but police at the scene noted that John's clay pipe had been found, disintegrated in the impact of the shot, beside the space where his head had been. Was it an effort to reinforce the idea of darkness at the scene, and thus her inability to recall any details of the murderer, or the genuine effect of trauma on the memory? Either way, police considered the information they had quite enough to arrest Mary on the Sunday following the murder.

District Inspector Cary sent a case report to Dublin Castle on 23 December:

I have to report that on this day Mary Moylan widow of the murdered man was arrested on suspicion and lodged in Galway Gaol. I am making minute and careful inquiry from the information I have received from the people of the neighbourhood. I am of the opinion that Moylan was murdered at the instigation of his wife by Michael Downey, now in custody.

Downey was very intimate with Mrs Moylan during her husband's absence in America and was very often in her company. Moylan expressed himself as being very displeased with her conduct and the way the neighbours looked at it. Tom Browne, the other man arrested, was discharged last night, there being no evidence against him. As Tom Browne had some dispute about a farm with a man named James Browne, I believe that Moylan was not shot in mistake for Tom Browne but that the notice placed (as Mrs Moylan states) on her husband's body was put there to induce that belief and lead the police astray.

Tom Browne wears an entirely different dress to that usually worn by Moylan. The gun with which the murder was committed has not yet been found, though a rigorous search is being carried out for it.

The report finished by recounting the inquest verdict that Moylan had been shot, but by whom they did not know. At this point (though you wouldn't have known it from the media reports), the inspector and his men had all but ruled out the idea that the note found on John Moylan's body was a true indication of anything other than a ploy to distract the constabulary.

The arrest of Mary was an important step in building something resembling a case. The agrarian theme and greed for land were somewhat tied in with the alleged criminal intimacy between the two; with John out of the way and an opportunity to wed Mary, Michael Downey stood to greatly improve his lot in a very short space of time. The press, owing mainly to the circumstantial nature of the evidence, were only given snippets. The fact that Mary was even arrested didn't hit papers until the 26th, three days later.

Mary was booked into Galway Gaol the same day as the above police report, 23 December. She became prisoner number 936, and her prison records give us a picture of a 35-year-old 'farmer's widow', who stood at 5 feet and 2.5 inches, had brown hair to match her eyes and a pale complexion. As it was with the only other person in custody for her husband's murder, in the column for education, 'nil' is written in black ink.

At close of business on Sunday, it seemed police were forming a strong idea of what they felt happened. But all they had were rumours of an affair, a threatening letter and two suspects, neither of whom could have actually read the foreboding notice, let alone written it.

9

A LUCKY BREAK

C hristmas came early for the constabulary in 1883. One day early.

At first light on a chilly Christmas Eve morning, 50 policemen gathered on the fields at the crime scene at Clonboo and began to comb, as they had done relentlessly, through the overgrowth. It was the fourth day of the Clonboo murder investigation, and while a strong case for a motive was being built, quietly, by investigators, it was time to bring home some hard evidence. On the same morning, some headway in that respect was being made; an analyst in Dublin was receiving his first consignment of materials for testing. The corduroys, a vial of muddied water from the bucket and the wadding used in the shot that killed Moylan had all been signed off, though by a person unbeknownst to Inspector Murphy, and sent to the doctors. A constable named Coffey had carried the package, and the results would be highly anticipated.

As for the search back west, a 'needle in a haystack' didn't cover it; hedges, long grass, walls of ivy and any amount of bushes, shrubs, rocks and trees could easily cover the gun that killed John Moylan – especially if hidden by one who knew the terrain better than the visiting peelers. And that's assuming the perpetrator was Michael Downey. That's also assuming he didn't take off immediately to Galway city to sell the gun, or throw it into one of the other innumerable hiding spots in between.

It was about 4 pm when the discovery was made. A constable approached a wall to the side of a field, about half a mile from the murder scene and between 200 and 250 yards from Michael Downey's front door. Reaching up to the top of the wall, he grasped a gun: single-barrelled, fully cocked and displaying suspect stains along the barrel. Inspector Cary, in his report, noted that the weapon 'had the appearance, when I carefully examined it, of having been recently discharged'. The wall of ivy was picked apart, and police discovered some other items of interest: a pair of top boots, apparently American-made, and two stockings, one stuffed into each of the boots.

Police had interviewed another Clonboo man named Denis Hynes, who had said he had dealings with Downey regarding the purchase of a gun a number of months beforehand. They knocked the door of the public house run by Hynes on Christmas Eve, not long after the discovery. The helpful acquaintance of Downey's quickly identified the gun as belonging to the accused labourer, remarking that he remembered the gun well, because the last time he saw it, the screw of the hammer had been lost and replaced by a wooden one.

Inspector Cary also had an unlikely aid in linking the stockings to Downey: his 10-year-old brother, John. They were shown to the boy, who quickly took them in his hands – on two separate occasions – openly telling the police that he remembered the stockings well; they belonged to his brother, Michael. The boots, too, were confirmed by his siblings as having belonged to Michael, according to at least one report, while another went further, and said they had been a present for the young man from John Moylan – perhaps a sign of appreciation for the hard work he had put in on his farm in his absence, no doubt relayed to him by Mary. While at Downey's house, police told reporters, they checked the place under the floorboards where witnesses in the know had told them Downey often kept his gun. They found the hatch empty.

On Christmas Day, a constable named James D'Arcy got his orders. He was to proceed on the first possible train on St Stephen's Day to Athlone, then Dublin, pending approval from Dublin, carrying with him the gun discovered in the bush. His first destination was the laboratory of Dr Cameron, the City Analyst. It was recommended, then, that the gun be taken to a gunsmith to confirm the inspector's hunch about the weapon's recent use. As it happened, Dr Cameron was sick during late December. The forensic work in the Clonboo murder case went the way of Dr Edwin Lapper, at 36 Highfield Road, Rathgar.

While Downey and Moylan were still remanded in Galway Gaol under questioning, Murphy wasted little time in putting the plan in motion to firm up the physical evidence. He wrote the following order to the undersecretary on Christmas Day:

> There are spots on the barrel which bear greatly the appearance of blood, and I think it be well they should be submitted to analysis. It would also, I think, be well to produce the gun to some eminent gun maker to have it examined so as to have the evidence of an expert as to how recently it was probably discharged. If you decide on having it examined the man ought to explain to the gun smith the circumstances under which it was found – in the open air, &c.

Constable D'Arcy spent about a day in Dublin, keeping a close eye on the merchandise and awaiting his sanction from Dublin Castle. Carrying his precious parcel, he had already incurred an unexpected delay when he arrived to the capital; as the illness and unavailability of Dr Cameron became clear, arrangements were made to have Dr Lapper stand in. But, it being so soon after Christmas, D'Arcy had to adapt the plan a bit. First stop: Dawson Street; Rathgar could wait.

It was the morning of 27 December when D'Arcy first put the gun into the hands of an expert. The delayed policeman walked up Dawson Street, past Morrison's Hotel and the offices of Firmin & Sons, a button and military ornament manufacturers, past a clothiers' establishment, and two solicitors, finally arriving to No 9, the premises of Trulock & Harriss Gun & Rifle Manufacturers. The first man he met was one of the store's namesakes: John Harriss. On opening the parcel, Harriss discovered a badly worn, single-shot gun, with its ramrod jammed into the barrel – certainly the mechanical Frankenstein recalled by Denis Hynes and absolutely showing signs of its recent stint of exposure – dutifully relayed to him by the waiting constable. Beyond its general wear and tear, Harriss could see one thing quite clearly: it had recently been fired.

The following memo soon arrived to Dublin Castle, addressed to Jenkinson and handwritten on 'Trulock & Harriss' headed paper:

Sir,

I reply to your second letter just received I have to state that in my opinion the gun in question appears to have been recently discharged, judging by the appearance of the breech and the mag.

I am, Sir, Your obedient servant,
John Harriss

In his full report, attached to the above letter in the case file, Harriss details the damage he found to the gun. 'I found a broken ramrod and took out the breech and found the remaining portion of the ramrod in the barrel and attached to it was a piece of rag, which I think was put in evidently for the purpose of cleaning,' he wrote on the same day of the examination. His theory was that in an attempt to remove dirt and gunpowder from the barrel, the owner of the gun had evidently jammed a piece of rag down the barrel with the ramrod; the long, thin probe had then slipped through the rag and wedged the entire lot in tightly. In an attempt to pull it back out, the rod had broken, and there it had stayed.

A report from Dr Lapper on 31 December confirmed what police had already suspected. The stains upon the barrel, stock and ramrod were blood – mammalian.

※

All week, the vultures had circled a carcass they knew was plentiful. Eventually, police decided to throw them a string of gristle, letting a little more information out to the curious media. Correspondents from all over the country had been arriving since the night of the murder, and it was becoming harder to give them answers without jeopardising what was, so far, a fragile case. At the same time, it couldn't be denied that police were looking to pin this on Michael Downey and, as of Sunday the 23rd, Mary.

They found the farmer's widow to be a tough nut to crack. Their theory, that she had something to do with her husband's murder, presumably to get him out of the way to allow Downey and herself the full run of the land, demanded that she be cunning. Too cunning, perhaps, to willingly plunge herself into the middle of the case by overly cooperating with police. This was part of the reason the police decided to arrest Mary – a little time in Galway Gaol, they surmised, wouldn't do their search for information any harm. Throughout the week she strenuously denied any improper involvement with her younger neighbour. It's unsurprising, perhaps, the angle and hint of salacious detail delivered to the media at the end of the week, one day before she was due to appear before the magistrate alongside Downey.

The hearing was scheduled for Saturday morning.

Thirsty following a familiar drought from constables, the *Freeman's Journal* took all they could when Inspectors Cary and Murphy finally threw them a bone. On 28 December, under the headline 'The Late Murder in Galway', the paper's reporter managed to do three things in his report: 1) assure the public that the police were working hard and had their man, 2) avoid divulging any details over the hard evidence and 3) leave no doubt over the salacious goings-on in the house of Mary Moylan and, subsequently, what kind of character she was. 'All that has come to light points in the one direction,' read the report, 'but at the same time it is to be remembered that the evidence obtained up to the present is altogether circumstantial.'

The inspectors had been kind to the reporter; the American boots, the socks and even the finding of the gun were relayed in the story. The report mentions Mary's recollection of there being two shots, but delivers a fatal blow to her credibility: 'The woman's evidence, however, was of such an extraordinary character that a discrepancy of this sort seems only to afford to the police further confirmation of her complicity in the murder.' The clay pipe, too, got a mention. 'It was proved that Moylan had put his pipe into his pocket before leaving his father-in-law's house; no pipe was found in any of his pockets after death, and Mrs Moylan was very positive in her statement that her husband did not resume smoking after he left her father's house…'

The tone in all articles regarding Mrs Moylan, from that point on, was unmissable. Insinuations of 'criminal intimacy' and 'spending a lot of time' with the accused man were weighed heavily against the portrayal of John Moylan, a man who had left the west of Ireland and sent back a small fortune for the upkeep of his farm. Police relayed these feelings to Mrs Moylan. It becomes clear from reading the police reports that they made sure to let her know just what rumours were being spread about her.

Mrs Moylan, the time for telling the truth is now. You could leave here, you wouldn't have to stay in a cell any longer. You were seen with him on the day, we know you were. You weren't washing clothes, you left your house to see him. Your concern shouldn't be of your neighbour's thoughts; they already know the story of your nights spent with him. It was from your neighbours we obtained the information. Think of your boys.

Mary was feeling the pressure. Certainly, the conditions of Galway Gaol in the late 19th century would have been a far cry from the comfort she was used to.

The Crown looks favourably on those who help it seek justice. Set straight the record. Mary, make a statement to clear your name, if you have no guilt.

On Friday, the day before the hearing, Resident Magistrate Reed had arrived in Galway to meet with George Bolton, the Crown Solicitor. On Saturday, the men met with Mr Lyster and district inspectors Lennon and Cary at the gaol, in anticipation of the arrival before them of Mary Moylan and Michael Downey.

Newspaper reports surrounding this hearing were slightly delayed, and some were inaccurate, stating that Tom Browne was still in custody, when in fact he had been released days prior. It isn't surprising that details were slightly scattered in the media; the proceedings were held in private. That shouldn't have mattered too much – at this point, all police were seeking was more time to question the last two people they had in custody. Their theory of infidelity and some concoction of a love triangle was well and good, but key evidence had not yet come back from the analysts; and, as inspector Cary wrote in his notes the following day to Dublin Castle, the writer of the letter had still not been traced.

Opening the hearing, Bolton, the Crown Solicitor, told the magistrates he did not want to go into any evidence, due to the fact the Crown was seeking only a remand. With nothing else to be heard, Lyster moved to end the hearing and grant the remand. Just as the preparations to return the prisoners to their cells began, the widow said she had a statement to make.

It was Michael, she said. Michael Downey, who murdered her husband, John Moylan, in Clonboo, County Galway on the 19th of that month. She couldn't be mistaken – she knew Downey, and had clearly seen his features, heard him speak and remonstrated with him when he put his hands on her, casting her aside as he moved to take the fatal shot. She didn't try to jump over the body in an effort to save John, she said, for fear of her life.

Her entire testimony until now, including the detailed story featuring the red-faced, long-bearded man, had been a thinly veiled ruse to shield him – but not for any nefarious reason arising from improper relations, she insisted. Michael was a criminal and she was terrified; had she told the truth about what happened to her beloved husband, her five children would have been without two parents, rather than just their father. On the night, she said Downey had sworn that an accomplice of his would kill her if she told the police.

Reed did not believe her entirely. Scribbled in brackets in the margin of his report, for the benefit of the undersecretary, are the thought of the police on the existence of the mystery comrade: 'We consider Downey committed the murder unaided by a second man.'

But there was more. Michael Downey, she said, had been a leading member of a secret society which she said was active in the locality two years beforehand. It was this, above all, that made her afraid to give the evidence which she now solemnly swore was true. Michael's involvement in an agrarian secret society would not have been a wild accusation; such groups had a long history in Galway, stretching back to the Houghers in the early 1700s. Certainly, a labourer such as Downey would have been a prime candidate.

Mary was released from custody and signed over as a witness for the Crown. The official deposition was then taken in front of Michael Downey, who no doubt wore the fretful expression often credited to him by newspaper reporters throughout his hearings. As was the custom at such events, he was given an opportunity to cross-examine her; an opportunity, perhaps, which he should have been more cautious to grab. 'He cross examined her upon some points of the deposition,' wrote Reed in his report, 'and when doing so made some admissions confirmatory of the evidence and very damaging to himself.' Downey, caught off guard, challenged Mary openly about her insistence that nothing romantic had transpired between the pair.

'Was there anything between you and me, that I would go to shoot your husband?' Downey asked. To which Mary replied: 'I don't think there was.' 'Mary,' said Downey, 'I'll put you from swearing, I'll tell what sort of woman you are.'

Downey admitted, under oath, to owning two unlicensed firearms, a gun and a revolver, 'and even stated that he broke the ramrod of his gun and left a portion of the rod in the barrel trying to clean it' – though he insisted he was not in charge of it on the night of the murder and that he did not commit the crime.

The mystery of the broken ramrod was beginning to clear itself up. As for the revolver, he told them where they could find it – such was his innocence of the crime, he said, he had nothing to hide from the police having possession of either gun. Downey, in his haste, also admitted to owning a mask – this wasn't reported in newspapers, but the magistrate says that the widow had first cited a possible disguise over the perpetrator's face as the reason for her inability to see his features above his nose. In any case, Downey said in cross-examination, he had given the mask away. He was further remanded until 5 January 1884, and the hearing wound up just before midnight.

The magistrate concluded his report to Dublin Castle by outlining his plans for bringing the case home, namely, a couple of days touring the houses and boreens of Clonboo and doing what investigators had done so well: knocking on doors. More witnesses were to be collected – anyone, he said, with a tangential connection to Downey and the murdered man. This time out, the writer of the threatening letter was being sought, and for that, the police needed samples of writing for comparison. As many as they could get.

Reed couldn't hide his satisfaction. Playing hardball with Mary Moylan had worked perfectly: 'The arrest of Mary Moylan has answered the purpose I intended – she would never have told the truth had she not been imprisoned. She was made aware we had proof of her criminal intimacy with Michael

Downey – that also had an excellent effect in (pressing) her to tell the truth.'

The neighbours' rumours and the time spent extracting gossip from hushed lips had produced a result. However, as had already been picked up by reporters, the woman's word and reputation were hard to rely on by the time she solemnly swore she remembered the killer's face. She had consistently told lies from the moment of the killing – why should now be any different? By the end of December, police had already interviewed dozens of people in Clonboo, with at least one source saying Mary was spotted at a local well with Downey on the morning of the murder. The widow, on the other hand, apparently didn't change her testimony regarding any secret meetings with Downey.

On the morning of 30 December, as Cary sent his usual update to Dublin, County Inspector Murphy, Mr Lyster, Mr Bolton and District Inspector Lennon arrived to Galway Gaol, apparently to tie some loose ends. Downey was only on remand, and there was still a case to finalise. When the men convened in the prison office, a number of prison officials met them with news of their own.

Michael Downey, quiet since being brought back to his cell less than a day beforehand, had broken his silence. He wanted to speak to a policeman. The room was cleared but for Mr Lyster, the magistrate, and Downey was brought before him. 'You are not obliged to say anything,' Lyster customarily cautioned a haggard-looking Michael Downey. 'But whatever you say will be taken down in writing and may be given in evidence against you.' According to Lyster's notes, Downey then launched into his statement.

I had a gun and revolver without licence for any of them, about six weeks after John Moylan came home from America I was three days threshing with him. Himself and his wife were fighting afterwards, on the same evening John Moylan put on his clothes and walked up the road and stand there awhile I was putting on my own clothes. My boreen waistcoat.

'I don't know at all,' said Mrs Moylan to me, 'what I'll do. I'm afraid he'll kill me – asking me every day where did I put all the money he sent me.'

'Don't be fighting, you,' said I to her, 'He sent a great deal of money home to you.'

'The devil have the same man,' said she. 'I'm killed with him.'

About two or three weeks after that, he went to Galway with Tom Small of Cregduff. I was passing up the road and she, Mrs Moylan, calls me into her house. We were talking about everything, but not about her husband, till one of the little boys went out. When he came she got tea ready and when it was ready I stand up and I walk over and caught a little spade. When she was going to draw the tea out I was going. Before that a little while another woman came in, James Harren's wife Mrs Harren.

When I was going to walk out Mrs Moylan caught me and said: 'The devil a bit you will leave this till you take some of the tea.' I was striving to go out and she won't let me go. After that about three or four o'clock in the evening of the same day, I was walking down the road after setting a trap for rabbits up behind that house, she called me in again and said this with me: 'I don't know what will I do with that man, If I can get anyone to kill him in any way I'll pay for it.'

'Stop Mary,' said I. 'Why will you do that with your husband?'

Says she, 'I rather have him killed than be killed myself. If you will do it,' said she, 'I'll pay you very well for it.'

'I don't care,' said I, 'for all the money in Ireland, I won't do that, and don't do it you, either,' said I.

'Do you know,' she said, 'them long boots you have?'

'I do,' says I, 'very well.'

'Give them to me,' says she, 'and the gun and I'll give them back to you again in any place you'll mark for me. We had a pound,' says she, 'before he came home and when he was threshing the oats I stole some of it from him. And I'm striving,' says she, 'to make up two pounds and I'll get a man and if you'll go along with him I'll give the two pounds to the two of you.'

'Well I won't go there,' says I.

'Well if you go there,' says she, 'you will get more than a pound.'

'Well I won't go there,' says I. 'Where will you get the money?' says I to her.

'Stop you big ape,' said she, 'if I had him killed I'd get a great deal of money.'

Then I went down home and stopped there. I went up the road this morning the man was killed on the same night – when John Moylan's wife saw me she followed me up the road and she told me this way: 'John went to Baranna [Barna] this day', says the wife to me 'and I will go to Cregduff,' says she, 'and I told the little boys to let him to follow me up to Cregduff tonight when he came home from Baranna. But look at now,' says she, ''tis good for you to [go] along with the man I had, I got a man for to shoot him, you have a gun and a revolver,' says she, 'let one of you have the gun and the other the revolver.'

'Well I won't go there,' says I, 'and I have no ammunition for the revolver, and if I had itself I won't go on it.'

'Well you'll give me the gun,' says she. I gave her the gun after, very near the place where they bring water from, in a bag of guano. I brought the bag of guano home with me after leaving the gun and boots. She was not at the place when I left the gun and boots in it and I went down then and I was afraid someone saw the gun in it and I brought a trap with me. When she saw me going up, she followed me up and I was standing back there with the wall, she called me up and she drew a little bottle out of her breast.

'Let you have some of this,' says she, 'there's good stuff in it.'

'I don't care what kind of stuff is in it,' says I. 'I won't take it at all.'

She then drew out a small little bookeen, and said, 'Kiss this and swear not to speak about this and about the gun in all your life and any place you'll mark for me now you'll get the gun in it in the evening.'

'That will do,' says I, 'leave it back in that big wall, John Burke's wall,' says I.

'But don't tell it to anyone,' said the woman to me, 'about that you gave the gun to me. If you do, I'll tell it to the police that you have a gun and a revolver and you will be in for it,' says she.

'Where did you get that you got in the bottle?' says I.

'Oh, it's good stuff,' says she.

I jumped outside the wall then and I ran down as quick as I can the small rodeen. I did not know anything about John Moylan and his wife no more than that till the police came to me and searched the house and arrested me. I have my sister and another old man that can swear I did not leave my own house that night from about half past four o'clock till after ten. I don't know [about the killing] that night or anything about it. No more I have to say this time. When he was going to pay the rent he had not the rent entirely – he sent one of the little boys to Baranna and I think he got it there, say the woman to me. That's all I have to say.

Signed, Michael Downey
Father before me at Galway Prison this thirtieth day of December 1883.

Downey's bombshell statement echoed, somewhat, what the police and half of Annaghdown already suspected – that Mary Moylan had something to do with the murder.

Murphy's report on this break in the case arrived to Mr Jenkinson's desk on the same day as the notes detailing Mary Moylan's discharge. It was confirmatory in a number of ways; even if Downey denied killing John, he had admitted knowing about the murder, owning the murder weapon and meeting Mary that day at the well. In the margins of the report, a day later on 31 December, Reed gave due weight to the development, while also pointing out that not all the dots connected. Vitally, there is one familiar dead-end which cannot be reconciled with any testimony so far. 'This is a further successful issue in this case,' he wrote, continuing:

I consider we have now sufficient evidence against the accused to obtain a conviction from a jury against Michael Downey. But I shall not be satisfied till we clear up the mystery connected with the threatening letter and discover the writer. I expect we shall make a most complete case of this. Downey's statement is inconsistent in important points with facts proved by other evidence and with his admission made on Saturday. But this statement proves that he knew of the murder and corroborates Mary Moylan's evidence historically.

He knew at this point there was little doubt Mary was aware of the impending death of her husband. He said it himself; she probably instigated its commission.

Downey was up again on 5 January, having been remanded for another week. That day, yet another letter arrived to Dublin Castle – dated 2 January, it bore Dr Lapper's seal. It appeared the analysis on the other items was complete. Through examination of the trousers, a bottle of water from the bucket in which they were steeping and the wadding in the gun, Dr Lapper found the following:

> The trousers were saturated with water. No blood stains were visible on them but discovered mammalian blood in the water that drained off the garment. The dirty water was in a semi-putrid condition and contained blood of a mammalian character. The wadding consisted of a number of pieces of brown paper, hardened ... by dried blood on the removal of which, with one exception, they appeared to be composed of the same description of thin brown paper, the other fragment was much thicker, coarser in texture, colored dark blue upon one surface and light brown on the other.

After a run-through of depositions at his hearing Downey was again remanded for a week. His guilt was all but certain, as far as the authorities were concerned.

Writings in the margins of the remand report remarked that there was 'little doubt' they had their man. The Crown Solicitor, Bolton, writing from his room at the Railway Hotel in Galway, was confident of securing a conviction.

In his words, 'Downey was a calculating ruffian and enough has transpired to satisfy me his motive was to get possession of Moylan's farm and to get … compensation for the widow which would afterwards come through her into his hands.' Little sympathy for the idea of coercion, it seems.

Reed, the magistrate, was optimistic about discovering the writer of the letter. The pool of possible candidates was becoming narrower, he wrote in his report after Downey's statement. It was clear, he said, that Mary Moylan had some hand in the deed.

10

LOOSE ENDS

T he next 48 hours would be a busy time for the officials. A day after Reed's report was sent, a team of constables was combing the house and lands of Michael Downey, as they had done, endlessly, for days. The accused had admitted to owning two unlicensed firearms. One was still missing.

It was constable Patrick Tobin who made the discovery. Searching the brickwork of a stone wall surrounding a small patch of potatoes, he came across a hard steel object, wrapped in flannel. Unfurling the bundle, he revealed the missing revolver; 'it was not loaded, and had not the appearance of having been recently used.' It was a six-chamber revolver – unlike the single-shot gun which police believed was used in the murder. There was no ammunition to be found. It appeared to inspectors that Dr Lapper's services would be needed again.

On the 9th, the procession of policemen with wooden boxes arriving to Dr Lapper's door continued, when he had a call from Inspector Darcy, who brought with him a shirt, hat, the boots, a coat and a waistcoat belonging to Michael. Separately, on the same day, Tobin presented the revolver to the doctor. Within two days, the analysis was completed. Stains upon the soles – and right heel – of the 'American' boots proved to be mammalian blood, and the same was found on the outside of the left wrist of the shirt. 'I found a stain of a similar kind that had evidently been washed,' wrote Dr Lapper, 'a faint smear upon the inside of the front – a few specks like flea marks on and above the right wristband – and a few small bloodstains upon the back and front of lower portion.' As for the rest of the articles – they were clean.

In all respects bar the letter, the case was complete. Ignoring the supplementary evidence, including the widow's testimony, Reed believed he could quite easily get Downey on accessory to murder, based solely on his statement made to Lyster. But he wanted the full conviction. Cary was dispatched to Dublin, carrying two writing samples gleaned from door-to-door inquiries. They had not yet covered the entire area of investigation, but there was enough to start handwriting expert John Shaw Peake about his work. The results of that analysis came back quickly. No match. For the police, it meant a return to the drawing board: knocking doors with pencils and sheets of paper.

On 14 January Downey came, again, before Lyster – two days later than had been previously planned. Depositions were read to a 'careworn and haggard' Downey – a process, by now, with which he was familiar. He made his same statement, implicating Mary and the other man she had mentioned. A court date was set at the next assizes in March, secured at last, but the same problem remained. 'No further advance has yet been made towards discovering the writer of the letter found on body of deceased': the scrawled note on the police report margin on the day the court date was set, which was nearly becoming pro forma at that stage, was something of an understatement.

Things had been going so well, but Peake's handwriting analysis was a speedbump. Tempers and patience in Clonboo were wearing thin – both among the community, and within the local police force. The next block came on the Sunday morning – 13 January – this time, from the pulpit of the local church:

> I beg to state that on this date immediately after last mass the rev Lawrence Ansboro when addressing the congregation said he would tell them not to write any more for the police. Some of them were too efficient, and that they had no authority to make them write without an order from a magistrate. He said all the people wrote nearly alike and if the expert said their writing was like the letter they would be put to trouble. He did not want to prevent the police from getting the writer.

The above account, taken by a local sergeant named Mullane, was a canary down the mine of local cooperation which the police had enjoyed – at some expense. Fortunately for the authorities, by the time the reverend issued his advice, they had garnered samples from 'most' of the main suspects, according to Inspector Murphy, who replied on the 19th. In this case, it seemed like the local policeman had caused the trouble in the first place.

'I fear Sergeant Mullane has acted very indiscreetly in this matter,' he wrote, 'and caused the remarks of the priest.' It had reached Murphy's attention that Mullane, the sergeant at Clonboo, had, of his own accord, paid a visit to the post office at Corrandulla, nearby. The office was 'kept by a woman of high respectability and who would give every aid to the police'. Mullane's business was with her son, from whom he extracted a handwriting sample. It seems the local officer was, perhaps, a little heavy-handed. The woman went straight to the priest, who carried her message on the pulpit.

'Sergeant Mullane acted, I think, with too much zeal, unchecked by prudence,' wrote Murphy in his diagnosis of the dynamic between the local constabulary, which had sprouted amid the highest-profile case they had ever been assigned to. 'Too much competition' between the local constables at Clonboo after the 'heavy work' was completed, was his conclusion.

Murphy's action on the matter cast a dim view of the local police: 'they were only doing mischief by endeavouring to outry [sic] each other and I have directed all to return to their stations, except Sergeant Dalton, who can, I think, still be useful'.

And he wasn't wrong. For three days, Dalton painstakingly knocked doors in Galway city, and successfully traced the movements of Mary Moylan through the town on the Saturday before the murder – the last day she was known to have left Clonboo. The details, listed in Murphy's report on 22 January, are innocuous – she ate in one house, then stopped in another to shelter from a shower. Crucially, she did not leave the company of her husband once. She had repeatedly denied, even after turning witness for the Crown, knowing the source of the letter. It appeared, as far as Dalton's findings showed, that she may have been telling the truth. Dalton was assigned to do the same for Downey's movements – and to inquire about the 'society men' who had come to the attention of police.

Sergeant Mullane's faux pas, at a different stage of the investigation, could have been fatal to finding out the writer of the letter. But internal police memos show that Inspector Cary, by 22 January, had been the first to hatch the opinion that the letter was written in Cregduff. Cary set men on tracing the movements of John Browne, one of the many farmers who had been questioned on the night John Moylan died, and who was 'very much interested' in the land dispute with Tom Browne.

Then came another break. As with the previous jumps forward, Downey seemed all too eager to help police. On the evening of 3 February, as he had done once before, the prisoner summoned a warder. He had a statement to make. Mr Lyster gave him the caution, and Downey began an add-on to his previous drama, this time with more actors.

'There were four men on that night, the night John Moylan was killed,' he said. 'Martin O' Hara of Ballinasheehy and John Collins from Park over in the Bay and Pat Kearns of Toonrane, who was a soldier, and myself.' The men had murder on the agenda that night, but John was not the target – on the contrary, he was a dangerous man to tangle with:

> The four of us went that night, watched Tom Browne to kill him, the four of us were sworn to kill that man; Moylan was joined in the Fenians and we did not like to kill him, but we had too much drink taken. Kearns did not know Tom Browne very well. When Moylan was come to the stile Kearns asked two times: 'Is that Tom Browne? Is that Tom Browne?' And Moylan did not speak. Kearns fired with Moylan on the minute and I ran over the wall the moment that Kearns turned out from the wall after having shotten this man.

Downey added that it wasn't until he saw Mary Moylan that he realised what had happened:

> We caught Kearns that way catching the breast of his coat and he gave me the gun back and I thought it was Browne was [shot] this time and I went outside the wall and I knew Moylan's wife crying. Martin O'Hara was going to shoot the wife and I said: 'Tis too much done before,' said

I and I drew a letter out of my breast and threw it there and went away then and we did not see any of them no more. Martin O'Hara was with me too near Moylan's house, he went home and I break the ramrod in my gun and stick a rag back in it and throw it up on a wall with ivy and put the boots and the stockings up in the same way and went away home.

Then he came to one aspect of the story investigators were eager to clear up:

It was John Browne of Cregduff wrote that letter for me in my house. When he was writing that letter, Pat Allen came in and I brought Pat Allen down to an old house where there was an ass and gave the ass three or four shakes of straw. After the letter was written John Browne, Pat Allen and myself went up to Denis Hynes' and stay there til after 8 o'clock. John Browne had the letter in his pocket and he gave it to me near Fahey's house when I came down from Denis Hynes'.

If Downey was to be believed, and it was all a case of mistaken identity, wrapped up in Fenianism and secret societies – perhaps not everything Mary Moylan said was a lie?

'We had this plan to kill Tom Browne done for three or four weeks before that,' Downey continued, well and truly spilling his guts:

There was nine or ten of us joined with Fenians sworn to kill any man that would be asking land, I was the head of them, the names of them were William Browne of Park, William Hughes – who fired at Shaughnessy and who went into England shortly afterwards. Pat Collins, brother of John Collins of the Bay, and George Browne of Cregduff. Tom Browne was his uncle.

One of the men, Pat Collins, had fled to Australia after the shooting to which Downey referred – at a man named Shaughnessy. William Hughes, who Downey claimed had pulled the trigger, fled shortly afterwards to England. Tom Browne was to be another hit for the gang, supposedly led by Downey.

'Tom Browne was to be shotted because he was asking for land,' explained Downey, continuing:

> If I had been standing where Kearns was standing at the stile, Moylan would not have been shot, as I knew him very well, but Kearns asked him two times – 'Is that Tom Browne?' and he thought it was Browne was in it. We heard Tom Browne about two hours before that coughing in James Browne's land and we were watching him.
>
> It was I asked John Browne to write the letter and I saw him write it. I was going to post the letter this night and my sister saw three men out in my garden and one of them asked is Michael within. 'No,' says my sister and when I came in I went out into the garden and went away with them. I want to see Sergeant Dalton in here to tell him where he will get two revolvers and the stamp of the gun that shot Shaughnessy. Martin O'Hara was going to shoot the wife with a revolver he had and I said 'It is too much done before'. Collins and I each had a stone each in our hands but we did not fire any of the stones.

Lyster, armed – at the very least – with a new roster of men to question, read the statement back to Downey, who signed it with his mark.

Murphy rubbished most of the claims, but was excited about the identification of John Browne as the letter writer. Pat Allen, John Browne and Michael Downey had been to Denis Hynes', a public house in Clonboo, on the evening of the murder. That much he knew as fact, and it was those men he wished to speak to next.

Inspector Cary arrived early to Pat Allen's house on 5 February. To his surprise, he found the man quite at ease. Allen spoke with clarity and without hesitation. Cary quickly surmised he was telling the truth.

After threshing at his own house on the evening before the murder, Allen agreed he went to Downey's between 5 and 6 o'clock, where old Peter Collins was sitting in the kitchen. Downey emerged from his bedroom with a few handfuls of straw, thrown down from the loft, and he and Downey went out to feed the donkey – an odd request, as Downey had never before asked him to feed the ass, but he went along with it. Only upon returning did he see

John Browne sitting beside the kitchen fire at Downey's, and the three went to Denis Hynes' to play cards. Himself, Downey, Owen Casey, Denis Hynes and John Hannon played away into the evening. The group left in dribs and drabs – he couldn't recall the order – though he recalled John Hannon salting a pig in the public house.

Cary, in his questioning of Allen, had not mentioned John Browne's name. Allen had paved over that crack himself. He had no doubt, he said in a secret internal memo, that Downey's odd, spontaneous request for help feeding a donkey – not a two-man job – was a ruse to hide the fact that John Browne was concealed in the bedroom. When the pair came back, he was at the table, after all.

Police quickly formed the opinion that Downey – unable to read or write himself – had used John Browne as a pawn to write the letter, leveraging his existing dispute with Tom Browne. 'I believe the truth to be as we initially concluded,' he reported, 'that Downey got this letter written for the pretended purpose of intimidating Tom Browne and then adapted to his own purposes.'

The next stop for police was John Browne's. It was a sergeant named Reynolds who found him first, and before the constable opened his mouth, Browne launched into an explanation of his movements that night. 'I was in Downey's on Tuesday evening,' he declared, without provocation, 'but I went there to ask him if he wanted me to bring any turnips to Galway for him on Saturday.' Notwithstanding the gripping turnip story, police figured Pat Allen had filled him in about the investigation. It didn't matter; all they wanted, really, was another writing specimen. He gave them two. The specimens were sent at once to Mr Peake in Dublin, whom Inspector Cary discovered was ill. The expert vowed to do it, but they would have to wait.

Just over a month later, on the back of Downey's most recent statement authorities rounded up the key players for a special court sitting. They were brought before Lyster.

John Browne was examined. He flatly denied any involvement, but knew of the dispute the authorities referred to – it had arisen among several of the Brownes in Cregduff:

I never at any time wrote a letter for Downey. He never asked me to write a letter threatening Tom Browne or any other person. I did not write the letter which was found on John Moylan's body and know nothing at all about it. I did not give any letter to Downey opposite Fahy's, not any other place, on the 18th December 1883 or at any other time. I never saw any pencil with Downey. I said that Tom Browne was working for James Browne's land – Willie Browne and Tom Browne were not as friendly with one another as they used to be.

He said he didn't know the precise details of the dispute, but that 'it was the common report of the neighbourhood that Tom Browne was looking for James Browne's land'. His own beef with Tom Browne was in loyalty to his friend, Willie. John said he had not visited Tom for some time.

Turnips. That is why he was at Downey's house on the night of the 18th – nothing more. His name was signed in an unpractised, familiar cursive.

Winifred Browne, daughter of Michael Browne, another head of a Browne household who lived in the same village as Tom, had also been in Hynes' pub, and deposed seeing John and Michael near Fahey's. On noticing Winifred approaching on the road, John and Michael moved away, as if to have a private conversation. 'I knew they did not want my presence while they were speaking; they were speaking in a very low tone of voice.' She often heard Willie say that Tom was after his father's land. John was close friends with Willie, and Michael Downey was 'a great friend and comrade of John Browne'. They had been hanging out more often in the week before the murder, Winifred said, as Michael had been working with John.

Patrick Kearns, the man Downey blamed for firing the fatal shot, was examined the next day, on the 13th. A decorated soldier of 21 years, he lived in Toonrane, about a half mile from Clonboo, with his aunt, wife and child. He had returned from the 9th Regiment about a year before John Moylan's murder, and said he had never before laid eyes on Michael Downey. He had barely ever been to Clonboo, except to buy groceries at Fahey's.

On the night of the murder, he had played cards with a group of strangers at a house belonging to a man named James Lemand in Drumgriffin. John Collins was there, too, though he did not play. They left the house and met

John Moylan's brother and another man on the road; they were on their way to fetch the priest. Moylan, they were told, had been killed. Kearns denied knowing his supposed accomplice, Martin O'Hara, and said he had never seen John Moylan before in his life, either. 'I do not belong to any secret society and no person ever asked me to join such,' he concluded.

Martin O'Hara wasn't exactly sure of his age, but he reckoned he was about 24. On the night he supposedly nearly shot Mary Moylan but for Downey's intervention, he said he went to the house of a friend, one Michael Madden. He left at about 8 o'clock, went straight home, and ate supper with his parents and siblings. It wasn't until the next day that news of the murder reached their house. Truth be told, he hadn't left his house, nor the village of Ballinageehy, in a month, owing to a nasty cold, he claimed. Then, the refrain as per Kearns: 'I am not and never have been a member of the Fenian Society – and was never asked by anyone to join it. I did not see Downey, John Allen or Kearns the day Moylan was killed – I did not see any of them for at least four weeks before the murder.' He was at home that night, and was barely acquainted with the men he supposedly conspired with. He had no part in any of it, he insisted.

Finally, John Collins confirmed he and Kearns had gone to Lemand's to play cards with a number of other people, and that he himself did not play. Downey didn't cross his path that night, nor for six weeks previous, and he never saw Martin O'Hara that day, either. On the way home, they met with John's brother, on his way to the priest, just as Kearns had said.

Pinned to the front of Collins's deposition is a note from Lyster, which said the following part of the statement must not be connected to Collins, as per an agreement he struck with the man. Collins came clean about his own Fenian ties, and Downey's: 'I heard Downey was then head of the Fenians. I was sworn in as a Fenian about three or for years ago by John and William Hughes, who went to America.' His own brother, Pat, had fled to America, but as far as he knew, Kearns was not a Fenian, and there was no Fenian presence in his village.

It was faith, Collins said, that brought him out of the Fenians, after the local priest refused to give him absolution. He then joined the Society of the Sacred Heart of Jesus. None of the men at the card game were Fenians, though he heard Martin O'Hara was sworn in. Fenianism, he said, had been forced upon him: 'they told me the whole parish had joined then, and that I would stand in danger if I did not join'.

Lyster, in his own judgement, didn't believe Downey had any accomplices that night, but was sure John Browne wrote the letter, despite his own testimony. Winifred Browne's account, and the men's odd behaviour, led him to that conclusion. John Collins, for his cooperation, was not to be associated with the testimony he gave about his own Fenian membership. Bolton, the Crown Solicitor, agreed with the local constabulary that John Browne was duped by Downey into writing the letter, and that John had no part in the murder.

On the same day Lyster penned his conclusion, the results of the handwriting analysis were signed by Mr Peake in Dublin. The expert adopted the opinion 'that the notice was written by the writer of the specimen signed "John Browne"'.

An application by the defence council saw Downey's trial deferred, and he was rescheduled to appear at the summer assizes. The prosecution would have to wait, again. But at long last, they were ready for trial.

11

WELCOME TO GALWAY GAOL

'**A** black and foreboding pile of granite on the banks of the River Corrib.' This blunt description of Galway Gaol by F.J. Higginbottom in his book *The Vivid Life: A Journalist's Career* may best convey the sight that met Michael Downey the first day he was conveyed to its cells.

Galway Gaol as Michael Downey would have found it was a large, dominating structure at Nun's Island in the centre of the city, where the present-day cathedral stands. Between about 1804 and 1810, two gaols were established on the site: the Town Prison and the County Prison. In the 1840s, it was proposed that the gaols be joined, sparking a lengthy merger that completed in about 1870.

The main entrance of Galway Goal.

Irish prisons around the time of Downey's incarceration were enjoying at least one positive trend: the number of juveniles had declined slowly in the years preceding the report for 1884/85 (1882/83: 1,085; 1883/84: 959; 1884/85: 835). Juveniles were recorded by the General Prison Board (GPB) as anyone under 16 years of age.

Some of those incarcerated were children, and in many cases they were so young as to be shown mercy and sent elsewhere. The GPB report states:

> we regret to state that occasionally Magistrates have, during the past year, committed to prison juveniles of such tender age that in some instances it has been the duty of the Board to report the fact to the Executive with a view of having such children released and sent to an Industrial School. It is needless to point out how cruel and improper it is to commit children of such tender age to prison, as it is quite impossible to subject them to prison discipline, or to make them fully comprehend the cause of such treatment on the part of the authorities, while on the other hand the custody of such a charge places the prison officers in a most awkward predicament.

Owing to what the prison board considered to be a greater concentration and uniformity of treatment among prisoners, the administration of prison punishments for offences amounting to insubordination had also fallen. Some restraint measures, at their most extreme, included leather muffs, handcuffs and a 'canvas jacket with long sleeves stitched to mattress'.

Education for prisoners remained thin on the ground, and a scarcity of teachers meant the opportunity to assign them to 'secular education' duties was out of the question in many facilities – particularly smaller, local prisons. 'Lunatics' and the criminally insane were becoming an issue across the board for prison guards, who did not have the training, nor the experience, to deal with the ever-increasing amount of insane convicts, who should have been elsewhere assigned. The board was at pains to point out, 'as it had done before, the illegality of committing lunatics to gaol'. The practice had seen an increase in recent years, owing, the board felt, to an ignorance of the law among magistrates. Around this time, an inconsistent approach to the treatment of lunatics exposed wholly different expert opinions on those convicts.

The mid-1800s was a time of industriousness among gaol officials, and the physical structures built by inmates were a cause of pride in yearly reports. In Galway during the report period for 1884/85, inmates had constructed a female prison from an old disused block, containing 22 cells, three matrons' rooms and a Roman Catholic chapel (as well as the latter's decorative fittings). A Protestant chapel had also been established, along with a mess room, scullery, general store, laundry room and other amenities associated with the new female cells. It was certainly a considerable amount of work – 'performed at a minimum cost'. The necessary plumbing work was also completed, as were general repairs about the buildings, including improvements to the roof of the officers' mess room roof, gas fittings, bells, gongs, bolts, bars, windows and other fittings.

By the time Downey arrived Galway Gaol had a large section smothered in scaffolding amid construction works. A large building operation was underway to convert an old chapel into 14 new cells, and because the work was done by convicts, and involved carrying huge amounts of rubble out of the grounds, a worry arose about security.

To quell the unease surrounding a potential mass escape, the governor of the prison wrote to Dublin Castle requesting the temporary employ of two retired RIC members for a couple of months, to stand in as temporary warders. That was in July 1883, but the same two men would be rehired a number of times after the work stalled. One roadblock came from the Roman Catholic bishop; while the chapel was being excavated, he insisted a seperate temporary chapel be built for Protestants to pray in. Eventually, the 'temporary', two-month staffers were kept on, at £1 1s 0d a week plus expenses, until 1 November 1884.

Prisoners in the late 19th century were assigned to other work according to their skills; blacksmiths and other iron workers were put to use, as were carpenters. Inmates could also be assigned to woodchopping for the Board of Public Works, and in Dublin, a basket-making initiative was in full swing by the summer of 1885, benefiting the General Post Office. Galwegian prisoners under hard labour broke stones, whitewashed buildings, picked fibre, sewed, knitted, tailored and ground meal, among a host of other menial tasks.

Smaller disciplinary quirks cropped up in the mid-1880s, graffiti chief among them. In a circular to prison officials on 8 September 1884, Richard Clegg, chief clerk to the governors in charge of prisons, wrote that

> much scribbling on walls of cells, prison furniture, school and library books exists. You are hereby requested to have, at once, all such writings erased, and to inform the officers in charge of prisoners that it is their duty to bring all such breaches of Prison rules to the immediate notice of their superior officers, otherwise they will be held responsible for the injury thus done to prison property.

A few months later, a toilet paper rationing regime was put in place after convicts began writing messages on it.

At the end of the report period, March to March 1884/85, there were a total of 37,829 (24,323:12,506 male:female) prisoners conveyed to Irish prisons. This figure included long-term prisoners, repeat offenders, people awaiting trial, 'drunkards' and people under short sentences for breach of harsh vagrancy laws – a common one being falling asleep in public. Galway accounted for 870 lodgings, 601 males to 269 females.

Galway prisoners 1884/85 age breakdown

Age	Male	Female	Total
Under 12	3	1	4
12–16	15	1	16
16–21	125	84	209
21–31	272	103	375
31–41	116	57	173
41+	70	23	93
			870

The majority of prisoners in the gaol that year were 'wholly illiterate' at 386 (273:113 male:female). Those who could read and write numbered 320 (222:98), while 200 could 'read imperfectly' (142:58). The vast majority were Roman Catholic. A short line in the GPB report for that year has one cold statistic: during the course of 1884, there were three suicides by hanging. Regrettably for Dr Richard Kinkead, the medical officer at the prison, it was these cases that gave him his understanding of the mechanics of execution by hanging. One such case, involving 'TB', as he was named by Kinkead and in official documentation, was particularly harrowing.

Dr Kinkead had his hands on the boy's chest, rhythmically trying to bring him back to life. Little was happening. The neck was already stiff with rigor mortis. As Kinkead and his colleague, Dr Lynham, tried to apply live-saving pressure on the teenager's body, the upper torso began to arch backwards, slowly, ever stiffening. 'Quite dead,' Kinkead concluded.

The 18-year-old had been found hanging in his cell by a warder at about 2.30 pm, in an apparent suicide. TB had been committed on 11 August 1884, and he was found dead on the 16th. His crime had been to steal a loaf of bread, some tea and sugar.

Prison doctors in the late 19th century weren't always allowed to perform post-mortems on executed prisoners – though they could be ordered to by the coroner – due to their apparently compromised position. This was an assumption Dr Kinkead was at pains to disagree with. Equally, prison doctors couldn't examine people who took their own lives by hanging without the express permission of the prisoner's family. This wasn't Dr Kinkead's first taste of red tape during his time at Galway Gaol, but that didn't make it any less frustrating.

'Consequently, in cases of executions,' he wrote, 'I have been unable to make a post-mortem examination, unless by order of the coroner. The body having passed to the custody of the sheriff I have felt I had no power as a prison officer to interfere with it.'

A circular from Dublin Castle had specified the Lord Lieutenant's view that post-mortems of prisoners should not be done by prison doctors. Kinkead, if deprived of the experience, definitely welcomed the clarity. However, the coroner could still order him to do a prisoner's autopsy, and because the coroner was a judge, his orders had nothing to do with directives from the

Lord Lieutenant, or even the Home Office. Faced with two different orders, the medical officer was often 'placed between the hammer and the anville [sic]', as Kinkead saw it. Coupled with restrictions brought in earlier in the century via the Anatomy Act – simply put – it could be hard for a prison doctor to get his hands on a body.

It was cases like that of the young man above, and a handful of executions he was present at, that gave the doctor a shred of expertise, and professional opinion, in the field of 'lawful' hanging.

'At about 2.10 pm, after the dinner tins had been removed, he rang his bell and was let out to the closet, where he remained about three minutes and returned to his cell,' wrote the doctor of the day the teenager died. 'Ten minutes later the warder, on looking through the trap in the cell door, saw him standing in a curious position against the wall under the window of his cell, which was immediately opposite the door. He at once went into the cell, and found him partially suspended by one of his braces to the chain of his window.'

The doctor himself was sceptical as to whether it was a real attempt at suicide, as no knot had been tied in the cloth that took the boy's life. Also, his feet were touching the ground when he asphyxiated. 'Taking the entire circumstances into consideration, I believe the intention was to make a feigned attempt, knowing that the result would be his being placed in association in charge of two other prisoners.'

Kinkead studied the details of TB's death. He ran his own experiment on the chain, half in disbelief that a folded piece of cloth without a knot could hang a person – but apparently it could. The rough texture and downward force had, in the moment the boy died, bound it tight enough to cut off his air supply. The case was detailed in a run-through of six executions and three suicidal hangings, published in *The Lancet* in April 1886, which helped to form Kinkead's professional view on the subject.

TB's death was tragic, compared to others he outlined. But tragedy wasn't a stranger to the doctor. That wasn't remarkable for a prison surgeon and medical officer. But death, it seems, followed the doctor beyond the walls of Galway Gaol. In his later life, it wouldn't be the memory of obscene death faces or tragic discoveries that gave him pause for thought. Trips past Lough Corrib were no doubt tough for Kinkead – one of his two dead sons had drowned in its waters. The other, a soldier and Kinkead's last surviving son with his wife, Emma, would die in action during the First World War. The young captain, who earned a medical degree himself, was killed at Klein Zillebeke during the First Battle of Ypres, his final resting place.

Born to a Protestant reverend, Francis Kinkead, in Ballina in 1844, nothing remarkable pops up in the early life of the medic charged with the upkeep of Michael Downey, among the other hungry, sick and often mentally unstable inmates of Galway Gaol. Kinkead was educated at Rossall College in Fleetwood, Arlington House in Portlaoise, Trinity College Dublin and the Royal College of Surgeons of Ireland. Through his Dublin practice, he earned a reputation as an excellent obstetrician. In 1876, a midwifery professorship in Queen's College Galway brought him back west, and ultimately to the gaol.

His early years teaching were bogged down by red tape. It was difficult, prior to legislation in the 1890s, to get access to hospitals for practical assessments and work. It often involved backhanders and winks and nods – evidently something Kinkead didn't take up as well from his predecessor, Professor Doherty. Established links with hospital management – however unofficial – fell, meaning his midwifery students were forced to go abroad for practical training, usually to London, Liverpool or Edinburgh. Another difficulty in accessing midwifery patients lay in the habits of Galway women, it appears, who were reluctant to present themselves at medical facilities. 'It is very difficult in the West of Ireland to get women to go into the hospital,' he's quoted as saying in the *Galway Express* in 1904.

As well as midwifery, he dabbled in general surgery, which was not uncommon among specialists at the time. But the prison gave Kinkead access to death on a different scale. He may have been prevented from performing as many post-mortems on bodies that had hanged as he would have preferred, but that didn't stop him weighing in. Thus, James Berry would find out when he came to Galway in January 1885, he was a bit of a critic.

The doctor, in a *Lancet* article, detailed his examination of the body of another inmate, one he identified as 'TK'. His face was barely recognisable, but the typical aftermath of a hanging was rarely much different, according to doctors at the time. This was another suicide, one which he had been granted rare permission to see through to post-mortem.

'When I saw the body rigor mortis had commenced in neck and upper extremities,' Kinkead wrote. 'The face was swollen and livid. The right eye closed, the left half open and prominent. The tongue, black, swollen, and protruded, was pressed against the upper jaw; the limbs were livid; the surface of the body was congested and the hands clenched.' TK, incidentally, had been a 32-year-old farmer, incarcerated on a murder conviction on 21 January 1884. He took his own life six months later, on 1 July.

Kinkead clearly could never get his head around the rule that kept his hands tied after a convict's execution. Surely it was he, above any other county practitioner, who should best understand the mechanism of death that occurred so regularly in his domain? Dr John Rowland Gibson, in an address to a committee on hanging, highlighted the absurdity of the rule when he recalled that during his 27 years at the Newgate Prison, he witnessed 40 hangings and performed just one post-mortem.

The need for objectivity, an independent operator, was the reason for the rule, but as Kinkead was at pains to point out, he himself had nothing to do with the hanging, and nothing to gain from fudging the particulars. Hanging was the work of the sheriff, and once the death notice was handed to the governor of the prison ahead of the execution, gaol officials had nothing to do, legally, with the proceedings, beyond hosting the affair. The sheriff was not under the remit of the prison. 'It cannot be too clearly understood,' wrote the doctor, 'that [prison officers] have nothing whatever to do with an execution beyond assisting the sheriff and acting as witnesses, and that the entire responsibility rests with the sheriff'.

In one respect, James Berry and Richard Kinkead had at least one thing in common: William Marwood introduced them both to execution, so to speak. Three years before Marwood's death and before James Berry would even consider writing the application letter for the job of executioner, the Galway doctor got his first up-close experience of a 'real' hanging.

It was January 1880, and Kinkead was about to see the long drop in action for the first time. The prisoner was robust, a bit of a brute, a 'tall, powerfully-built fellow' by the doctor's estimation, who 'met his death with great fortitude.' In his writings, Kinkead does away with the ceremony of the execution; he is only concerned, really, with the result. He noted that

Marwood had used the long-drop method, placing the knot under the chin, draping the slack of the rope down the length of the prisoner's back. When the deed was done, the body was left to hang for the normal time. An hour and a half later, assisted by his colleague Dr Pye, he performed a post-mortem.

The doctor's notes on this autopsy reveal technical details and stark realities of the process, far beyond any hangman's notes. On a brief examination of the convict, he noted that faeces had not been passed, but that there had been an emission of seminal fluid, which was not uncommon. The doctor's description of the internal damage caused to connective tissues, blood vessels and organs, perhaps best demonstrates the devastating effect of Marwood's method:

> On dissecting the neck, we found most of the tissues torn through, the body of the third cervical vertebra was broken diagonally across and separated for at least two inches and a half to three inches from the remaining portion, the spinal cord was torn through, and in fact the head was retained in connexion with the trunk merely by the skin, which was not even abraded, a few muscular shreds, and the vessels on the right side.
>
> The trachea and oesophagus, the carotid artery and jugular vein on the left side, were torn through, and the tissues were emphysematous. On opening the thorax, nothing particularly abnormal was discovered in the lungs; they were slightly congested, but not to a very appreciable extent; the left heart was empty and firmly contracted, but on the right side both auricle and ventricle were full of frothy blood, the air escaping from the ruptured trachea having been evidently sucked down through the jugular vein.

The doctor never considered the question of capital punishment himself – or rather it was beyond his remit as doctor to publicly declare his conclusions. 'I do not enter on the question or express any opinion as to whether it is expedient or inexpedient, right or wrong, that capital punishment should exist,' he wrote. 'But surely so long as the penalty of death is exacted it is the bounden duty of the State to see the provision made for executions shall be as perfect as possible, so that they may be rapid, painless, and free from the possibility of mistake.'

Regardless, he thought if it were to be done it should be done properly, for the benefit of everyone involved. 'That any bungling should take place or any delay occur through the inexperience or awkwardness of the executioner, or that through his avarice he should be able to dispense with needful assistance, would be to add great cruelty to the punishment; yet under the present system this is not only likely to occur, but has actually happened.'

Of course, hangings were only a small part of Dr Kinkead's remit.

12

TWO VIEWS OF THE CITY

T he health of the prisoners on entry, and particularly the diet, was wanting. In general, sick prisoners were treated with sympathy by prison authorities at Galway. Geraldine Curtin, the author of *The Women of Galway Jail*, outlined a case in April 1887 of a man who was released from Galway Gaol because he had been 'fretting and not eating food'. At the time of his release, he had served one third of a six-month sentence for assault occasioning actual bodily harm. On another occasion in 1891, a 94-year-old woman was released nine days into a three-month sentence for having illicit spirits. During her time in the prison, she was fed on an 'invalid diet', and on discharge, was accompanied home by a prison officer.

Galway in the late 19th century was poor, and the diet afforded to prisoners in workhouses and prisons was often far superior to that on the outside. To that end, committing a small crime – such as breaking a window – to provoke a custodial sentence was often a bid for better, more regular nourishment. Prisoners often gained weight while in custody – or 'gained flesh', as per Dr Kinkead's phraseology. Often, that hindered the work of the hangman; stories were told of prisoners gaining up to 10 or 11 pounds between the day of their first weighing and execution. Quite a difference, when it came to measuring out the correct length of rope.

The food consisted of meagre portions of meal and milk for breakfast, followed by bread and a pint of milk for dinner. Those serving longer sentences had vegetable soup, tea and bread for supper, while a stint of a month or longer would merit meat soup on Sundays and Thursdays. In the cases of prisoners serving shorter sentences, a fasting period between 3 pm and 9 am the following morning was par for the course. The diet, in the earlier part of the century, had been better, but was brought to beneath the nutritional quality of the workhouses. This was to remove the incentive for workhouse inmates to attempt to earn a place at the gaol.

Still awaiting trial by the middle of 1884, Michael Downey was feeling the pinch. In December, when he was first lodged in the County Gaol, an official form sent to Dublin Castle had listed his behaviour as 'good' and his health as 'good'.

In late June a correspondence was struck up concerning Downey's health, with a relaxation of his dietary and exercise allotment being sought. Exercise was a matter taken seriously by prison officials; a December 1884 circular by Richard Clegg, chief clerk, reminded officials at gaols that untried prisoners, in particular, were to be granted their exercise, rain or shine. If the weather didn't allow for it, they either had to arrange for exercise within the confines of the prison buildings, under cover, or ensure they got outdoor activities within the same 24-hour period. The general recommendation to better welfare seemed to be popular that month; within weeks, recommendations were issued with a view to stopping prisoners drinking impure water out of cisterns. A new rest interval was also introduced for prisoners under bread and water punishment – a strict diet of bread and water which was imposed, usually, for three days at a time.

In Downey's case, a medical report on his health had indicated he needed a better dietary allotment than was allowed to him under his registered prisoner class; after all, he had not yet been convicted of anything, and was merely awaiting trial. Around the same time, a man named William Moran who was lodged in Sligo Gaol, awaiting trial for assault, was granted an extra pint of milk and one hour's exercise per day – though the governor of the gaol was at pains to ensure the relaxation wouldn't impede any discipline: 'I beg to state that these extras will not interfere in any way with the proper discipline of the prisoner.'

In June, having seen the request, Dr Kinkead wrote in his journal: 'Read letter from GPB 23/6/8 re: Michael Downey and report that I recommend that he get 1 pint milk and 1 lb white bread, an hour or two additional exercise. I shall be glad to know if this man's name is to be entered in the continuous treatment book as sick.' This was transcribed and sent to Dublin Castle.

In response, the GPB chairman granted the relaxation: 'In accordance with direction contained in letter dated 25th June 1884, I have the honor to recommend that prisoner Michael Downey be given the extra diet specified by the medical officer, and an additional hour for exercise daily.'

The summer of 1884 was a hard time for Michael Downey, despite the small relaxation. Meanwhile, another young man was enjoying the freedom of the city.

Thomas Parry, a man about Downey's age, basked in the sun as he walked hand in hand with his beloved along the new pavement in front of her stepfather's hotel on Eyre Square, and west over the slick cobbles towards the river Corrib, just a few hundred yards from the prison.

For four days in July 1884, Parry thought himself the luckiest man alive. Amid the din and bustle of the Galway Races, love prevailed, and Jealousy lost. In fact, Jealousy, at 12 stone 4 lbs, came second to the Warriors Vase for the Queen's Plate on the Wednesday; the latter won in a canter.

Parry, a 27-year-old steward working in Edenderry, had been engaged to 19-year-old Galwegian Alice Burns for about seven months. Chance had brought them together; they had met just over a year beforehand, in April 1883, while both working at the house of Irish lawyer Major Thomas Braddell

A view of the Royal Hotel, Eyre Square

in Wexford, where Parry's family lived. Prior to that, he had worked as an assistant to his father, William, who had been a shepherd for Lord Ashtown until the employer's death in 1882.

The two had a short whirlwind romance that led to the engagement. Parry, smitten, had spared no time in buying a beautiful ring, well beyond the financial boundary of a steward with no salary owed. Alice would eventually return to her native Galway, where she took up a job as a barmaid in the well-known Royal Hotel on Eyre Square. Her stepfather, George Mack, owned the business. Alice's mother had married the popular proprietor after Alice's father died some years beforehand. All that was left of the young woman's family, besides her mother, were her sister, Bessie, and a niece named Fanny Rickaby. In the summer of 1884, they were living and working together in the hotel.

When Alice moved back to Galway, Parry saw little point in remaining in Braddell's. His behaviour, too, had changed. In the absence of his beloved, he became irrational. Impulsive. Compounded with frayed nerves – a result of a nasty bout of sunstroke the previous summer – he left Wexford, and the home he still shared with his parents and sister. He received a glowing reference from the Major and others in the area, being described roundly as a sharp, conscientious worker. 'Thomas Parry is a smart, intelligent young man with a good hand and keeps accounts well,' wrote the rector of Kilflynn, John F. Luther.

On the back of his experience in Wexford, Parry easily found work as a steward and stock manager on the lands of Miss Elizabeth Newsom in Edenderry. It was there he sent and received – mostly sent – letters and gifts to Alice in the painful months prior to their reunion. Parry longed to be with her again, and during Race Week in Galway, 1884, he got his wish.

Arriving to the station, Parry laid eyes on a city in transformation. Galway was certainly a poor county, and post-famine emigration and, more recently, land war and agitation, had left many rural areas in a bad way.

A foot and mouth outbreak at the beginning of the year saw the Galway Town Improvement Commissioners forced to write to the Lord Lieutenant, asking for licences to be reinstated for the Oranmore and Clarinbridge markets, owing to 'serious loss and inconvenience to the trading community', but the request was declined by the veterinary department. Meanwhile, progress marched on elsewhere; the same committee put in motion the first orders for a fire engine, lengths of hose and trained men to establish an efficient fire brigade for the city. Progress indeed, though it wasn't until the bitter end of 1884, in November, that they ordered a bell for the engine.

Eyre Square was in a state of constant improvement. It was beginning to feel new. Multiple motions for paving different sections of it appear that summer and in the years before and after Parry's lovers' jaunt in Galway; by the end of 1884, the local authorities would move to order a further 20 tonnes of kerbstones for the city. Two large, now-famous Crimean War cannons that stood in the square had begun to sink into the earth, and quick intervention was needed to reinforce the foundation on which they perched.

From the start of the visit, Parry felt ill at ease. George Mack, an affluent, protective stepfather in his late 40s, seemed to take an instant disliking to him. Thomas Parry had long known about Alice's stepfather's distaste for their engagement; the elder man had told him as much in a letter just a couple of months before, in May. Simply put, he 'didn't approve'. Mack's rejection seemed a little at odds with favourable depictions of the young man. Repeatedly described as well-dressed and respectable-looking, it usually came as a surprise to new acquaintances that Parry wasn't working at something in the city. Yet, despite his notable presentability, Parry was quite cash poor. As the days wore on, any air of peasantry Parry dared to betray was greeted by a snarky comment, or perhaps a steely glance from Mack, caught from the corner of his eye.

Salthill and its beautiful strand brought moments of respite. Each morning, Alice and Parry, and sometimes Bessie and Fanny, would take the tram from outside the hotel to the shimmering waters. The tram ride, at first, had whipped Parry from his loving bliss; it was cluttered in areas, and in poor condition in patches, mostly out towards the coast. Its condition would eventually prompt the town commissioners to issue a summons to the tramway company, ordering them to clean it up.

That summer, bathers at the popular spot had new bye-laws to contend with, first announced in March by John Redington, sub-sheriff at the gaol, and Blake, the solicitor. The rules wouldn't have impacted Thomas and Alice's day trips, though some people fell foul of the rules towards the end of the summer.

In August the town commissioners were told: 'Sgt Reynolds reported that he found certain persons bathing at Blackrock without drawers, contrary to the bye-laws of the Town Commissioners on the subject'. They were dealt with at the petty sessions. The next summer, 1885, would see the first springboard installed at the popular diving spot.

Part of the reason Parry enjoyed those mornings was the downtime from Mr Mack, who preferred to bathe a little later, usually 8 am or 9 am, by which point Parry would be eating breakfast in the main hall. Like ships in the night. That was, until he invited Parry out to attend his own dip one of the mornings.

An awkward venture turned into interrogation, as Mack made clear, again, his opinion of Parry and his engagement to precious Alice. He wondered about Parry's means. How much did he make? Did he have anything owed from Miss Newsom? How could he expect to provide for a family under such circumstances?

Parry had no money owed to him. He had spent it on Mack's stepdaughter; when he wasn't sending her gifts or buying hefty engagement rings, he was paying for his train fare to see her in Galway, or, as had happened shortly before, paying Alice's fare to Dublin to stay with her aunt.

Perhaps Mack spotted the glimpse of Parry's fury, for a moment, at being heckled and degraded. Parry did not deal with such abuse well. Perhaps Mack already had his mind made up. Whether Parry didn't have the means, or Mack simply spotted a better match for Alice, is impossible to know. Either way, as they rode the tram back to the centre of the city in silence, Parry likely realised this had been his last chance at an audition. Undoubtedly, he had failed.

Parry knew something had changed during those four or five days. His mind whirred as he ascended the steps of the station, Alice by his side, George Mack a distance away. Ever watchful. A lump of clay sat in the young steward's chest, clinging to his ribs as the thought of leaving his sweetheart alone with the corruptive forces of her influential stepfather. Mack gave her everything; a living, shelter. Parry would have to have faith in the power of her love for him, but he couldn't shake the feeling, as they ended their parting embrace, that maybe she could slip away.

The young man stiffened his upper lip, told Alice he would write, and boarded the train back to Edenderry. The train pulled out and he felt, already, like he was missing a limb. As he watched Galway's low fields and the coastline disappear, he dared not think about how long it could be until he saw her again.

He need not have fretted. It wouldn't be long.

13

HIGHWAYS AND BYWAYS

T homas Parry wasn't the only one with uncomfortable memories of his time in Galway. If James Berry considered Ireland a bad assignment, Galway was a step worse. It wasn't often Berry admitted to feeling frightened carrying out his duty, but one episode during a journey west was enough to give him 'one or two cold shivers'.

'I knew that amongst some of the lower classes [in Ireland] there was a feeling of hatred against myself on account of my occupation,' wrote Berry, detailing a journey to Galway from Dublin that left him needing a stiff drink at the halfway mark. Four moonlighters had been condemned to hang and the £40 commission, expenses aside, was enough to coax Berry through his apprehension.

Berry's uneasiness started when four other men sat in his compartment as the train left the capital. Somewhere between Dublin and Mullingar, a political discussion became heated and just as the train left Kilcullen, the Irishmen 'began to fight most violently, using their sticks and fists to such an extent that all their faces were soon covered with blood'. To Berry's surprise, the fight cooled as quickly as it had begun. As the train pulled into Mullingar, the men traded apologies and wiped blood from each other's faces.

The fracas was enough to wobble Berry. He alighted at Mullingar and found a place within the station to get a drink to steady his nerves. The fight, he later wrote, 'had somewhat upset me, although I took no part in it.' On the platform, his attention was drawn to two rough-looking characters. They stood by the train, chatting with the four men who had fought in close quarters with Berry just minutes before. Berry, keen to remove himself from the scene – he had managed to conceal his identity so far – made his way to the washroom. The two men followed. They were anxious to meet Berry and carry on a conversation. They insisted, with force, that he accompany them for a drink; he agreed, for fear of causing more friction.

The strangers, in a distinct brogue Berry would later caricature when recounting the story, chatted with the executioner, telling him they were going to Galway. The conversation turned sharply, and the Bradford man was asked if he knew whether or not the English hangman – 'Barry' – was aboard. He did not, of course. 'Like two shadows', the men followed Berry back onto the platform and into his compartment, bringing with them a sinister tension which the Bradford man found hard to ignore. Despite the fact he was well-armed – he often carried a revolver, sometimes two – there was nothing he feared more than having to kill in self-defence. Dread, to him, was the idea of being convicted for murder and having to meet a man in his own line of work.

Some relief came moments later, when two plain-clothes Royal Irish Constabulary officers boarded the train. The carriage was made up of two compartments, divided by a low partition – the officers sat in the other half of the carriage; the two men, who were now haranguing Berry, had their backs to them. The two strangers didn't seem to notice the RIC men, who were paying close attention. According to Berry, the journey between Mullingar and Athenry was marked by rapid-fire questioning; strong efforts to pull information were met with brief, yet polite, answers from Berry, who veered at any pitfall that might give rise to an opinion. As the train pulled into Athenry, his two companions moved to the other side of the compartment, and in a barrage of whispers they presumably thought were silent, debated whether or not Berry was 'Barry'. Berry hovered his hand over the weapon in his pocket – perhaps his only ally aboard the train.

'One of them got quite excited, pointed out that I was an Englishman, that I came from the North of England, that there was no one else in the train that looked like an executioner, that my tale about being a poultry-buyer was "all a loie," and finally that I had a scar on my cheek which "proved it intoirely, begorra!"' Berry later wrote, adding that the men, at length, reached the conclusion that Berry, a gentleman by all appearance, couldn't possibly be the 'murderer and blaggard' they sought.

The train, at last, pulled into Galway. With a consciously casual swing of his arm, Berry propped his hand on the window ledge and dangled a handkerchief into the breeze. At this prearranged signal, the policemen assigned to escort him safely from Galway Station assembled, and were standing at the door as Berry marched off the train. As he did, he cast a final glance back, spotting his two stalkers 'gesticulating wildly' as they realised their mistake.

Berry asked the constabulary about the two men, and was told they were bad news – 'two of the roughest characters in Galway', in fact. Berry's attention quickly turned to a different set of rough Galway characters, namely the moonlighters set to ascend the scaffold in the coming days.

While hangings were relatively common, reprieves were, too. As the execution dates approached, one by one, the men were shown mercy, which usually meant life imprisonment or penal servitude. In the meantime, owing to safety concerns, the governor of Galway Gaol made Berry reside within the prison walls. Berry found this frustrating. 'I was kept waiting more than a week in Galway gaol, with nothing more lively to do than to read the newspapers,' he later wrote, his frustration pouring through the lines, 'and to walk about in the dreary prison yard, because the governor did not consider that it would be safe for me to venture outside. I was heartily glad when the last reprieve arrived and I was free to return home.'

When eventually he was allowed to leave, he took the midnight train out of Galway. The service was not a busy one, and as a result he had an entire compartment to himself. As he did many times before, he made himself comfortable, hoping to catch some sleep in the coming hours. And so part two of his Galway nightmare began. It was at Mullingar, again, that the tension arose. He noticed a man on the platform peer into his compartment, then go to the trouble of walking the entire length of the train, once it had stopped, so he could sit with Berry. This was unusual – there were still other empty compartments on the train.

A 'heavy swell Yankee' sat before Berry, speaking friendly words in a strong American accent. The hangman's attempts at feigning sleep didn't deter his new companion. He kept his eyelids half open as he fielded questions on Irish politics, where he lived, what his business was, where he was staying in Dublin. Berry managed to get a decent look at the American. Besides a wide-brimmed slouch hat atop his head, a long cape and an ornate, silver-mounted bag, Berry clocked the unmistakable outline of a revolver in his coat.

Berry said his name was Aykroyd, and avoided most of the other questions. He admitted to being from the North of England – at least that way, he didn't have to mask his own obvious accent as he dipped under the more sensitive queries. After a short time, his unfortunate suspicions about the concealed revolver were confirmed. The American drew his weapon, but only to examine it – in a careless way, Berry thought. Buoyed by the fact his own weapon was 'built for business and twice the size' of his fellow traveller's, Berry took his out, and pretended to do his own inspection. 'Can I take a look at your gun?' the American asked. Berry declined – the use of the word 'gun' annoying him somewhat – and put it back in his coat, the barrel secretly covering the stranger until the pair reached Dublin. They didn't speak much after that.

When they arrived in the capital, Berry got into a car and gave the driver the name of his hotel. The next unhappy chapter of anxiety immediately followed as the American jumped in alongside him, saying he, too, would stay at Berry's hotel. Arriving at the accommodation, he went quickly to his room. The next morning, when 'Aykroyd' descended the stairs and entered the breakfast room after washing up, he discovered the American talking to the waitress. In his unmistakable drawl, he was asking if she knew Mr Berry, to which she truthfully answered that she did, as he often used that hotel. He asked if she had seen him that morning, and she said she hadn't. Berry later caught the waitress in the hallway on her way to the kitchen and filled her in on the situation.

The man, for the next few hours, became a plague. A shadow. Berry next found his new fan examining a letter addressed to 'Mr Berry', which had been left in the coffee room. Later, before Berry was due to catch his boat out of Ireland, the American suggested they go for a drink – and so they did, to Mooney's. Berry knew the bartender, and threw him what he described as 'a vigorous wink' on entry. The bartender kept up the ploy, and eventually Berry parted ways with the American, who seemed satisfied at long last. The pair traded bon voyages. The moment Berry left in a car for the port, the bartender – out of some compulsion of divilment – revealed that there was no such person as Aykroyd, and that the American had been sitting, all along, with the man he sought.

A chase ensued, as Berry tried to make his ferry and the American tried to catch him. 'As the ship swung out from the quay-side, a car, driven at red-hot speed, came dashing along, and the passenger, whom I recognised as my American, gesticulated wildly, as if he wanted the vessel to stop,' Berry later wrote. 'But we swung out with steam and tide, and he drove some distance along the quay-sides wildly but vainly waving his hands.'

The next time Berry was at Mooney's, the same bartender relayed the story. Berry never saw the American again. While Atholl says Berry would later tell this story – and others, for that matter – with somewhat dramatic flair and conviction that the man was pursuing him for his blood, the likelihood was that the American was curious to meet an executioner, or better yet, purchase some souvenirs. Berry would hardly take that chance for a few shillings. This time out, Berry's suspicions could possibly have saved his life, or cost him a generous increase on his standard rate.

Ireland, for all its unhinged train journeys and shouty country crowds, wasn't all bad. Dublin, in a way, was a tonic. Anonymity seeped through the cobbles, between the upturned collars and shouting sellers, drunks, prostitutes and businessmen. A sanctuary of peace for the travelling hangman. Efforts to stay hidden could truly be relaxed, however momentarily.

And making new friends wasn't hard. On the third or fourth time passing through a city, the same faces appear. James Berry was a creature of routine and habit; he liked certain hotels and public houses. The people he met would buy a fake name without hesitation, out of gullibility or indifference, it didn't matter. This sort probably wouldn't have flinched had he told them what was in the bag.

On one occasion in August 1884, as he arrived into Dublin from Wexford having executed James Tobin, he intended to wind down. Tobin's murder case had been quite well known in the region. He had served 18 years in the Royal Artillery before being discharged with two good conduct badges. That reputation soon faltered, as he was convicted in 1882 for having assaulted and robbed a pensioner. He was sentenced then to six months, to which he replied: 'the next cock I kill won't crow'.

Tobin spent the next two years as a tramp, before brutally murdering an 84-year-old farmer's wife near Rathdrum in May 1884. He had approached the farmhouse in the middle of the day, making sure she was alone. Her husband discovered her body later that day; the woman was lying in the yard, 'sweltering with blood and quite dead'.

The case had gripped the south-east, not least because Tobin's execution would have been just the third at the gaol in Wexford in 50 years. His sentencing hearing had caused a particular stir, when he indignantly replied to his death sentence: 'My Lord, you and everyone of you will have my blood on your heads.' On entering prison, he had been a difficult prisoner, but like so many others, he had repented for the sake of his soul as the execution date approached, listening closely to the sermon of the Roman Catholic chaplain.

Berry, who rarely wrote in concern with a condemned person's guilt, often wondered about the veracity of these divine eureka moments – there just seemed to be so many. The prisoner, in any case, was Berry's to hang. It was one of his first visits to the island in an official capacity and, all things considered, it went quite well. Sitting in his lodgings a day later in Dublin, he appreciated not being the centre of attention. Those quiet, stolen, in-between times gave an opportunity for headspace.

It was also in these down days and travel days when Berry could have some fun, if the conditions were right. For a man who constantly complained about the 'peep show' of his situation, he didn't shy away from mischief, should it raise its head. Gallows humour was well and good, if a bit of a myth, but the crushing weight of anxiety at the prospect of being found out meant levity wasn't often on the agenda. When it was, it made sense to grab it. Pretending he was another person was a skill he honed to a fine point. 'Aykroyd' was his usual alias. Other than that, frightening old men by handing them his business card was another of his favourite pastimes. Fear of a sinister reaction and political tension forced him into silence on Irish railways, but it could be said that his only dissuasion on British ones was discomfort at being a sideshow. His fellow countrymen lacked the venom of the Irish.

'I always try to remain unknown while travelling, but there is a certain class of people who will always crowd round, as if an executioner were a peep-show,' he wrote, recalling a time when his presence was so well known on a Durham-bound train that he had to give up pretending. Except, that is, to one man.

Berry had caught a connection at York, having been forced to engage in a bit of verbal parrying with three rough-looking men who had crowded his compartment. It went well. Successfully incognito, and convincingly 'Aykroyd', he moved to his connecting train. His broad frame didn't fit the narrow train walkway, and he shimmied sideways, gladstone bag clutched at the rear, searching for an empty carriage.

As he began to run out of options, his gaze was at last met by the bright eyes of a kindly face. A 'benevolent-looking old gentleman', as he put it. Unfortunately, distinctive scars, a distinctive bag and the fuel of whispered rumours had more or less blown his cover with every other passenger on the train. It hadn't helped that he'd just marched up a sizeable chunk of the train, peering into carriages. Short of swinging his hanging rope around his head like a lasso, he had done quite enough to broadcast his presence.

Berry sat his bag on the seat across from the old man. They engaged in idle 'hellos' and Berry reached across the carriage, pulling closed the door with a rattle. He turned to peer out the window, watching the bustle of the station as the train prepared to depart, steam filling the platform. No need for a hand clasped on the revolver this time, he thought, as he closed his eyes.

Tranquility didn't last long. Snapping quickly out of his trance at the voice of an annoyingly eager young man, his hand shot instinctively to the metal bulge in his coat pocket. His tension dissolved on turning to the carriage window, where he saw the stupidly happy face of a young porter, mouth agog, with a small crowd of people gathered at the door behind him. The old man was instantly confused.

'What was that?' Berry asked, not catching the porter's opening bit.

'I said,' replied the porter. 'Make sure you give him the right tightener!' A small satisfied laugh escaped his lips after landing his odd attempt at jocularity. A silly one, Berry thought.

The porter ran off, giggling, and the people at the door dispersed. 'Strange,' said the old man, mystified, looking to 'Aykroyd'. 'What do you expect all of that was about?'

In response, Berry did his best 'Heavens, I haven't the slightest clue' head shake and shoulder shrug combo. 'I'm quite unable to imagine what he meant,' he replied. They laughed it off.

At Darlington, the fun started again. The train ground, noisily, to a halt. The sound of passengers again filled the walkway on the train, the bustle of cases and bumping of bodies outside Berry's carriage a sign of the mass passenger tradeover. This time, a crowd gathered near the carriage of the two men, chatting loudly about the mystery hangman aboard the train. However, this time, none knew what James Berry looked like.

'What is it?' asked the old man, highly curious at the commotion and the procession of heads on swivels that appeared in their carriage. 'The hangman, Berry,' one replied, falling over himself to spread the gossip. 'They say he's aboard the train, headed for Durham!' The small group moved on to another carriage, eager to get a look at the creature, and Berry could hear a distant, murmured copy of the conversation he'd just had.

The prospect captivated the old man, and he became excited. 'The hangman! On this train.' He surveyed walkers-by, wide-eyed. 'Do you suppose you'd know him, if you saw him, Aykroyd?'

Berry had to hold back a laugh. He formed his face into something resembling an earnest consideration, and cast an eye outside the carriage, looking for a suitable patsy. It was an odd feeling, trying to pick out what he thought a layperson should think he himself looked like. More odd, still, considering he had spent so much time and energy trying to destigmatise the profession. However, a charade was a charade. He quickly found a ragged, wild-enough creature hunched in his seat. A 'low-looking character', he would say. 'Possibly him?' Berry gestured to his plausible hangman.

'Yes!' the old man chimed, happy at the revelation. 'The hangman would look very much like him!' he agreed. The old man's quick acceptance of the wretch as being James Berry didn't sit extremely well. *He must have read a so-called portrait in one of the newspapers*, he thought. Sure, he had a scar on his face, but the papers tended to run with a thing like that.

With a bit of a thrill in the air, the two again struck up conversation. Berry seems to have been quite taken with the older man and his attentive company; no doubt the liaison reminded him of his long, meandering chats with William Marwood about the marvel of hanging – before the gladstone bag, before the Italian silk, before Aykroyd. The train pulled into Durham and Berry stood to leave, but his new friend was staying on board.

'Aykroyd, your card? Should I be in Bradford...' the man smiled at him attentively as Berry plunged his hand deep into his coat and obeyed the request. He was, Berry later said, surprised, to say the least. 'This story has been much warped and magnified, and has even been made the subject of a leading article which takes me to task for "glorifying my gruesome calling" and shocking some respectable people by giving them my cards,' he wrote in his diaries, defending his actions. Yet not really offering an alternative explanation.

But back in Dublin, after his Wexford hanging, those antics weren't on the cards, though he would again pull on the Aykroyd mask for an evening of entertainment. Sometimes, at his most reluctant to engage with the public, he was known to bring members of his family with him to hangings. *A man travelling with his family surely couldn't be suspected of being a hangman*, he reasoned. And, to be fair, he was correct in this assumption. Still, it was a rare thing to put them under the stress – and, to Berry's mind, the danger – of travelling across the Irish sea. This time, he was going solo. He missed Sarah, and had one night left to spend in Dublin before going back to England for another appointment.

He left his boarding house and walked the quays, listening to the music of the sailors' shouts and wandering the windy, cobbled roads south of the Liffey. It was evening, but he wasn't hungry; Wexford Prison had been nothing short of a culinary delight. On his way out that morning, he had received a hearty commendation from the governor of the prison, and a heartier breakfast of ham and eggs. His mind, instead, was on an appointment he had to keep – a casual acquaintance he knew from previous trips. So casual, in fact, the man didn't know his real name, or indeed what he did on his trips from England.

'Aykroyd!' The name took a second to register, as it always did, piercing through the hum as he approached the Gaiety Theatre at the top of Grafton Street, a busy city-centre thoroughfare he had strolled invisibly down. People were lined up at the box office; *Carmen* had been enjoying a fiercely popular run. With nothing else to do and his fees already collected, Berry had decided a night of culture might be just the best medicine for a man who needed to disappear.

Sitting in the dark, mesmerised by what he would say was a fantastic show, Berry wasn't a hangman, or a freak. He was Aykroyd, a businessman in a sharp tweed suit, with no gladstone bag or tools of death to speak of. Most invisible.

14

RETURN TO SENDER

Thomas's heart ached.

Traipsing around Mrs Newsom's and performing his usual duties as stock manager and steward, albeit with less than his usual vigour, at least occupied him. But he longed for Alice. To see her face, to touch her, to finally be married. He had trouble putting it into words, but he had certainly tried, as evidenced by the reams of paper he had sent his beloved in letters.

Mr Mack, her stepfather, had tried his utmost to ruin their time together in Galway during the races. It was a futile effort. Staying at the Royal had not been ideal, but any fleeting memory of an angry glance from the rich old codger was wiped away with scenes of the glimmering water in the early mornings at Salthill, and Alice gliding effortlessly through the gentle waves. Try as he might, Mr Mack was not going to stop this wedding.

At least his honesty could be respected – he made no odds about telling Parry what he thought of their marriage. It mattered little to the 27-year-old; what did matter were Alice's recent letters.

For the last week or ten days, drink had been Parry's comfort. Bottles of whiskey and porter replaced the warmth that had sapped out of the words in Alice's letters. She wrote him quite often, and he could see she was being careless, as he put it. Maybe Mack was getting to her after all; he had her ear night and day, whereas Parry only had the periodic grasp of the written letter and whatever credit the many presents he sent her earned – along with the fact that she still wore the engagement ring.

But he couldn't shake the feeling that she was turning away. In one letter she said she had been called a 'flirt' – but there was nothing true about it. His heart broke at the words. 'Whether it is true or not,' he had written, perhaps in haste, in his reply, 'you ought be ashamed.'

He was tired on 28 July 1884. The light hung in the sky as late as it could, casting a warm, orange glow over Edenderry. June was well past, and he knew the summer was coming to an end. So tired was he as he climbed the steps to his lodgings that he nearly missed the parcel near his door, wrapped and quartered with twine.

There was no return address, but he recognised the handwriting at once. He grabbed his precious bundle and ran to his room, closing the door behind him and ignoring a distant voice following him up the stairs, asking him some question or other. As he pulled the string, he could almost smell her scent. He unfolded the paper, revealing a bundle of letters. A bundle, he thought. Imagine the time she took.

He looked through them, eyes flitting over the familiar curves and dots, over 'beloved's and 'I love you's. Those seconds of light delirium turned quickly dark, and a harsh knot formed in his stomach as the hallmarks of his own handwriting came through the fog. His letters. Months of them. Bundled up and returned. As he began to shuffle through them, pace quickening with his heartbeat, something with weight to it fell from between the pages and landed on the thin, hard mattress of his bed: Alice's engagement ring.

Numb, he slowly turned his gaze from the simple circle to the final envelope, pristine in comparison to its well-travelled bedfellows. He peeled it open and read, in disbelief, Alice's writing. A mist descended and Parry remained very still, his own letters clutched in his fist. After opening the package containing his now ex-fiancée's engagement ring, Parry sat on the bed for a long time, then took to pacing. Mentally, he hadn't felt himself since a bout of sunstroke the previous summer. Under an unusually punishing sun, he had spent the day cleaning machinery; after that, he was bed-bound for three days and unwell for another seven. His constant drinking of late hadn't helped. By all accounts he was an intelligent and nice young man, but his temper was quick and his nerves easily shattered; it took a few minutes before the fog cleared and a plan could be formed. Alice. He needed to speak to Alice.

Glancing around the room, his bright, brown eyes unblinking, he did some mental calculations. He had, perhaps, just enough for a train ticket.

No salary was owed to him, and he had spent all but a pittance on gifts for Alice, not to mention the ring. *It must have been Mack in her ear. Or another man?* He couldn't entertain that now; the thought threatened to send him into a spiral. Now was the time to be organised. After gathering himself for a moment in his room, he prepared to go to Galway. It was late, and logic said to wait until the morning. But it couldn't wait.

Getting leave from his duties at such short notice had been easier than he thought. It was a blur, but he recalled beckoning Ed Peyton – his master and the man who had hired him at Miss Newsom's – to the garden. There, he had Alice's package laid out: scraps of letters, the odd small gift. The ring. Every token of his love, unmercifully bundled up and packed onto a mail train. Ed surveyed him closely as he spoke; his scattered sentences, flushed face – the man was beside himself. Without any protest, he gave Parry the time off.

Parry returned to his room and dressed smartly. Looking his best was an imperative. And there was no time to pack a bag. He reached, instead, between a cluster of empty bottles for a small, cloth-wrapped bundle he'd had for six months, untouched. One last present for Alice. Edenderry to Galway was a little over 110 miles. He'd better get going.

The train zipped through the night. Thomas Parry sat aboard, breathing heavily, eyes fixed forward. The grief pulsing through him was difficult to contain. It splashed flecks of red on his cheeks and beads of sweat on his brow. Thoughts came fast, unorganised. Controlling his arms and legs was a constant effort; he tensed up, clutching the small, hard package on his lap. He focused on the plan: *Salthill for 6.30, breakfast for 8. Salthill for 6.30, breakfast for 8.*

It was after midnight on 29 July 1884 when Parry arrived in Galway. His excitable state had somewhat subsided, quietened by the grumbling of his stomach. He only realised as he crossed Eyre Square how long it had been since he had eaten anything. Approaching the Imperial Hotel, he had to remain small. The Royal, next door, housed his beloved. He knew its rooms and hallways well and ideally he would have lodged in there, though he couldn't guarantee how his presence would be welcomed. The Imperial would do. Out of eagerness, he considered simply asking for her at reception, though Mr Mack would likely object and she would be long asleep by now. He could wait until morning to speak to her – the plan would work. Luckily, the streets were all but deserted. The perfect time of night for a man who didn't want to be seen.

Thomas Nolan, the manager of the Imperial, didn't ask many questions beyond what train Parry had arrived by. More importantly, he hadn't recognised him from the near week he had spent living next door earlier that summer. He had the space, and he was happy to book the young man in and serve him some food. Parry ordered two bottles of porter, which he quaffed steadily with his meal. When he'd finished, he called for a half glass of whiskey to chase. That dispatched, he ordered another. He tipped the waiter and retired to his room for the night.

Sleep didn't come to him. *Salthill for 6.30.* He lay down and tried his best to drift off. *Breakfast for 8.* Fits of passion ignited him each time his mind approached peace. *Salthill for 6.30.* Restless, he took a sheet of paper from the bureau and penned a letter to his father, William, by lamplight. *Breakfast for 8.* He folded the letter, slid it into his coat pocket, and lay back down on the bed.

What would he say when he saw her? He loved her so. But the ring, 'the flirt'. Mack wanted someone better for her. The fool. She wouldn't get away with it.

Morning came. Parry sat on his bed, dazed. His perishing thirst had returned. The clock face read 6 o'clock – *Salthill for 6.30.* His eyes, dazzled by the glare from the window and foggy from the whiskey, took a moment to focus. His gaze landed on the wrapped-up bundle on the table beside his bed – his only luggage. Alice was awake by now, in the building next door. Feet away. Part one of her morning schedule approached: swimming at Salthill with her sister, Bessie, at 6.30. He had gone there with her himself; he basked in the memory, thinking of Alice up to her waist, splashing playfully at her sister, catching him looking. The smile she gave still melted his heart. He'd been so lucky.

The breakfast room in the Imperial was well tended to. Thomas Nolan, he found, was up ahead of him, pleasantly greeting the stream of guests who must have risen for the first train. He caught Parry's eye and wandered over.

'Ah, good morning,' all smiles, 'how did you sleep?'

'Excellently, thank you. Could I trouble you for some grog?'

If Nolan judged him for his order, Parry hadn't noticed. He was looking about at the guests and through the front window of the hotel, into Eyre Square.

'Mr Nolan, when does the first train leave?' Parry's eyes were fixed on the road outside.

'Half past six. Why, there's Mrs Mack going for it now – her husband owns the Royal Hotel, next door,' replied Mr Nolan, pointing at Alice's mother as she crossed by the window.

'I know them better than you,' Parry replied, 'and that is not the party I want to see.'

The grog didn't quite hit the spot. Parry ordered a whiskey shortly after, and another near 8 am to settle his nerves. *Breakfast for 8.* Part two of his beloved's morning schedule was coming down the line – at this hour every day, before Alice began her own duties at the hotel, she breakfasted. This, he decided, would be the ideal time to greet her, as it coincided with another key player in the drama: Mr Mack.

The old fool would depart for Salthill himself usually at about 8 am. Parry distinctly recalled the unpleasant invitation for a morning dip with Mr Mack, which he'd felt compelled to accept during his recent visit. Torturous, intense minutes spent away from Alice. The invite, he supposed, was to gauge him as to his suitability to marry Alice. Parry cared little about his opinion, let alone trying to perform for him. In any case, the swim proved useful in one way; Parry now knew when Mr Mack would be away on the morning of 29 July. One fewer obstacle.

The clock closed in on 8. Parry rose and patted the pockets of his coat to ensure he'd remembered his package and the note to his father. He paid his bill, and left the Imperial Hotel for the last time, treading slowly down the steps into Eyre Square.

His heart, broken, raced pathetically in his chest. He took a calm walk through the ever-growing crowds of people on the path. One thing began to trouble him: Mr Mack. Parry was fairly certain he would be safely at Salthill by now, and Alice sitting down to breakfast. But what if they were away? What if Mack delayed his swim today, or felt ill and didn't go at all? Was he about to be disgraced and ejected from the hotel? Was his embarrassment to be compounded? To hedge his bets, he decided to go in a back entrance, through the ballroom – an entrance he'd seen used once or twice by staff. Walking calmly around the edge of the building, he quietly climbed a set of large stone steps leading to the door he sought. He took a deep breath, put his hand on the large handle, and pulled. Nothing. Locked. It would have to be another door.

Turning around and descending the steps, he saw a young man named James Murphy washing a car in the yard. He didn't recognise it. Possibly it was Mr Mack's, possibly a guest's.

'Excuse me,' he said to the worker, 'is Mr Mack in?'

'No, sir,' replied the young man. 'He's now at Salthill.'

How predictable. Perfect.

Parry, buoyed with his correct guess and a plan back on track, asked the young man to accompany him inside the hotel with the steady voice and confidence of a guest who'd lost his way.

They arrived to the hall door, which led directly to the breakfast room. It was busy, busier than the Imperial had been. Parry entered and his eyes panned the room slowly. Then his heart stopped.

Alice had her back to him, though he would recognise her hair and neck – beautiful – through the darkest night. He stood for a moment, ignoring the worker who had led him this far. There were two girls with Alice – one he recognised as her sister, Bessie Burns, and the other was her young niece, Fanny Rickaby.

You've come this far. What are you going to say?

His heart leapt, his face froze. Slowly, he approached the table.

'Excuse me, ladies.' They each looked up from their plates. It took Alice a moment to realise what was happening. Her mouth opened in disbelief as Thomas Parry shook hands with her two companions, then with her. His ears rang; rage filled him. *Where are your manners?*

'I am sorry to have disturbed your breakfast,' he offered, turning to face Alice. The pain bubbled up – Salthill, the letters, Mr Mack. The ring. *Why?*

'Why, Alice?' He kept it steady. 'Why did you give me up?'

Alice's mouth opened again, her eyes glued to her ex-fiancé. She muttered, under her breath, a reply that nobody heard, except Thomas Parry.

'We will see,' he said softly. Reaching into his pocket, Parry's fingers found the cold handle of the loaded revolver he had carried with him 100 miles. He gripped it tightly. All in a moment, the gun was drawn and aimed, point-blank, at Alice.

The shot rang out through the breakfast room, piercing the low rumble of chat and clinking glasses. Pandemonium ensued. The dining hall exploded into screams and a blur of movement. Alice stood, bleeding and screeching, and scrambled for the door. Bessie and Fanny ran for a different exit at the opposite end of the room. Murphy, who had remained outside the door and had a head start on the throngs pouring out, broke into a sprint, heading for the police barracks.

Parry remained collected and walked after Alice. His beloved made it as far as the passage leading to the room. Then Parry shot again. She lay still, face down on the floor. Her breath grew shallow. Parry walked to her side, aimed again, and shot her twice more in the back. One of the final pellets passed directly through her heart. Next, he turned the revolver on himself, pointing at his abdomen, and squeezed the trigger.

The bullet ripped through Parry's flannel shirt with ease, yet he remained standing. Unsure of how to proceed, he walked up one flight of stairs, then down another, then casually left the building, descending the steps at the front of the hotel.

James O'Halloran, who had been working next door at the saddlery when he heard the shots, arrived to the front door of the Royal just as Parry emerged, dazed and covered in gunpowder. The weapon hung loosely in his hand. O'Halloran immediately snatched the pistol from him and tackled him to the ground, pinning him down with the help of another passer-by named Donnellan. Parry said nothing, and didn't struggle.

Inside, Bessie and Fanny had returned to Alice's body. She was carried into a room and a doctor was called for, but she was already dead. Thomas F. Brady, the head of the fisheries department who happened to be staying at the Royal, had been descending the main stairs at the moment of the shooting, and had seen the lifeless body of the proprietor's stepdaughter carried from the bloodied floor of the passage.

Brady exited the front door of the hotel, descended the steps and marched up to where Parry was being restrained. 'You ruffian,' he spat at Parry, who turned his head to face him, 'you have shot her!'

'I am damned glad of it,' Parry replied without a beat. 'That is what I came for.'

Murphy was sweating when he arrived at Prospect Hill barracks, shouting about guns and blood. He was hard to calm down. Constable Conden deciphered the basics and took off for Eyre Square, where he found a dishevelled man being held by two others on the new pavement in front of the Royal Hotel. Another man stood nearby, sheepishly holding a revolver out to the policeman. Five barrels discharged.

Back at the barracks, Parry wasn't shying away from his actions. Far from it. He wanted no delay in meeting James Berry. 'I have come 112 miles to do it,' he declared to constables. 'I have shot her. I would not let any girl play on me. She was engaged to me for some months. She refused my letters and my engagement ring.' The pieces of the puzzle were all there. Home run. At 1 pm on the day Alice Burns was killed, an inquest was held by the coroner, Robert Stephens.

Bessie Burns, Alice's sister, gave the play-by-play of the brief, lethal exchange. Dr MacConnell of Glenamaddy, who had been first to respond, said he examined Ms Burns after the shooting, and discovered a ball under the skin, directly over the breastbone. He held the post-mortem examination, along with Dr Valentine Browne, another physician who taught at the university. According to a report from the *Ballinrobe Chronicle*, 'Dr Browne stated he had found four pistol or gunshot wounds on the body, and had extracted two of the bullets; death must have been almost instantaneous.' One of the bullets had entered her side, and passed directly through Alice's heart. There was another wound evident, but he did not pursue the course of the bullet, 'as the lady was not undressed,' wrote a reporter for the *Irish Times*. George Mack was examined, but could offer little assistance; 'his evidence only went to show that deceased was alive when he left the hotel at 8 o'clock in the morning, and dead when he returned at 9'. But, of course that was the case. Such was Parry's plan.

The official inquest verdict is contained in the police report that evening, written by District Inspector Lennon – who was evidently having a busy year for homicides. 'The deceased died on Tuesday 29 July 1884 at Eyre Square Galway from the effects of pistol shot wounds wilfully inflicted on her.' It was Lennon who ordered Parry to appear before Resident Magistrate P.T. Lyster, directly after the short inquest. At about 1.30 pm, Parry made a statement admitting his guilt, and 'expressing his willingness to suffer for the deed'. He was remanded until 3 pm the next day.

Parry was then loaded into an outside car. The impact of his actions on the townspeople, though the murder was just hours beforehand, was already clear. Crowds gathered around the car and a heavy police escort kept the mob – thousands in number – at bay. Mr Mack was well known, but his 19-year-old niece had been extremely popular in the area. 'Great regret is felt in Galway,' wrote one reporter, 'where Miss Burns was a general favourite.'

The next day, before Judge Murphy, a true bill was handed in by a grand jury against Thomas Parry, meaning he was to be sent forward for trial at the present assizes, which were ongoing at the time of the killing. A reporter for the *Freeman's Journal* described Parry as 'a young man of middle height and respectable but somewhat commonplace appearance, preserved undisturbed composure, but evidently by a strong effort of his will'.

Parry pulled, with effort, the same strained poker face as his trial was postponed until the next assizes, due to there being no time to establish a defence case and on application from his legal representatives. Elizabeth Newsom, his employer, had already arrived in Galway. Parry was well connected, and a team of 'professional gentlemen' – from lawyers to doctors – were ready to stand in. 'The prisoner himself is, it is stated, most anxious to plead guilty and to be hanged forthwith,' reads a *Connacht Telegraph* report. 'His only regret, he has publicly stated, is that he did not succeed in shooting himself. He says he would prefer death by shooting to death by hanging.' At the hearing, Parry told the court he gave Alice no time, and he wanted none. He showed no mercy, and wanted none himself.

Top right: Murder by a Sweetheart – Galway. *The Illustrated Police News*, 9 August 1884.

Papers rightly pointed out the 'great excitement' the case had drummed up in Galway. It was evident in the press, too: 'SHOCKING TRAGEDY IN GALWAY'; 'MURDER AND ATTEMPTED SUICIDE'; 'DREADFUL MURDER IN GALWAY – KILLING HIS SWEETHEART'. The above three headlines (*Ballinrobe Chronicle, Freeman's Journal, Kerry Sentinel*) denote well the fever that engulfed newspapers.

It was a busy weekend at the courts. The delaying of Thomas Parry's case until the next assizes somewhat took press focus from other proceedings happening at the same time. Namely, the Clonboo murder trial.

Downey's day in court had come. At the summer assizes in Galway, as with any high-profile murder case, crowds gathered at the courthouse. Not quite the throng that formed the procession when Thomas Parry left the courthouse two days beforehand, but quite a stir nonetheless.

Michael Downey had lost weight, but not his resolve – he insisted the prosecution had the wrong man. On Friday 1 August 1884, just as papers nationwide received details of the postponement of the Eyre Square sweetheart assassination trial, Downey was indicted for the wilful murder of John Moylan at Clonboo nearly eight months before, on 19 December 1883.

Mr Taylor addressed the jury for Michael Downey, and Charles Edward 'The MacDermot' replied on the part of the Crown, reading through the evidence gathered at length by the inspectors in Galway and substantiated with expert opinion. The case was heard before Mr Justice Johnson.

An *Irish Times* reporter present at the hearing recorded the judge's charge to the jury, whose duty, he said,

was to give a verdict according to the evidence, which must be clear and conclusive, leaving no reasonable doubt, such as would exist in the important concerns of life on the minds of the jury. If the jury were satisfied that guilt was brought home to the prisoner it was their bounden duty to convict him, but if not they were bound to acquit him.

It was about 1.40 pm when the jury retired. 'The jury cannot agree,' was the unwelcome address from the foreman to the judge about an hour later. The judge asked if there was anything that could be done to assist them, to which the foreman replied. 'No, my lord, and there is no chance of our agreeing.'

'You must again retire, gentlemen,' he ordered, and they went out again. They were a long time gone. Tension filled the courtroom as the result began to look inevitable – 'no chance of agreeing' was a strong statement from a foreman. When they came back, after what the reporter described as a lengthy absence, they still disagreed.

The trial of Michael Downey was, again, put forward until the next assizes. 'This concluded the business of the assizes and the learned judges left for Dublin.'

Another frustration for the prosecutors. If they wanted to see Michael Downey – and now Thomas Parry – brought to justice, they would have to wait until winter.

15

THE MADNESS OF THOMAS PARRY

T homas Parry shot Alice Burns. He admitted as much himself, with zeal. Building his defence case wasn't a matter of disputing the course of events, it was about absolving him of responsibility and proving his insanity.

By the time of the census report for 1881 (the nearest to the killing of Alice Burns), instances of 'lunatics' had greatly reduced, partly owing to a number of redefinitions in the preceding decade. At the beginning of the 1880s, there were a total of 9,774 lunatics in the census, with a fairly even breakdown of 4,857:4,917 male:female. The vast majority, 7,547, were housed in the district asylums; 1,284 were in the workhouses; while 943 were classed 'at large'. The number of 'idiots' was 8,639, with a gender breakdown of 4,674:3,965. Of the total, 4,548 were 'at large', 1,896 were in asylums and 2,195 were in workhouses. Zero lunatics or idiots were reported as being in prison, though the General Prison Board (GBP) would have strongly refuted that by the time Thomas Parry made it to Galway Gaol.

Of the 'lunatics' and 'idiots' in the institutions and in society, the most popular job was labourer, followed by servant. Some of the disorders listed as fitting into the categories were: mania; melancholia; monomania; epilepsy; idiocy; idiocy and epilepsy; dementia; dementia and epilepsy. An illuminating section of the lunacy and idiocy section of the report lists the 'causes thereof'. Here are the top causes, in order of prevalence:

Total of 4,159 cause listed: 1,748 'moral or mental' causes, 1,540 physical, 871 hereditary:

Moral & mental

1   Grief 485

2   Terror 293

3   Religious excitement 293

4   Reverse of fortune 199

5   Love and jealousy 141

6   Disappointment 130

(No others reached 100 instances.)

Physical

1   Head injury 301

2   Intemperance 297

3   Epilepsy 284

4   Nervous system disease 192

5   Structure 189

(Again, no others reached 100.)

The 'lunatic' ratio in 1881 was 1:529 as per the general population. Leinster had the most at 1:482, followed closely by Munster (1:493), Ulster (1:625) and Connacht (1:729). Meath, as a county, had the most (1:299). Galway was relatively low at 1:710; it was up to the defence to show that Thomas Parry fit into that equation. Considering 'love and jealousy' was an official cause of insanity, it wasn't an unrealistic target.

The defence case for Parry, and the details of building it, cannot be gleaned from the police reports on the case, though the expense claims of his counsel, Mr O'Farrell, show the effort made to gather evidence for hereditary madness. O'Farrell visited, most remarkably, Limerick District Lunatic Asylum, where an uncle of Parry's, an elderly man named William Wilson, was a long-time patient. Incidentally, he had a hard time getting those expenses back.

From Parry's admission to Galway Gaol on 29 July, he was in close contact with Dr Kinkead. In early December, Dr Kinkead sent a lengthy report of his dealings with Parry, and his opinion on his state of mind.

Kinkead entered the room and looked over Parry. Physically, he looked fine for a man who had, hours before, shot his sweetheart in cold blood. About twenty-seven years old. Medium in stature, though thin and decidedly nervous-looking. He had bright eyes, but they were dark in colour. His ears were large. As a man, he didn't look like he was involved in anything outdoorsy. 'The type of a city artisan,' the doctor wrote, 'more than of one all his life following agricultural pursuits.'

The doctor sat beside Parry, who was quite calm. He asked him the basics – his name, his medical history. 'Cool and collected' were the doctor's first impressions. The answers Parry gave were impressively rational, and he was happy to give them. His family, the young man said, were healthy, though he had been suffering from heart palpitations for about six months.

Kinkead was aware of what had happened at the hotel. He knew, also, that the man had apparently shot himself. He asked Parry to undress and examined him. His clothes, Kinkead saw, bore the marks of having been involved in a shooting. Gunpowder flecked his waistcoat. Two shirts were taken from him – an outer made of linen and an inner flannel one. The outer shirt had a large hole in it, and was stained with powder – there were two holes in the flannel shirt, one slightly larger, denoting an exit.

But there appeared to be no entry wound on Parry. He had a cut – later referred to as a graze, on his left flank, above the navel. It was red, and had gunpowder in it. The direction of the shot that caused was 'from above, downward and outwards'.

Kinkead had already been through a number of suicide examinations that year. In his journal after the initial examination, it's clear he was taking no risks this time: 'This man to be carefully and constantly watched, both day and night, taking away braces, handkerchief, necktie and everything he could commit suicide with.'

Not long into his incarceration, Parry began complaining of disturbed sleep. 'I cannot say whether it was on his admission, but if not it was within the next day or two – he complained of headache, said he had suffered from it frequently for some time, and complained of not being able to sleep and stated that for some time previous to admission he had scarcely slept at all,' wrote Kinkead. Bromide of potassium, and after that a gin, followed by a bottle of porter at bedtime, and he was back on track, with the complaints diminishing and warders confirming he was sleeping soundly at lights-out.

On 3 or 4 August, Kinkead was called into the prison office and handed a note. The letter isn't included in any files and appears to have been posted at some point before the trial. However, one version of the letter – with some errors – was reported in newspapers:

My Dear Father,
I drop you a line to say I arrived here tonight. There is no occasion for me to tell you any further about my visit to Galway; but, thanks be to God, I never felt better than what I do at the present time. I told you before I am led to destruction by the way Alice has treated me. As far as she could deceive me she has done it, after a period of 15 months' engagement, and wearing the engagement ring the greatest part of the time.
I received a letter from her on Monday morning, 21st, saying she changed her mind and wished to give me up, but I will be sure no other fellow will have the chance of having her when she does not want me. I have no more to tell you, my dear father, only enclose you some of her letters to me, and you have already got the last one I received from her. So goodbye, my dear father, mother, brothers and sisters. May the Lord forgive her and me also and be merciful to us – I am your ever loving son.
Thomas Parry
To Mr William Parry, Coolmelagh, Clonegal, County Wexford

The above letter has some inconsistencies; the date he says he received the last letter from Alice, for instance, is incorrect. Nevertheless, it's the closest record to the actual note which Dr Kinkead held in his hand four days after Parry's admission to Galway Gaol. The most remarkable aspect, for the doctor, was its coldness. 'I read that letter attentively, on it there was no expression of sorrow, remorse, or anything which would lead to the belief that he was conscious of having done anything wrong,' wrote the doctor.

A second doctor, Mr Rice, was employed by Parry's defence team to look over the accused. Dr Kinkead, as medical officer, was present for both examinations, one in August, and the other in November. Parry's account of himself was connected and rational, and Mr Rice remarked to Kinkead that his statements could be depended on.

Kinkead recorded Parry's account:

That his health has been always good until July 1883 when he had a sun stroke. He knew it was a sunstroke because the doctor told him so. He got it when he was at work cleaning machinery – it affected him thus; he got headache and felt faint. Was able to go on about half a mile, had to go to bed at once and after going to bed, because unconscious, he did not know how long he was unconscious, might be an hour or two. His stomach was sick but he did not vomit – was confined to bed two days and a half, did not feel well for a week or ten days after – but able to go about his work – his head felt light and he was weak. Since then he suffered from headache and does so still.

At times has flashes of light before his eyes and head feels light. Can't smoke, the doctor told him not to smoke – but has done so and it makes his head light and feel as if he would fall.

Parry told the doctors he had been drinking heavily, and knew Alice was pulling away. Parry 'knew by her letters she was getting careless', and told the doctor about the letter on the 23rd, in which she told Parry she was called 'the flirt'. Finally, he received the break-up letter on the 28th, when he set out for Galway. 'He got the revolver to protect himself long before, did not get it for the purpose, it was six months loaded, did not load it for the purpose of shooting the girl, took it just as it was.'

The weight of his crime was gradually dawning on him. A religious childhood had ostensibly taught him good from evil, and he knew then – at the time of the examination with Rice and Kinkead – what he did was wrong.

He couldn't grasp it when he pulled the trigger – his mind had been in a whirl from the time he opened the letter. Yet he seemed to say he had the wherewithal to understand the repercussions: 'Said he did not think of being hanged for it, for he was determined to kill himself and if he was dead how could he be hanged? Had been there thereafter in prison and now knew it was wrong and was sorry.'

The man seemed sane. His composure was remarkable. But when the doctors approached the issue of finances and asked if he had any wages owed to him, a flash of rage exposed itself. There was no salary due to him – he had drawn it all. How could he have any money when he spent it all on her? he said. Was it likely he'd have any after buying her clothes, jewellery and paying her fare and his own to bring her to Dublin to her aunt, to come to Galway…

Kinkead paid close attention to the sudden change:

> Up to this point he was as indifferent as if he was talking of some one else, and he expressed sorrow and remorse beyond the mere admission; there was no sign of it … no evidence of feeling … but now, his eyes became bright, his face flushed and his voice became loud and angry as he rapidly detailed what he had done for her.

Two months went by. Parry's general health improved and 'he picked up flesh' – weight gain was common in prisons then, owing to a regular diet and less labour. From the time of imprisonment to the time of his trial he gained at least 1.5 stone. On 24 October, Parry had a visit from his brother, late in the evening.

Shortly after, the doctor was summoned to see the prisoner. He found Parry lying on his back in bed, deathly pale, his skin cold and moist. His body was weak, but his heart was beating through his chest and his pupils were dilated: the warders confirmed he had been worse before the doctor arrived. He seemed to have settled down, and it was treated as one of a handful of isolated health incidents. Official documents on Parry's well-being indicate his overall physical health was 'good' throughout his incarceration.

Kinkead pored over the evidence concerning the elusive inmate in Limerick. He was informed by Mr Rice, with O'Farrell having done his homework, of Parry's maternal uncle in the city's asylum. It was, in fact, his great uncle who had been housed in the facility; the medical officer confirmed in a letter that Wilson was being confined on the basis of 'homicidal tendencies'.

While on the train to the assizes in December, Dr Kinkead happened to sit near a man named Manley Palmer, who was heading to Carrick-on-Shannon for the same reason; he was to give evidence of a familial streak of madness. He was an old acquaintance of the family, and the doctor put great weight behind his testimony, which emerged officially later, at the trial.

Kinkead wrote extensively about the calculating manner of the murder itself, and Parry's complete lack of consideration as to what would happen to him. By all accounts, he had been a steady, upstanding young man, until the sunstroke, after which stories of impulsivity and incandescent rage popped up. His behaviour on the day defied all sense:

> He made no attempt to escape, but walked out and stood opposite the door. To any one who spoke to him, he said he was damned glad he had done it that he came 112 miles to do it and insisted that he had a bullet in his own body … The next day, the 30th, he made a statement that he did the deed he gave no mercy and he wanted none and hoped he would be tried at once.

From all of the information at his disposal, the doctor concluded that Parry was of unsound mind, and was so at the time he shot Alice Burns.

He listed his reasons in the initial report and later writings about the case:

1. The family history.
2. His behaviour on the day and following the attack.
3. The sun stroke – 'excluding the family history sunstroke alone would be quite sufficient to produce insanity – it is well known that various forms of insanity follow sunstroke …'
4. The physical symptoms, including a headache following the attack, coupled with rantings and sleep trouble. The doctor also pointed to

the flashes of light, which were often an indicator of 'serious mental disturbance'.

5. Change in disposition, according to his family, particularly towards his mother, to whom he had always been affectionate, and after the sunstroke had threatened to shoot dead in an argument.

6. A 'powerful passion' acting in a brain injured by sunstroke.

7. A sudden giving way to alcohol – 'for a week or ten days prior to the murder he was drinking day and night. This is well known, that a sudden crave for stimulant in a previously temperate man is precisely indicative of insanity.' When he was weaned from the drink, he became more temperate.

8. His letter and statement showing an 'utter incapability to understand' the guilt of his conduct or the enormity of his crime. Alice's 'crime' of breaking up with him, or acting in a way he deemed unworthy, was seemingly placed on the same level as his own.

9. Dr Kinkead's own close observation over 14 documented interactions.

10. The suicide attempt. Parry was religious, 'yet on the very morning of the crime, with the determination of [committing] it and killing himself fixed in his head he writes to his father: "Thanks be to God I never felt better in my life" – a blasphemy too appalling to be compatible with sanity'. The marks on his clothes told the doctor the suicide attempt was genuine. 'Some authorities hold that suicide is always a proof of insanity. I know not, but it most frequently is, and in the cases where it is a sane action, there is some good logical reason why it is deliberately chosen … and I think [it shows] a disbelief in the doctrines of christianity.'

11. Finally, Parry never said he was insane. He understood that his friends, through letters to authorities, had proposed the idea and that it was being pursued by his defence team. 'Yet never by word or deed does he try to lead me or any prison officer to believe he was not of perfectly sound mind,' wrote Kinkead. 'My experience agrees with that of authorities in insanity – that the really insane do not shame.'

Repeated descriptions of a 'cool and collected' murderer, and the calculated plan and execution of the attack, did little to promote much sympathy for Parry. Dr Kinkead, on the other hand, had a nuanced view of insanity. At the same time, he knew it was a hard sell.

'The great difficulty in this case is the appearance of intellectual sanity – and it was only after the most careful consideration and investigation that I came to what I believe the true failure of his case,' he wrote of the case. 'The law only recognises knowledge as a test of responsibility – if a man knows that his act will cause death and that the consequences of his act is punishment – the law holds him responsible – but that test would convict the majority of the insane in asylums. Indeed, the whole management of asylums presupposes a knowledge of right and wrong.'

The mind, he insisted, was not merely intellect, but emotions, passions, compassion and judgement. The knowledge of what one is doing and the ability to restrain oneself were two different things. 'His memory may be perfect, may be abnormally so, he may argue logically, reason conclusively and yet be unable to appreciate the difference between trifling offences and heinous crime.'

Parry's insane mind magnified offences against him, according to the doctor. 'Passion is to the will what illusions are to the senses, and delusions are to the mind,' he said. 'The sane mind can control them, the unsound mind cannot.'

Kinkead was something of a specialist in insanity. As a lecturer in medical jurisprudence, he had to be. His conclusion, he said, was carefully thought out. Parry was not able to control his passions and was of unsound mind on the day he killed Alice Burns; his insanity was caused by sunstroke and hereditary weakness.

But Parry was fit to stand trial. It would be for a jury to decide whether or not Parry was insane at the time he killed Alice. Kinkead, unsurprisingly, was subpoenaed for the defence. If they were going to save Parry from Berry's rope, Kinkead was the best weapon they had.

16

AND JUSTICE FOR ALL

T he Connacht winter assizes at Carrick-on-Shannon, 1884, captured the attention of the county and the nation. Both Michael Downey and Thomas Parry – alleged perpetrators of two of the most remarkable murders in the county's recent history – were due before Justice Lawson. One after the other.

On 11 December, shortly after 10 am, Justice Lawson resumed the assizes. First up that day was Michael Downey, who took his place in the dock – a well-formed habit – nearly a year to the week after he allegedly gunned down John Moylan in cold blood on a lonely, dark boreen in Clonboo. Serjeant Robinson and The MacDermot appeared for the Crown, while Taylor, this time accompanied by O'Malley, appeared for the defence, instructed by Concannon.

Mary Moylan was examined. Her life had virtually been on hold since the proceedings began, and she had been under police protection for nearly a year, at some expense. She gave the story she had deposed a year earlier when she traded her way out of gaol: the man in the dark, Michael Downey's face, her poor husband's limp body, his shattered face.

Judge Lawson read Mary's evidence for the jury, and commented on a single, remarkable document in the chain of evidence – the long-sweated-over threatening letter – 'which was relied on by the Crown as to the guilt of the prisoner, for it did not admit of doubt that the person who left this document on the breast of the murdered man was the person guilty of the murder'.

The judge moved first to absolve the Smalls – Mary's family – from any wrongdoing. They were never seriously considered for the crime, as per the internal police memos, but no doubt ill feeling had come their way in the wake of revelations about Mary's behaviour.

At the centre of this case was a salacious rumour, which served the rubberneckers above all. A lonely woman. The younger, fit man next door. The poor, absentee farmer. It had it all, but nothing, of course, could be proved. The absence of a child throughout the alleged fornicating was raised as a possible pin with which to pop the gossip bubble, though that in itself didn't settle much. On that, the judge had his part to say, according to a report in the *Irish Times*:

> Referring to the suggestion that in the absence of Moylan in America improper relations had been formed between the prisoner and Mary Moylan, he observed that during the two and a half years the deceased was away no child was born. That was a circumstance as to which he not think it necessary they should form any conclusion; but, though they might have their suspicions, this, at all events, was certain, that the prisoner made himself quite at home in Moylan's house in Moylan's absence and once or twice he slept in the house.

The purpose of the judge's address on Mary's evidence, he said, was to attach the appropriate history about her testimony, in order that the jury could determine its credit, adding that,

> as to the first great discrepancy in this woman's testimony, if she had not been a dreadful woman and privy to this transaction, she would immediately after the murder have told that Michael Downey was the murderer of her husband if he were; but though the police sergeant and others were there seen after the murder she never mentioned to them the name of the prisoner.

Mary's reputation, convicted or not, was shattered at this point. Further than her obfuscation of the true identity of the murderer, the judge lambasted her testimony in the inquest as a 'tissue of falsehood'. Furthermore:

When she was arrested she made a clean breast of it, and in distinct, positive and express terms said that the prisoner was the man who murdered her husband. If this case rested on the testimony of Mary Moylan, or even mainly on her testimony, he would not recommend them to find the prisoner guilty. He did not say that she was an accomplice, but she was a person who swore one thing one day, and another thing another day, and was therefore not entitled to receive any credence from a jury.

But it was on other evidence that the jury were directed to make their decision. The fact that they were seen speaking at the well on the day of the murder. A flimsy alibi, constructed to make sure someone else saw him that night. The traces of blood in the water which trickled from the trousers. The gun. The American boots and socks concealed in the ivy wall, happened upon by a conscientious constable. A claim from Downey that had no substance to it, that he had been killing rabbits. It was difficult, the judge said, to reconcile all the facts with the innocence of the prisoner, regardless of the widow's testimony. Lawson then read out, line by line, the statements he made while in custody to Resident Magistrate Lyster, and his cross-examination of Mary Moylan.

The judge told the jury there was nothing to indicate unsoundness of mind on Downey's part. On the contrary, his statements showed a great deal of art; 'but when a man committed a crime he was subject to a great deal of infatuation, and he said and did things which led to the discovery of his crime'. Downey need only have taken advice – from anyone – and he would not have uttered his statements to the magistrate. That had been his real downfall.

Lawson charged the jury in the usual manner, reminding them that if they considered the evidence conclusive, they should find him guilty. If they had reasonable doubt, he had to be acquitted.

An hour and 15 minutes later the jury returned, as the last one had done, without a decision. Again, they were sent back. About 25 minutes after their second retreat, they emerged again, and with an air of deliberate forcefulness that didn't escape reporters' gazes, concluded they would not agree. It wasn't confirmed in official channels, but whispers in the courtroom indicated it was a 50-50 split.

Lawson, accepting the result, discharged the jury, admitting he wouldn't be justified in keeping them any longer. Downey's case was to be tried again, but there wouldn't be a delay this time – he was to appear before the same assizes, with a different jury.

Once again, on Monday 15 December 1884, Michael Downey, a physical shadow of his former self, entered the courtroom for his third trial for the murder of John Moylan. The courtroom was, again, packed – a trend that had been set the previous week, when the jury's split decision saw Downey spared.

The night before the third trial of Michael Downey, the prosecution notified the defence counsels they were planning to introduce two new witnesses: a local woman, Margaret Scahill, and a man named Feeny. Their names had not appeared in any previous witness lists, and their introduction was news to the court. Ultimately, to save time, Serjeant Robinson for the prosecution avoided the inevitable conflict and stood them down; their testimony, he said, was not vital. It's not clear exactly what they would have contributed, but their last-minute inclusion shows a wobble in the Crown Solicitor's previous steady assurance that they could convict Downey with ease.

Lawson took his seat on the bench at about 10.30 and a jury was empanelled, after a little back and forth and a number of exclusions. Again, Robinson and The MacDermot appeared for the Crown and Messrs O'Malley and Taylor defended. Serjeant Robinson laid out the case for the Crown, leaning more heavily this time on the disruption of marital bliss.

He painted a quaint picture. A small, industrious farmer left his family, with a heavy heart, to realise a little money to clear off a charge on his little farm. The money – £103 by his estimation over two years and nine months – reached his wife's hands, as he had promised. Meanwhile, a young, unmarried labourer who lived nearby struck up relations with the lonely wife. 'The prisoner kept his gun in the chimney of the room in which Mary Moylan slept and on two occasions, at all events, though his own house was convenient, he slept in Moylan's house,' he reasoned, according to a report in the *Irish Times*.

Criminal intimacy between the parties, he said, couldn't be proved. Why then, during Downey's cross-examination of Mary when she first accused him of murder, did he become so impassioned? Why did he ask her to say if there really was nothing between them? There was no child, certainly, but 'no doubt would remain on their minds that at all events such relations existed between the parties as should not have existed between a respectable married woman and a man who was not her husband'.

John returned, and heard the whispers. He ejected Downey and his sister out of the house. A week before the murder, the jury would hear that a man named Kelly was approached by Downey, and asked to procure some ammunition. Kelly declined. It was curious then that the slug found in Moylan's head was nothing more than a self-rounded ball of lead – a practice Downey often employed when he hunted wild geese. 'It would be proved,' he said, 'that the slug which was found in Moylan's head was not the class usually sold in shops. It was a piece of lead rolled up.'

The motive, he said, was simple. Money. Nine acres adjoining his own land. Moylan's wife. It would be proved that Downey, the day before Moylan was murdered, bought a pencil from a woman named Sarah Allen. Why would a man who could not read or write need a pencil? He submitted that it was part of the plan to form the threatening letter, found on the dead man's breast, to trick the police after the deed.

On the day of the murder, it would be proved Downey met Mary at a nearby well, while Moylan was away. She went to have tea between 3 and 4 o'clock at her father's house in Cregduff, her husband joined her a couple of hours later and during their walk home, at about 9 pm, he was hit with a single shot, 'which struck off the whole of his nose and entered his brain. Shot and slugs tore into his brain.'

Mary raised the alarm at her father's house and when the posse arrived to the body, she took care to make sure the note was preserved. How, in the midst of such a terrible deed, did she have the presence of mind to save key evidence? And why?

As for the threatening message itself? The object of this letter, he said, 'was to throw the constabulary off the scent and send them investigating some conspiracy against Thomas Browne'. To dispel any insistence by Downey to the contrary, he assured the jury that Moylan wasn't killed because of a breach of any secret society laws. He asked the jury to consider the trousers, steeped in a bucket, which were found when police arrived to Michael's house early the next morning. The other physical evidence – bloodstains, ballistics – was compelling.

Mary Moylan's false testimony at the inquest was nothing more than an attempt to shield a man with whom she had been in improper intimate relations. 'She knew that it was Michael Downey who, under his own hand, virtually admitted the deed. He denied that his was the hand that killed the man, but his gun was the gun with which the shot was fired,' Robinson told the jury, before reading Mary's cross-examination, including Downey's emotional interjection for the second time in his address: 'Was there anything between you and me, that I would go to shoot your husband?' She replied, 'I don't think there was.' Then he said, 'Mary, I'll put you from swearing – I'll tell what sort of a woman you are.' Serjeant Robinson then read Downey's statements, attempting to condemn others, and insisting he resisted the woman's temptation – 'not for all the money in Ireland.'

It was the defence's turn. In stepped Mr O'Malley. Beginning his address, he lambasted the authorities for not making available those men whom Downey named in his latter statement. Bolton, as we know now via the internal police documents, was out for Downey's blood – and considered him a 'ruffian'. The Crown Solicitor's zeal was not lost on the defence: 'He wished that Mr Bolton was there to be examined, that they might see whether any influence had been used to obtain from the prisoner the statements he had made.'

The evidence of Mary Moylan, as had been the tack of the defence and also acknowledged by the prosecution and judges so far, was unworthy of credit.

Before the day finished, the court heard from Michael Hannon, who deposed that Downey had called into his house at 10 pm on the night of the murder. Another witness for the defence, a boy named William Leenahan, swore he saw the prisoner skinning rabbits on the day of the murder. As for the trousers in the bucket? Downey's brother said they were being washed, by Bridget Downey, for Christmas.

With that, the trial was adjourned until the next day, 16 December 1884. It was 10.30 am in Carrick-on-Shannon when Justice Lawson took his seat. Downey, again, looked somewhat anxious, as was understandable.

Where Mr O'Malley had left off for the defence, Mr Taylor picked up, continuing on behalf of the prisoner. Though it had looked like the discrediting of Mary Moylan's testimony was finished, it was not. The jury 'could not set on the evidence of the woman Mary Moylan, for no eye saw the murder committed but hers, and she was a person whose testimony was utterly unworthy of credit. They should act on evidence given on oath, but what credit could they attach to the oath of such a woman?'

The defence council then referred, at length, to the evidence. There could be no doubt the money John Moylan sent home was squandered, and the dissatisfaction with his wife was clear, owing to her behaviour during his long absence. 'The wife in consequence wished to get him out of the way,' he put it, frankly. Again he ran through the evidence, explaining away Downey's supposed actions using the shaky foundation on which the accusations stood. He asked the jury not to be too quick to shed blood, and to consider whether the evidence was worthy of a guilty verdict. 'There was no evidence that he committed the murder except that of the woman whose mind plotted and whose heart wished for that dreadful occurrence,' he said. Flimsy proof, he insisted, should not be used to take away a man's life.

Next up was The MacDermot, who thoroughly discredited the outlandish theory proposed by the defence. Which was more likely? The defence counsel, it seems, had some choice words when Downey was again brought forward at the same assizes. MacDermot thought that 'unworthy' of the court, and reminded the jury that the Crown was only acting in society's best interest.

The sad picture again emerged; he recapped on 'poor Moylan', slaving away in America. 'Where did Downey spend his days, and sometimes his nights?' he asked. 'The very gun that was used in the commission of the murder, and which belonged to the prisoner, where did it spend its time? In the chimney of that woman's bedroom. Located there, it was the silent witness of that man and that woman's guilt. There could be no doubt of it.' He wondered aloud why the prisoner's counsel had not yet offered an explanation for that one.

MacDermot more or less reiterated the Crown's position from the day before; relatives of the deceased said Downey was in the house late at night, and the physical evidence and other testimony could only bring about a single rational conclusion. Mary knew of the letter, which had been traced to Downey, and knew of it at the time she spoke to Downey at the well. Mary was in on it. She loved Downey, there was no doubt about that. Had the deed not become uncovered, they would have been married.

Justice Lawson, for the last time, charged the jury, cycling again through the evidence and strongly directing their attention to the prosecution's account of events. The jury retired and came back at 2.30 pm, about an hour and 15 minutes later. The paper was handed down. The verdict was in: guilty. Third time's a charm.

As with many Victorian-era juries, there was a caveat: a plea for his life. 'We recommend him strongly to mercy on the ground of the temptation which had been held out to him by that unfortunate woman.'

Downey, who reporters had described as nervous, was calm and unmoved in the face of the verdict. Interested throughout the trial, he kept his emotions in check. As one reporter put it: 'Though he is scarcely 25 years of age he is a man of nerve, and, in fact, incapable of displaying emotion.'

Lawson addressed Downey, asking why he should not send him to the gallows. 'I have nothing at all to say; but I am innocent of the crime,' he replied, coolly, 'that is all I have to say.'

Lawson then gave his sentence:

> Michael Downey, you have been found guilty of the crime of murder and on evidence that left no doubt on the mind of anyone who attended, that you joined in a conspiracy with this woman to commit that crime, the murder of her husband, and that yours was the hand and yours was the gun that took away the life of that man. The circumstances of the case, and your own statement, have left no doubt of that. The jury have added to their verdict a recommendation of mercy on the ground that perhaps you were tempted by that woman to engage in this crime.

The judge warned him not to hold out any hope of mercy. 'You took away the life of that poor man,' he said, 'and for that deed your life has been justly forfeited to the law.' Lawson assumed the black cap and sentenced Downey to be hanged at Galway Gaol on 16 January 1885.

Downey piped up: 'My Lord, will you allow my people to visit me?'

His solicitor, Mr Concannon, explained to the judge that his sister and brother, whom the police had used deftly to help Downey's conviction, were in the public gallery.

'They may see him,' said the judge.

For a man supposedly unable to control his emotions, Thomas Parry's ability to remain calm was remarkable. Reporters often noted it – even describing the effort he must have exerted to seem so overwhelmingly underwhelmed. The day of his trial for the murder of his fiancée, Alice Burns, was no different.

Smartly presented as ever, Parry stood before Justice Lawson at Carrick-on-Shannon on 11 December 1884. The other high profile-murder case – that of Michael Downey – would end that day with a split decision. Parry's defence team hoped for better than that again.

Serjeant Robinson stated the case for the Crown; he appeared with The MacDermot, both instructed by Mr O'Farrell. For Parry was Mr Bodkin and Mr Taylor (instructed by Mr J.C. O'Farrell).

Robinson painted the picture for the jury. He spoke highly, at first, of Parry. The verdict was in, and it was undeniable that Parry was honest, trustworthy, intelligent. Truly a good character in every way. Until 29 July.

Robinson painstakingly went through the steps of the murder, from the disapproval of Alice's stepfather, Mr Mack, to her sending Parry the letter, to Parry boarding the train and perpetrating the terrible act with orchestrated precision. The exact reason why Alice had broken it off with Parry wasn't known – disapproval from her stepfather, his lack of means to marry, or perhaps she found someone she liked better. Did she see something in him during the Race Week visit that didn't sit well?

The truth? It didn't matter. 'She wrote that letter by which she freed herself from this engagement, as she had a right to do, for in many ways women had not the same advantages as men had, and it was right that a woman should consider whether the man who had won her affections, to whom she was engaged for life, was capable of retaining them,' said Robinson.

Galway was a seaport, Robinson reminded the jury. A beautiful place with 'splendid bathing in its neighbourhood'. It was his knowledge of that, and his former fiancée's fancy of an early swim, that had aided him in his task. He shot her, in cold blood, with a room full of witnesses. When accosted, he admitted to the deed, and said he was 'damned glad of it'. Robinson then read out the letter to his father, as studied by Kinkead months previously, which left little doubt, he said, as to the man's intentions.

Insanity, he understood, was the position of the defence. The jury should pay close attention to this tactic; the defence were not refuting any of the facts he had relayed. Robinson reminded them of the law: 'A person who was presumed to be sane and responsible unless the contrary was plainly made out to the jury. The question here would be, whether this man at the time he committed the deed knew what he was doing wrong.'

The MacDermot, for the Crown, then examined his witnesses. 'I knew the prisoner,' said Bessie Burns, Alice's sister and the closest witness to the deed on the morning. She continued:

He stayed at the hotel during the Race Week at Galway. He was engaged to my sister: she wore an engagement ring. On the 29th of July my sister and I got up at 6 o'clock. We used to bathe at Salthill every morning at 6.30am, going to town by the train – he knew this, for he came with us one morning. We had returned and were at breakfast. He knew that we breakfasted at that hour. Mr Mack went to bathe at 8 o'clock – the prisoner went with him one morning.

On this morning of the 29th of July, he came in while we were at breakfast – my sister, myself and Fanny Rickaby. He shook hands with the three of us, and was sorry to disturb us. He then asked Alice why she threw him over, I could not tell her reply. He said 'We will see' and drew a revolver and fired at her. She rushed to the door and he fired again – we rushed out by the other door and heard two more shots. We found Alice lying in the passage. He went up one stairs and then down another – she died in a few minutes.

Bessie was asked if Alice had burned the letters sent to her by Parry. She didn't know. Fanny Rickaby, the young niece at the table, gave the same evidence as Bessie. Thomas F. Brady, Fishery Commissioner, remembered the scene well. 'When I was coming down the stairs, I heard screams,' he recalled. 'A woman was lying in the passage. I saw the prisoner in the hands of two men – I said, "You ruffian, you have shot the woman." He said, "I am damned glad of it, that is what I came for."'

James Murphy, the unwitting aid in Parry's plan who gave him access to the building, recalled his interaction with Parry. Murphy had been minding his business, washing a car when

> Parry came into the yard, he was going up the stone steps to the ballroom but the door was fastened. He asked me if Mack was in or not. I said he was gone to Salthill. He said 'Come in, I want you' – we went in at the hall door. He went into the room where Miss Burns was. I stood outside. He shook hands with the three ladies. He then fired at Miss Burns – I ran for the police.

Thomas Nolan, manager of the Imperial Hotel, gave evidence of Parry's stay the night before, detailing his movements – including his various drinks and food orders, and particularly the fortifying grog and whiskey he ordered before paying his bill and walking next door.

The first policeman on the scene, Constable Condon, said Parry was a willing confessor. 'Murphy came for me to the Barracks and I went to Mack's Hotel and found Parry in charge of two men, O'Halloran and Donnellan, they have up the prisoner and the revolver to me,' said the constable, continuing:

> I cautioned Parry and took him to the barrack. He said he did it, and came to do it. 'She deceived me and I shot her – she was engaged to me for 8 months and wore my ring, and then wrote to say she would not have anything more to do with me. I would not let any girl play upon me – I came 112 miles to shoot her.'

James O'Halloran, the passerby who held onto Parry until the authorities came, perhaps didn't get the plaudits he deserved in news columns already satiated with bloody detail. 'I heard the shots and saw the prisoner come down the steps,' recalled the man. 'I snatched the pistol from him and collared him.'

Dr Valentine Browne next took the stand. Dr Browne was a colleague of Dr Kinkead's at Queen's University Galway, where he held the professorship of surgery since 1849. It was he who performed the post-mortem, along with Dr McConnell. 'She received a wound on the left side,' he began. 'The bullet penetrated and remained in the body. Another bullet had struck the shoulder blade and the spine, and the fourth went right through the heart.' After the post-mortem, he went to the prison, where Parry had already met Dr Kinkead. 'I then went to the barracks and examined the prisoner,' said Dr Browne, adding that

It was told to me that he had wounded himself. There was a scratch on his skin and the bullet went through his flannel shirts. I said to him if he had intended to shoot himself he could not have done it in that way – he said he came 112 miles to shoot her, and had shot her, and that he made no secret about it.

The prisoner then stuffed into the doctor's hand a letter – the one read by Dr Kinkead a few days later. But, for reasons he didn't clarify, he did not care to read it. The constable at the barrack showed Dr Browne the revolver at that time, and noted all five chambers were empty. Parry, shackled, had piped up in the background: 'There are four of them in her body anyhow!'

Bodkin moved to clarify something for the defence; was Parry insisting he had shot himself, when he bore only a light cut? 'No,' replied the doctor, making it clear that the accused was very much in tune with reality. 'Parry did not insist there was a bullet in himself, he knew very well there was no bullet in him. I saw him a second time in the petty sessions office, he seemed very cool. He said some of his friends wanted to defend him, but he wanted no defence. He said he showed no mercy, and wanted none.'

George Mack, the grieving stepfather whose disapproval of Parry could not have guessed at his murderous potential, spoke next. 'I knew him,' he said, through tears. 'He stayed 4 or 5 days at the hotel as a guest of the family. I disapproved of the engagement and wrote to him in May.' Parry remained poker-faced, staring solidly through the courtroom. Neither Bessie's testimony, nor Fanny's, nor Mr Mack's was going to crack the mask. In all but body, he wasn't there.

Philip Lyster, in perhaps his busiest year for murders since becoming resident magistrate, took the stand and confirmed Parry's self-condemning words: 'I committed the deed, I gave no mercy.' A plan of the hotel was produced, and the points of the murder were plotted out for the benefit of the jury.

To this backdrop of undeniable events, Mr Bodkin addressed the jury in defence of Thomas Parry. 'I ask you not for sympathy for the prisoner, but for the cool excise of your judgement,' he began in an earnest bid to fight an uphill battle. 'This young girl, in the flower of her youth, met with a bloody and violent death, yet this is a case in which reason should dominate over sympathy, and the question for the jury is whether the prisoner is responsible for the deed.'

The facts couldn't be denied. But was a man responsible for his actions if he couldn't control them? Bodkin willingly accepted 'the honest, candid, fair and erudite exposition of the law given by the learned Serjeant who opened the case for the Crown'. But did Parry realise what he had done? Did he truly understand the difference between right and wrong when he met his former sweetheart at the Royal Hotel that morning? It was up to the jury to consider what insanity really was, and the legal responsibility of those branded with its name. He would refer to the highest authorities on the subject.

'It runs in the blood' in Parry's case, explained Bodkin. 'It will be proved that though the prisoner's father's hands had never been stained with blood, there were times when, had he committed a crime, a jury would have found him innocent.' A flinch from Parry in the courtroom at the mention of his father.

Bodkin mentioned the institutionalised relative and promised a comprehensive review of Parry's mental state from Dr Kinkead, then his primary medical caretaker. Parry was not a stable man, though it wasn't his fault; he was a sunstroke sufferer with a genetic proclivity for madness, who threatened to shoot his mother at the drop of a hat.

The objective, to construct an enduring, long-standing history of mental illness, began with testimony from Manley Palmer. He was an old friend of William, Thomas's father. He didn't know the younger Parry, but of his father he had quite a lot to say: 'I knew prisoner's father. He was a shepherd of Colonel White. His character and demeanour were excellent,' said Palmer. Dr Kinkead, sitting in court, had heard the upcoming story once before, on the train to the present assizes after he coincidentally sat beside the man:

About 20 years ago I saw Parry [senior] walking down the road very fast. He had no coat or hat on him – he vaulted into the field and back again into the road. I called him but he took no notice, but passed down the road. I saw him held by 5 constables two hours after. The doctor came subsequently and his head was shaved. This was 25 years ago. He left our part of the country six years after that and I lost sight of him. I never saw anything wrong with him except on this occasion. It may have been caused by drink, but he used not to drink.

The best William Townsend could say for Thomas Parry was that he was a 'sober man'. Townsend was a land agent with Lord Ashtown, and a former colleague of Parry's. Otherwise, he was impulsive. Rude and insolent, he thought. Yet he seemed trustworthy. 'I could not get on with him,' explained the man. 'He was quick and impulsive, but his character was good.'

Intelligent, determined and energetic. Fine parting appraisals from the agent, before Parry's doctor, a man named Rogers, gave a brief overview of Parry's sunstroke, on which much of the defence case lay. It was a bad dose, in the summer of 1883. Three times he was called to Parry's bedside at his father's house in Wexford, where he clearly saw the sunstroke had affected his nerves. 'This nervousness might be increased by any kind of passion,' he said, adding the caveat that it would not be a permanent affliction.

Evidently, his nerves were still shot the following Christmas, when he threatened to shoot his mother. She had chastised him for performing work she considered demeaning. How could he stoop so low? Then, he broke. Catherine, his sister, told the court: 'My mother was angry with him for bringing parcels for Major Braddell, and that he should not be demeaning himself. She abused him. He got very angry and threatened to go for the gun and shoot her. He got very angry. I was frightened and took hold of him – he came back and sat down.'

Another squirm from the impenetrable Parry as his sister recalled the episode. It had taken him a while to calm down on that day, nearly a year to the week before the court date. Parry had stood up slowly, remained silent, and left the house.

William, Parry's father, took up the story there. He had been such a mannerly, intelligent young man before the sunstroke. But that day, he barely recognised him. 'I met him after he had threatened to shoot his mother,' the elder Parry told the court, 'but I was not present. He looked so excited and wild, I was afraid to speak to him.'

The younger Parry watched his father closely as he spoke to the court.

'I went into the house and asked what was the matter with Thomas,' William continued in a quiet voice, recalling that after he heard the story he was resolved to hand his son over to the police. The safety of his family was paramount. 'I wanted him locked up as mad. But I was dissuaded by my wife and daughter. It would have brought disgrace to the family,' said the elder Parry.

A whimper raised to a cry that echoed through the courtroom. Whatever strength the younger Parry had shown in casting a stony face for the press representatives dissolved. His father's words melted him. He wept in the courtroom, loudly and for the first time. Thomas, of course, had not heard that part of the story before. Judge Lawson quickly ruled the father's latter opinion, regarding his son's institutionalisation, was inadmissible.

Parry's deviant behaviour was amplified with a textbook case of animal cruelty, courtesy of the next witness, Edward Peyton. As an agent for Parry's employer, Miss Newsom, he had hired Parry as a steward, having read three glowing references. It was Peyton who granted Parry leave to travel to Galway, seeing he was in an 'excited' state. 'In July, he came into the yard one day and called his dog, it crawled over to him and he kicked it cruelly,' he recalled, to a murmur in the court. 'I cried out to him and he stopped.' *What type of dog was it, Mr Peyton? Did he give a reason for thrashing it?* 'It was a sheep dog, he told me the dog had misbehaved and it came to him expecting to be punished.'

Then, a speedbump. The defence, having painted a sufficiently bleak picture of Parry's demeanour following the sunstroke, moved to have the medical officer of Limerick Lunatic Asylum give evidence regarding Parry's maternal uncle. The doctor was in the courtroom and stood on hearing his name, but Justice Lawson intervened. It was absolutely unconnected, and inadmissible. An expensed journey from Limerick or no, the evidence was ruled out.

It was a bad blow, and the loss of a piece of key evidence that was quite difficult to muster in the first place. The defence were down, but by no means out. Dr Kinkead was called to present the backbone of the medical evidence for Parry's insanity. The key exchange began. Needless to say, it was tetchy.

On the first day Kinkead saw him, Parry seemed 'perfectly cool and collected, answered questions rationally, but, on the whole case, the impression I formed was that the prisoner did not realise the position in which he was'. A small uptick of noise in the public gallery followed such an esteemed backing for the 'sweetheart killer'. Kinkead continued, saying that he had formed his opinion 'from the prisoner's family history and from the fact that he had received sunstroke. I came to the conclusion that the prisoner did not know he was doing wrong, though he knew what the legal consequences of the act would be.'

Serjeant Robinson, not keen to let Kinkead's conclusion go unchallenged, stepped in to cross-examine. He asked him, first, of his credentials. 'I was in 1870 District Registrar of the Probate Court in Tuam,' explained the doctor. 'In 1876 I was appointed professor of midwifery in the Queen's College, Galway. In 1879 I was appointed to the prison in Galway.'

Kinkead explained his duties as per his role at the prison, including the protocols for suspected insanity in a patient. 'It is my duty if a prisoner is insane to state so in my journal,' he began, before being cut off by Robinson.

'And did you, in this case? Record his insanity in your journal, I mean.'

A short pause from the doctor. 'I never did state in my journal that prisoner was insane.'

'Do you mean to say that you did not think it your duty to state that this man was insane, if you believed him insane?'

'I had not decided at that time.'

Robinson, countered: 'And are you aware, Dr Kinkead, that two persons in that prison had hanged themselves?'

Another pause. Longer this time. Of course he remembered. TK, the 18-year-old whom he desperately tried to save with his bare hands, had only been in gaol for six days. Despite the flagrant attempt to insinuate a negligence of some kind, he resisted the bait. 'I made a report on 3rd December 1884 that though fit to plead, he was insane at the commission of the offence. Dr Rice was employed by his friends to examine him,' Dr Kinkead explained, in a measured tone, continuing:

I saw him twice with Dr Rice, saw him in August, I said he appeared intellectually sane. I asked him did he know he was killing the woman, he said he did. But I do not think he knew it was morally wrong. He wrote to his father 3 days after, and said 'May the lord forgive her as I forgive her'. This shows he did not know he was acting morally wrong.

Robinson, now becoming frank: 'Will you swear he did not knew at the time that he was shooting this girl he was committing murder?'

'I don't think he did,' said the doctor, truthfully. 'I don't think he knew he was committing sin. I think he had no power of restraining himself and that he had formed an entirely wrong conclusion of the case.'

The Crown, in rebuttal, recalled Valentine Browne, who could not have been more succinct. 'I believe the prisoner was thoroughly sane, he showed no symptoms of insanity.'

Dr Rice, who had been sent by friends of Parry – likely his employer, Miss Newsom – said he examined him on two occasions. On the first, he came to the conclusion that he was perfectly sane and collected. 'We saw him again on the 10th November and came to no conclusion, except that he showed no signs of insanity, he was most accurate in all his answers. After hearing all the evidence today, I could not come to the conclusion that he was insane,' Rice conceded. 'I could say no more than that it was possible.'

The medical evidence on which the defence was so reliant was already outnumbered. Then, the Crown called Dr Bradshaw, surgeon to the Country Leitrim Infirmary. As it happened, he had also been the sole medical attendant at a Sierra Leone lunatic asylum for 14 years. An expert, in every sense of the word. 'I have seen and examined prisoner on Saturday and Sunday,' he told Robinson as the court fell silent. He continued:

> I questioned him. He answered perfectly and quietly. He said he had been deceived by her and came down determined to shoot her, and did so – he said he had a sunstroke which had him up for two days and one night.
>
> He was as sound in mind as I am myself. I went again in the evening and he answered me quite correctly. Next morning I went again I asked him if he knew what he was doing, he said: 'I did know what I was doing and I meant to do it, and I knew my responsibility.' I asked him was he sorry. He said he was sorry.

Then came the predictable 'My conclusion is that he was perfectly sane when he committed the crime.'

And so ended the witness testimony. Mr Taylor addressed the jury, contending that they should bring a verdict holding that the prisoner was not responsible for his actions. MacDermot replied to the contrary: Parry was a remorseless, unmerciful executioner and the soundness of his mind had the backing of three doctors, to the defence's one. Then, the twist of the knife: 'Dr Kinkead insulted the intelligence of the jury when he said he did not think that the man knew he was doing wrong.'

Justice Lawson then charged the jury. For his part, he said it was a strong proposition to suppose a sane man had, 'by some mysterious stroke' become insane for one moment, and was therefore not responsible. The question of guilt, he said, was the jury's alone.

After a two-hour deliberation, the verdict was in. Thomas Parry was found guilty of the murder of Alice Burns, with a strong recommendation to mercy 'on the ground that he was exasperated at the time' due to the letters sent to him by the deceased.

The judge turned to Parry, telling him that the verdict was the expectation of any person of ordinary sense and intelligence: 'The law has been more merciful to you than you have been to her. In a moment, you despatched her and sent her before her God. You have been defenced by most able counsel, who had offered everything that ingenuity could suggest in support of the plea of insanity.'

The law had given him time to prepare a defence, Lawson said. Now it was time for Parry to prepare to meet his God. He was asked if he had anything to say.

'I have nothing to say only that I am sorry for it, but my mind was not in a sound state when I did it,' replied Parry.

'I am very glad to hear you express that, and I trust that the short period that will be allowed to you in this world, you will make your peace, and endeavour to obtain forgiveness from your Maker.'

Lawson assumed the black cap and sentenced Thomas Parry to hang on 13 January at Galway Gaol.

Parry then spoke in a firm voice, now laced with sadness. 'I would be thankful if you would allow me to see my people before I leave this. They live far away from here.'

'Certainly,' said the judge.

17

A LAST GRASP AT FREEDOM

James Berry read the names in the Saturday papers with a lump in his chest. Whatever about having to travel to Ireland – a lengthy stay was a stressful prospect.

Despite his growing reputation, he was still required, each time, to apply to the sheriff of any Irish gaol for the pleasure. As he filled in the appropriate blanks in his pro-forma letter, he noticed a clash of dates. His eyes widened. In fact, he could not perform the hanging of Thomas Parry on the 13th, as he was already engaged in England. Excellent news. For him, that is. It was terrible news for Richard Chester, his assistant, whom he planned to send in his stead. Chester would be fine, he thought. Probably. Berry sent the letter and got the approval; he would travel to Galway for the 16th, and take care of Michael Downey, while Chester would take care of Thomas Parry on the 13th.

Try as he might to plan in advance, nothing was guaranteed in the weeks following a sentencing. Berry knew a barrage of reprieve letters and petitions would soon appear. He might well travel to Galway, only to leave with the £5 consolation prize. Sometimes, Berry welcomed a late reprieve for a repentant man. Other times, it was an obscenity. This divergence stems from a simple belief: not all murderers were made equal.

'To the ordinary Englishman a murderer is a murderer and nothing else. He is a vile creature who has taken life, and who by law, divine and national, must die because of his deed. He is a creature different from the rest of humanity, a fiend, a monster, who has outraged Justice, and must die like a dog,' wrote Berry in his diaries. 'To me, a murderer is a study. He is a man who has done an ill deed, who may or may not be naturally vicious; who may or may not be really responsible for his actions; who may or may not be devoutly penitent.'

Berry believed that for some criminals, the fear of death was the only thing which could curtail their passions. He continued:

> But I have sometimes thought that amongst those whom I have executed, for crimes which they have undoubtedly committed, there were men to whom their crime was a trouble more terrible than death; men who had not premeditated murder, who had taken no pleasure in it and expected no profit from it, and who, if they could by any means have been set at liberty, had within them the making of model citizens.
>
> Logically, and as a matter of conviction, I feel that if one sheddeth man's blood, by man should his blood be shed; but as a matter of sentiment, I sometimes feel sorry that certain murderers can not go free.

But this was often the case. Any conviction for a capital murder brought with it bags of letters to the Lord Lieutenant, seeking a reprieve. Crowds gathered at prison gates to pray for late mercy, for all but the most heinous murderers; people, generally, pulled for salvation. Berry believed in the right of reprieve for those who deserved it, yet he couldn't shake the feeling that heartless murderers would often walk free, just because 'they possess interesting personalities or influential friends, while others are executed who have a better plea for mercy, but no one to present it'. Some petitions were better than others.

In the case of his upcoming Galway projects, the reprieve cycle was no different. In the days and weeks following his sentence – after three trials – Michael Downey received memorials (petitions for reprieve) signed by dozens of people. The main plea for mercy was written by the defence solicitor, Henry Concannon. The signatures on that document show some staple Annaghdown names; the lines are dotted with Smalls and Brownes throughout. The memorial is an ornately written, six-point argument, which leans heavily on the influence Mary Moylan exerted on the young labourer. It was the common case for the defence and prosecution that Mary had a hand in plotting the murder. Colcannon concluded: 'I respectfully submit to Your Excellency, that the case is one which would justify an extension of the prerogative of mercy by giving effect to the recommendation of the jury, appearing as it does that the main criminal is at large, and that she induced the prisoner to murder her husband.'

In his own submission to the Lord Lieutenant, James Anthony Lawson, the judge who presided over Downey's trial, laid out the facts of the case. The wife certainly had a hand in the plot, but there was nothing, in his eyes, that should prevent Downey from going to the gallows.

In Downey's case, documents show that officials considered it 'most regrettable' that Mary Moylan should escape punishment. Nevertheless, it was ruled about two weeks after sentencing that the course of law had to be carried out. Michael Downey was to keep his date with James Berry.

And as for Thomas Parry? That was an entirely different issue.

Dr Kinkead was professionally wounded, and frustrated at having been denounced so emphatically at trial. In a submission after the trial adding to his earlier medical notes, he took issue with certain aspects of the proceedings. Firstly, the ruling out of the evidence concerning Parry's uncle was astounding to him.

'Evidence was available that the prisoner's mother's brother was an imbecile and that his uncle was in Limerick Asylum insane with homicidal tendencies,' he wrote. 'The doctor of the asylum was in court, but the court would not permit him to be called.' Furthermore, evidence had been conclusively heard that Parry was suffering sunstroke, and the effects on temperament were well documented. Evidence was heard that before the illness, Parry was 'exemplary in his habits, sober, quiet and good tempered. He was only once known to have taken too much drink that was at a wedding and the only evidence as to anything like bad temper was that of one witness who said he was impulsive.'

Evidence from the man who saw the same madness in Parry's father was unfairly curtailed, the doctor thought. 'Being subpoenaed by the defence as an expert I left for the assizes on the 6th December,' Kinkead recalled, continuing:

On the morning of the 8th while on the train I heard a gentleman, Manley Palmer, state that he knew Parry's father well and that he saw him mad about 25 years ago. That he perfectly recollected the circumstances; that he saw him running down the road without hat or coat on, vaulting over the walls, from the field to the road at each side – that as he came close to him. He was so close that Parry must have heard and seen him, and as Parry took no notice and looked so queer, he went home.

Palmer later saw Parry senior in the charge of the police, 'held down by four or five of them and that he heard them remark how strong a mad man was'. Palmer had seen Parry in the house he was brought to, with his head shaved and blistered, and knew he was attended by a doctor. He was ill for a week or ten days, he said, though he did not witness it.

The problem here, as far as the doctor could see, was that his extended illness and Parry senior's medical attention were inadmissible. Only what Palmer had seen – the 'queer behaviour' – was allowed to be entered into evidence. In itself, it didn't prove much.

Kinkead successfully cast doubt, too, over the medical practitioners' evidence. He did not mention Dr Rice, as he was present the days he examined Parry, but he did not give much credence to Dr Bradshaw's testimony. The mere position of having been a medical officer at a lunatic asylum, he said, was not, in itself, evidence. The man had only seen him twice, after the fact, and on one of those occasions it was a 'casual' visit. Bradshaw had, incorrectly as far as Kinkead could see, 'based his opinion on the accurate description which the prisoner gave of the details of the offence and on his taking whiskey the morning he killed the girl; that a man who had been insane, while he might remember his circumstances, could not recollect details.' If the case had been one of epilepsy or mania or dementia, Bradshaw might have had a point. But 'every authority on lunacy' agreed with Kinkead – that a memory for details did not automatically rule out insanity.

Though Dr Kinkead did not mention it, something of a controversy had surrounded the medical credentials of Dr Valentine Browne. Browne, by the time of the trial, was quite elderly. There was no doubt he had been a skilled surgeon and accomplished medical practitioner. Case in point, he was appointed surgeon to Galway County Infirmary in 1869, many years before the Queen's College Galway faculty were automatically appointed to that position.

But in about 1880, according to John Fleetwood's *History of Medicine in Ireland*, an allegation surfaced from a Latin professor named Thomas Maguire regarding Browne. Professor Maguire had become a fellow of Trinity College Dublin that year, and when he arrived in the capital, he asked his colleagues about Dr Browne, who he knew received his BA there in the 1830s. Valentine Browne, they told him, had died shortly after graduation.

The rumour that emerged was that Browne's cousin had received the BA, and that on his death, 'Valentine' had assumed his identity. He was, originally, a schoolteacher, or so the story went, from, of all places, Annaghdown, where the Brownes were rightly embroiled in the Clonboo murder drama. He undoubtedly achieved his medical training in the years following the 1830s, but the shadow hung over the initial BA.

According to correspondence on the issue between Professor Thomas Dillon and Professor John Fleetwood in the 1940s, the story went that Maguire apparently agreed not to expose him, on condition that Browne never attend a meeting of the Academic Council of the college again. Years later, in 1984, Professor James P. Murray of Galway concluded, after correspondence and research for his own book, that the allegation was likely false. It was certain that he was described in Aberdeen records as MRCS Ireland and BA TCD (1836). But if the rumour was true, he must have submitted his cousin's credentials to get a shot at that examination. Dr Kinkead didn't approach the issue at the time, though it is unlikely that he would not have heard about it.

There was also evidence to suggest that Dr Browne's own mental state was slipping at the time of the trial. Professor Murray's research unearthed a letter from the college president, Thomas Moffett, dated in the mid-1880s, in which he told a close friend in Australia that the ageing surgeon was 'very infirm'. He made no mention of any credential scandal in that letter. Dr Browne would die in office just two years after the trial, in 1887. In any case, for all of Dr Kinkead's criticism of the medical evidence for the Crown, he left Valentine's testimony well alone.

Apart from the vehement backing of Dr Kinkead, supporters of Parry's memorials numbered in the hundreds. Where Downey's file contains one main, large, petition, well written and scattered with a couple dozen signatures, Parry's file is packed. A template was used and distributed, with the same text outlining the case and the reasons for mercy.

But it wasn't just the number. Parry had friends in high places. Major Braddell of Wexford weighed in, calling Parry an 'honest, quiet and active' young man, with a 'most respectable' family to boot. (John O'Farrell, on behalf of Parry, wrote a plea for mercy similar to the one written by Concannon for Downey, enclosing sheets and sheets of references, from priests, landowners, gentlemen in Dublin, former and current employers.) The main memorial said Parry was 'honest, gentle, sober, upright, faithful and intelligent' until a bout of sunstroke which saw him succumb to 'strange paroxysms of passion', including attempting to shoot his mother. The facts suggested the strong passion, acting on weakened will and 'diseased intellect', brought about the tragedy, and Parry was not to blame.

Lawson, as he had done in the case of Downey, wrote to the Lord Lieutenant in an effort to rebut the outpouring of effusive memories, expressing his own belief that the verdict and sentencing were just. A report filed on 27 December noted the judge's frank conclusion. There was not, in his opinion, 'any evidence which would justify a jury in finding the prisoner insane. The jury recommended the prisoner to mercy because he acted under feelings of jealousy, but the judge cannot concur in that recommendation.'

The judge's word, which carried great weight in Downey's case, did not stick in Parry's. Whether it was the influence of a prominent doctor trying to make a point, the sheer volume of signatures, or the significance of those signing their names to pleas for mercy – or a combination of the above – the news came through that Parry's execution was to be delayed for one week, until 20 January. Dr Kinkead got his way. Parry was to be examined again. He had some support in the medical community; among the letters to reach Dublin Castle was one from Dr Robert McDonnell of 89 Merrion Square West, professing his high opinion of Dr Kinkead and suggesting an inquiry was necessary.

Somewhere in Bradford, a former shoe salesman muttered angrily under his breath.

The Lord Lieutenant issued an order to two doctors – Brady and Cruise – to travel to Galway to examine Parry. The feeling among his supporters at this point was optimistic, yet the orders for postponement were clear; this was a one-week reprieve to facilitate an examination, not an indication of a pardon. William Kaye, from Dublin Castle, wrote to Brady on 9 January 1885:

My Dear Doctor, I am directed by the Lord Lieutenant to acquaint you that he is desirous to have your opinion in conjunction with Dr Cruise as to the mental condition of a convict under sentence of death in Galway Prison, with a view to the medical examination of the convict. He has granted a reprieve for one week. If it will be convenient for you to undertake the examination of the convict the papers in the case will be sent to you. Be good enough also to see Dr Cruise, to whom I have also written an order that the earliest available day be fixed for the examination of the convict at Galway.

Both doctors accepted and were furnished with Kinkead's lengthy analysis before setting off for Galway Gaol, to give Thomas Parry his last chance at evading the scaffold, however little he himself wanted salvation.

One day after Parry's original hanging date and having examined the prisoner, Dr Brady and Dr Cruise wrote the following statement:

January 14th, 1885

In accordance with his excellency's command we have proceeded to Galway and investigated the mental condition of Thomas Parry, a convict now under sentence of death in the gaol there. We have studied the notes of the trial furnished to us – also Dr Kinkead's statement and have conferred with him – we have most carefully examined the prisoner, and the persons in contact with him at Galway. Notwithstanding Dr Kinkead's very important and carefully weighed report, we are of opinion that there is no reliable evidence to show that Thomas Parry is or was insane and consequently irresponsible. Either now – at the time of the murder, or previous to it.

In the following days, despite the spike of hope felt by Parry's friends, the ruling came through that the law would have to take its course. It seems power and influence could buy Parry a week, but not his life. This, in theory, would have pleased James Berry, who felt that this head-counting led people to wrongly endorse some pleas more than others, despite the crime. 'In many cases the people who draw up these petitions are people who object on principle to all capital punishment, but unfortunately the principle is entirely lost to sight when dealing with individual cases,' wrote Berry. 'The fact of big petitions being presented in one case, while no effort is made in another case with similar features, naturally leads uneducated people to think that there is uncertainty and injustice about the whole affair.'

On the other hand, this particular case would have annoyed the hangman. The upshot of the doctors' final verdict meant a reluctant, Ireland-shy James Berry now had time to attend both Parry and Downey at Galway. Of all places.

18

A DATE WITH MR BERRY

Berry had been truly hoping Parry would be reprieved, and winced as he put his name in his little black notebook, under Michael Downey's. Two men around his own age. At 32 on the morning he set out to meet them, Berry was just a little older.

As his train passed through Mullingar, he considered Chester. It was Thursday 15 January 1885; the poor man had been in Galway, twiddling his thumbs with the Irishmen, since the 12th. He may get used to it, Berry thought as he placed the pocketbook in his jacket, feeling the outline of his revolver. The job wouldn't be done until Parry's neck broke on the 20th.

Whatever about agrarian violence and Fenianism, it was the crowds in the Irish towns that irked Berry the most. What he'd give for a good old-fashioned English audience. A jolly laugh, and properly measured. 'Whenever I have been in actual contact with crowds in England,' Berry confided in his diary, 'their attitude has been friendly. In Ireland, such knots of people as may gather are usually the reverse. In England, if there is any sort of demonstration, it is a cheer; in Ireland it is hooting and groaning. But it is seldom, in England, that I meet with any personal demonstration.'

By and large, when the crowds liked Berry, Berry liked the crowds. In a purely scientific way, of course. 'Interesting studies' is how he termed those congregations at the gaol gates; he pondered about the way their voices rose and fell, how jubilation or derision carried on the air at the hoisting of the black flag and how, in an instant, he could gauge the public feeling towards a culprit. Irish crowds lacked that nuance. Scottish ones, too, for that matter.

It was a geographical exclusion zone, Berry would come to figure. The further you moved from London, the less people embraced hanging. And of course, any flexing of rule in Ireland was bound to be seen, in those times, as an act of political oppression, regardless of the crime. Berry, from his early days, predicted that hanging would be stopped in 'the Celtic countries' before England ever abandoned capital punishment.

It was early on 15 January 1885 when Berry's train pulled into Galway. No trouble this time. Whatever feeling of relief the Bradford man had was short-lived, however, and washed away at the sight of the crowds waiting outside the station. He was certainly used to 'fans' tracking his movements. Many studied the train timetables. But in this town, there was only one place to go to welcome the Dublin train.

The Clonboo murder case was due to come to a close the following morning. It was a highly anticipated execution, and a number of papers from all regions had published preview pieces ahead of the hanging, from a one-liner in the *Sligo Champion* the previous weekend to a longer piece in the *Freeman's Journal*. It excited the public. Quickly boarding a cab, Berry caught some of the insults, but the majority were saved for the short journey to the gaol. Galwegians followed for as long as they could, hurling abuse. 'Ketch' was a popular insult for hangmen in those days, stemming from a late 17th-century executioner named Jack Ketch, who famously, and very publicly, botched a couple of high-profile beheadings on Tower Hill in London. The first, that of Lord Russell in 1683, took so long and devolved into such a blood spectacle that Ketch publicly apologised. The second, of James Scott, First Duke of Monmouth, in 1685, was less extended, but took repeated blows. It was quite a feat to disgust crowds in those days, but the legend of his barbarity endured. Still, Berry had heard worse, and he could barely understand the rest. The accent wasn't his forte.

Berry met an unfriendly warder at the prison gate, though he wasn't much in the mood for chat himself. He was eager to go about his business, and perhaps walk about the town in the evening, as was his usual remedy for workplace frustration. On meeting Captain Mason, the military-mannered governor of Galway Gaol, he quickly realised that was an impossibility. 'One hour exercise in the yard, each day, Mr Berry,' the head of the prison told the stunned hangman. 'Out of concern for your safety, of course. Unless you'd like to venture back out to them?' The captain had a point, of course. As was evident by his reception, it was likely not a town through which he could amble idly about. Things had not been quite so rigorous in Wexford. His room would have to do. Still, he couldn't shake the feeling that the animosity from the streets towards the Crown's agents had seeped through the cracks of Galway Gaol's high walls.

The day got drastically worse from there. Berry's first sight of Chester's gaunt face was the canary down the mine of any potential pleasantness to be extracted from the building's thick, dull granite. Quickly, he discovered the source of his companion's pallor: the food. Berry's stories are punctuated with passages of culinary detail; he was a man who liked the smell of coffee and ham in the morning. Milk and bread and a drop of tepid tea didn't cut the mustard. All the more appalling was the enforcement of his stay in the prison; despite his most earnest pleas, he was forbidden from lodging in the town. 'Who are the prisoners, really?' he asked Chester. Chester didn't reply.

Berry's only for option staying sane in Galway was to go about his business. He met Richard Kinkead, who seemed to have quite a large chip on his shoulder. On the morning he met with the hangman, word would have just reached Parry that, despite the medical officer's opinion, he was actually sane and responsible for gunning down Alice Burns. It didn't matter much to Berry, who just needed Michael Downey's measurements and, in any case, respected the final word of the law. To second guess that would be to collapse the entire structure of justification for his grim job.

'He's gained flesh,' was the reply from Kinkead as he relayed the measurements on arrest, 'Parry, too.' Berry went quickly to the prison yard where he found the sole aspect of Galway Gaol to which he ever paid compliment. The scaffold he encountered there was one of the finest, if not the single best scaffold he had come across. 'Eight persons could be executed' in one go, he told a reporter that year. 'No improvements could be effected in its construction that I'm aware of.' Berry, satisfied with his weight tests, hung his ropes over the crossbeam and retired to his room, for an evening of forced conversation and choking down whatever slop was given to him.

Michael Downey knew his fate was sealed, which, in a way, meant he could come to terms with it. Parry was not afforded this certainty, but it seems from all accounts that he wanted to die, regardless. It had been the only failed stage of his meticulous plan.

Downey, now 25 years old, had turned to God, like an innumerable number of convicts before him. He spent his days in the company of the prison chaplain, Father Greaven, in deep and long prayer. Acceptance, it was widely said, had come to the young labourer with ease. 'Since conviction,' read a *Freeman's Journal* report, 'Downey has been fully resigned to his fate. He has paid diligent attention to the ministrations of the chaplain of the prison … who has spared no labour in preparing the unhappy man for eternity.'

Whatever about his acceptance of his fate, sleep was fleeting on the night before his execution. His last ever slumber was to be punctuated with the tossing and turning of a man all too aware of impending death. Downey rose at 6 am and was seen to by Father Greaven again, who celebrated Mass. Downey, as he had done previously, assisted. Meanwhile, James Berry filled a bag with cement in the courtyard, and performed one more run-through. All was in order.

Rest had abandoned Downey, as had his appetite. He was offered a breakfast, but he declined it. Instead, Dr Kinkead handed the young man a glass of wine. 'A stimulant,' he said. Shaking slightly, but ever stoic, Downey took the glass and drank deeply.

In the condemned cell, a few minutes before 8 am, the Clonboo murderer stood face to face with James Berry, the agent of his demise. An opera that had started more than a year beforehand, on a cold, misty night in a mucky boreen, was finally reaching its climax.

The two shook hands. Berry always asked for a confession. But whatever Downey said to Berry, or vice versa, in those last moments at the Galway Gaol was not recorded. The only other witness, the priest, never made statements about such moments.

Sub-sheriff John Redington had already handed Berry the death order. Downey was his now, and passed out of the hands of the prison. The Bradford man checked his watch and opened his gladstone bag, taking from it his pinion straps to tightly fasten Downey's arms. The legs would have to wait until the platform. It was time to go.

The procession formed and Michael Downey, flanked on either side by a prison warder, marched out ahead of Berry, who was followed closely by Chester. Kinkead, Captain Mason and a handful of other officials walked behind as the chaplain chanted the Litany for the Dead in front. The responses came strongly and clearly from Downey, who kept his head slightly bent throughout the entire melancholy march. 'The condemned man walked bravely,' wrote one reporter among the small gathering of press representatives, 'answering the responses in an audible voice.' Another recorded the remarkable way in which he 'bore himself with great calmness at the scaffold'.

Downey mounted the platform with one firm step, and his gaze wandered overhead. The Italian silk rope, suspended from the wide oak crossbeam, gave him little concern. Downey was slight and small at 5 foot 4, so there was lots of it. An unconcerned expression washed over his face, and he brought his gaze back down. Berry's watch ticked over to 8 am and, all in an instant, the hangman, coming up to Downey's side, pulled the noose tight to his neck, under the left ear, and dropped the white cap over his face. Chester, at the same time, fastened the leg pinions. Berry stepped aside to the right, touched the lever with his hand and Michael Downey, without a word, dropped into the void.

A slight thud escaped from the opening and the rope remained perfectly still. No squirming, no blood. A few minutes later, the black flag was hoisted high above the walls at Galway Gaol, signalling to the gathered crowd that it was time to go home.

⟶※⟵

Downey's corpse stayed hanging for an hour. You just couldn't be too sure. His body was then removed in preparation for the inquest, which began at 10.30 am before Mr C.G. Cottingham, County Coroner. The jury were first brought to examine the body, then returned to the inquest room.

Captain Mason, the governor, gave his official deposition – one of the last documents contained in Downey's file: 'The body the jury have now viewed is the body of Michael Downey, who has been sentenced to be executed on this day. I was present at the execution, which took place at 8 o'clock. Accused was 25 years of age, not married.' John Redington, the sub-sheriff, gave a similar statement, confirming that the sentence had been carried out.

The coroner then asked the jury if they considered they had sufficient evidence to enable them to arrive at a verdict. John McCormack, the fourth of 13 named jurors to be sworn in, piped up, according to an *Irish Times* report. He insisted they speak to the prison doctor, Kinkead.

'The doctor will not attend unless he is summoned,' explained Head Constable Wynne. Another juror, identified on the official papers as James Gildea, sought not to make a fuss. 'The doctor's evidence can be dispensed with,' he said, 'we have all seen the body.'

But McCormack was a stickler and, evidently, versed in the professional debates in the execution game: 'But we don't know how the man came by his death. Can we tell whether he died by dislocation or strangulation. The doctor's evidence is the only thing we have to rely on in coming to a verdict.'

The coroner said that if the jury wished, he would issue a summons for Kinkead's attendance.

'I require that,' said McCormack. He'd come this far. Why not?

The summons was issued and Dr Kinkead, likely confused at being dragged up, was sworn in: 'I am surgeon to her majesty's prison here, and was present at the execution of Michael Downey this morning, and from a superficial examination of the body, I would say that the bones of the vertebrae were separated, that spinal cord was torn, and that death was instantaneous.'

The verdict of the jury at the inquest was settled: 'We find that Michael Downey came by his death at HM Prison Galway on the 16th day of January 1885 and that his death was caused by the spinal cord being torn and the vertebrae separated, which was the result of hanging.'

Before the inquest finished, Inspector Lennon, evidently eager to see the constabulary's work pay off, asked: 'Did Downey make any statements previous to his execution?'

'Yes,' said Captain Mason, 'The chaplain handed me this …' He removed a small sheet of paper from his pocket. 'He stated Michael Downey wished to have it published …'

Berry returned to the confines of his room, not really up for the one-player game that was trying to have a conversation with Richard Chester. It was Friday morning; the gaol would be his home until Tuesday.

Parry's case for mercy had more uncertainty about it. Berry openly questioned the merit of hanging some men, as they seemed to be genuinely remorseful. Others were beasts, lifelong criminals. Dogs to be put down. But many were products of circumstance. Was it correct to treat them all the same? Berry himself favoured a graded system of murder conviction, with different penalties for different types of killings.

'On the whole, I think that our attitude towards murderers is based too much on sentiment and too little on reason,' he later wrote. 'Many people pity all murderers, whether they deserve it or not; many others condemn them body, soul and spirit, without considering to what extent they are the result of circumstances.' Many of Berry's culprits came through deplorable conditions,

> assailed by every sort of temptation, surrounded by an atmosphere of gay and hollow vice, cradled in misery and educated in wretchedness and sin, with little of the good and the beautiful entering into their lives to raise them, but with the accursed facility for obtaining drink to lure them down … in such deplorable circumstances, I say, that even an angel could hardly keep himself unspotted from such a world.

Regardless of the mere conditions of life, Berry recognised the implication of mental illness on a man's will. More so, he thought it worthy of great attention. At at time when many suffering with mental conditions – regardless of what the census said – were housed in prisons, Berry was brave enough to wonder 'whether it would not have been better for some of the murderers, as well as for society, if they had been placed under lifelong restraint years before their careers reached the murder stage'. Towards the end of his career, Berry mentioned a man named Rudge a number of times in this respect. After being sentenced to hang, he begged not for reprieve, but for the prison doctor to examine his brain after he died. There was something profoundly wrong with it, he had said.

In Parry's case, however, it was easy to consider him sane, following a single trial in which five doctors, to the defence's one, had said he was of sound mind. Further efforts to prove Parry was insane endured, even after the late re-examination by the two Dublin doctors. Superintendent Fitzgerald, a district inspector with the RIC in Mayo, wrote to the Lord Lieutenant on 15 January, mentioning that some years before, he had dealings with a family of Parrys that exhibited insane behaviour. He wasn't sure if there was any relation, but he thought it pertinent to raise, 'should [his] Excellency find, on inquiry, the convict is of the same family ...'

Meanwhile news reached the *Freeman's Journal* of Thomas Parry's demeanour in prison. In compliance with his death wish, the news that his hanging was to go ahead, despite the flash of hope, moved him little; 'He received the intelligence of his reprieve without betraying any emotion, and when subsequently informed that the law should take its course, he displayed no signs of regret or disappointment.'

On the night of Monday 19 January, the evening before his date with the executioner, the condemned man called for a pencil and paper. He was granted his request, and warders watched him closely; he had been on special suicide watch since the day he was booked by Constable Conden. Parry spent a few minutes hunched over his work in the corner of the cell, alternating between scribbling furiously and looking into space. Finishing his work, he returned the pencil with thanks and retired to bed. Not far away lay his rope, about 9 feet of it, already dutifully tested and coiled around the crossbeam in the prison yard.

Tuesday morning came. Berry and Chester sprang out of bed, brimming with the prospect of being able to go home and eat proper food. Berry went out to the prison yard to give the rope one last test.

Just feet away in his cell, Thomas Parry had slept reasonably well, though warders reported one or two breaks in his slumber, when he had evidently woken, but remained perfectly still and silent, staring into the blackness. A little after 6 am, he rose and dressed himself, without the offered assistance of the warders. Like Downey, he passed on breakfast, imbibing instead Dr Kinkead's fix-all for men facing the gallows: a glass of wine to settle the nerves. The Protestant chaplain, Rev. Canon O'Sullivan, arrived about an hour later, and the two prayed until about 7.45 am. At some point during these, the closing hours of Thomas Parry's life, he palmed the clergyman an important piece of paper, and gave him vital instructions.

As was customary, the governor handed the prisoners to the undersheriff, and he to Berry and Chester. The two Englishmen entered the cell, where Berry had a brief exchange with the condemned. 'The preliminary arrangement of pinioning the arms was then gone through,' wrote one reporter, 'and the mournful procession to the scaffold was formed.'

Governor Mason and Sub-sheriff Redington led the posse, followed by Rev. O'Sullivan, decked out for the occasion in surplice and stole and reading the appropriate droning psalm. Behind the clergyman, Parry walked with the assistance of a warder, held quite firmly at the arms by a nervous James Berry. Parry had proved himself unpredictable, and the Bradford man wasn't taking any chances. The culprit looked around himself absently, 'vaguely and wistfully', yet walked firm to the platform.

Berry placed Parry under the noose just before 8 am. The latter bent forward slightly, and in three clear, loud responses to Rev. O'Sullivan, proclaimed: 'Lord Jesus, receive my spirit; Lord Jesus, receive my spirit; Lord Jesus, receive my spirit.' So loud was his roar that an *Irish Times* reporter at the back of the yard could hear the cry clearly. Parry then stood erect and rigid, and awaited his fate. Chester went about strapping the arms. Berry fumbled slightly with the white cap as he removed it from his pocket.

The noose was tightened, a hurried glance was thrown over preparations. Berry placed his hand on the lever, and Thomas Parry dropped into oblivion. The gaol yard fell silent, save for the cold 'thud' of the rope doing its work, and the small crowd watched the rope sway gently.

Dr Kinkead gave evidence at the inquest later that morning, after Parry had been strung up for the appropriate amount of time, having 'made an external examination of the body. As well as I am able to judge from an external examination I am of opinion that the spinal column was dislocated in the neck and that death was instantaneous.'

Kinkead, Redington and O'Sullivan signed a declaration that the execution was carried out, and the verdict at the inquest rang of the same efficient finality shown at Downey's four days beforehand: 'death was caused by the dislocation of the spinal column, being the result of hanging'.

Berry and Chester made little delay in departing, after being paid appropriately by the undersheriff. Captain Mason caught the hangman at the gate; 'Thank you, Mr Berry,' he said, offering a hand. 'I would have been glad if the executions here had always been carried out the same way.' Berry of course thanked him, hiding his eagerness to leave the prison grounds.

Murderers murdered and died differently. But most had one thing in common: in nearly every case Berry saw to, they confessed. Many times, it came in the customary three-week delay between sentencing and climbing the scaffold. Often, a quiet word of confession reached Berry's ear in the moments before the death procession began.

One of the more common was the written confession, assembled in the days or moments before execution, directed to be read post-mortem. On his journey to Galway train station, in the company of Head Constable Wynne, Berry finally got the space to reflect on the two men now buried in the prison yard. Parry and Downey had a couple of things in common. Besides their location and the timing of their deaths, both men's defence teams sought to blame at least part of their actions on the behaviour of a woman. In the end, they had another, key common behaviour; they each confessed with a letter.

The following was read at the inquest of Michael Downey, handed to the governor of the gaol by the chaplain. Evidently not written by him, as he was unable to write, the document simply bears his haphazard 'X' at the bottom of the page:

I Michael Downey, under sentence of death for the murder of John Moylan, do publicly declare, on the eve of my execution, that I committed the crime for which I have been found guilty and sentenced to die. I am sorry for what I did and I hope that God in his mercy will forgive me. I wish to die in peace without blaming any person. I forgive all those who gave evidence against me. I wish also to thank the officials of the Galway Gaol for the great kindness and consideration they have shown me.

Michael Downey, X, his mark

Witness – Thomas Flannery

M. O'Connor

Parry, too, had made a statement. It was in his own handwriting, but is no longer present in his file.

Galway Prison, January 19th, 1885

(To be published)

I consider it my duty, now that my time in this world is coming to a close, to express my gratitude and thankfulness to my kind friends and to the general public, for the great kindness and sympathy shown to me by them.

In the first place, I wish to show my thankfulness for the great respect, kindness and attention shown to me since my committal to the Galway Prison by the governor and the prison officials; and I can only add that there was nothing left undone by those in authority over me to make my imprisonment as comfortable as the prison rules would allow.

I think it is only right for me, and my bounden duty, to do all in my power to remove from the public mind any doubt which they may retain as regards the state of my mind at the time I committed the dreadful deed which I am now about to suffer for, and my last declaration is that my mind was not right at the time, nor for a week previous, nor for some time afterwards.

Therefore my family and my friends may rest assured that the testimony of the learned and skilful gentleman, Dr Kinkead (Medical Officer Galway Prison), as to the state of my mind on the 29th of July 1884, was correct and right and I should be very sorry to leave this life without doing this justice to a kind and Christian gentleman.

I will now bring my last statement to a close by saying that I feel only too happy to suffer the great crime I have committed in the sight of Almighty God and also in the sight of man. I am heartily sorry for what I have done, and I feel satisfied that the Lord God Almighty will pardon and forgive me, as I truly forgive, and I trust that all those I have done an injury to will likewise forgive me, and I feel happy to say I have no ill will against anyone more than the child unborn.

Therefore I leave this world with a full confidence that I will have eternal happiness in the world to which I am fast approaching.

Weep not for me, my parents dear. Here I was not yours, but Christ's alone. He loves me best, and is taking me home. Amen.

Thomas Parry

***

Berry and Chester arrived just in time for the 11.30 am train out of Galway. The presence of the head constable seemed to have done the trick; one reporter commented that, as the men approached the station, 'They attracted no attention whatever.' Two plain-clothes RIC men were there to receive the men and accompany them back to Dublin. The men bade farewell to the head constable, and to Galway, and boarded the train.

They weren't long on board when a bright-eyed reporter from the *Freeman's Journal* approached the men and asked if he could chat with them on the journey. Berry, perhaps eager to vent, or even eager for a conversation, obliged. Openly, he chatted with the reporter, who noted that the Bradford man 'had less of the hangman and more respectability about him than any of his predecessors, and most assuredly he has more intelligence'. Nothing like the common hangman. He found, too, that Berry had some strong words for Galway Gaol.

'I am much better treated in English prisons than in Irish,' he divulged. 'In Galway, Chester and myself were locked up in a room and only allowed out for half an hour or an hour's daily exercise in one of the yards. In fact, we were treated almost as if we were prisoners, while the food supplied was of very inferior quality.'

Berry had been to Ireland before, not on business. He quite liked it. Other prisons weren't as bad as Galway: 'The only other Irish prison I have been in is Wexford, but they did not treat me in such a barbarous manner, as I may style it, as in Galway.' And for good measure he added, 'I always look upon a visit to Galway Jail as the worst punishment I am ever subjected to.' And so the train journey passed without incident, and the men made their way to the ferry terminal, with the reporter in tow.

'There's he is, the hangman, Ketch' – the Connacht brogue was unmistakable. It sent a shiver across Berry's skin. A trio of young, rowdy labourers who had come from Galway as he had now stood a short distance away, pointing. The small group had unhappily recognised the hangman from the train, and began chastising him as he stood waiting to board the boat out of Dublin, at the London and North Western terminals at the North Wall.

The hangman's posture took a dark change. His lips tightened, his hands sank deep into his coat pockets as he grasped hold of the loaded revolver. With a flare of unsteady anger, he pointed his plain-clothes police escort toward the men. 'If anyone attempts to interfere with me,' he spat, 'while I am travelling in the execution of my lawful duty, I would not think twice about blowing his brains out.'

But tempers died down and bloodshed was avoided. A couple of minutes later, he was aboard the boat en route to Holyhead. Berry's muscles relaxed and he released a slow, satisfied breath as the vessel stole out into the muddy waters of the Liffey.

19

EVERYBODY MAKES MISTAKES

Downey and Parry were buried and, as usual, the Bradford man had little time to dwell on their cases before his services were called upon again. By the beginning of 1885, Berry had garnered a quite good reputation for his efficiency, owing to a lack of major gaffes on his part.

But you can't win them all. Berry would learn that about a month after Parry fell through the trapdoor at Galway, when he undertook the hanging which clung to his reputation above any other blemish. It was the one that got away, so to speak.

If, in the late 19th century, you said 'James Berry', the reply would be 'John Lee'. Case in point, the *Western Times* article that reported James Berry's death – which came many years after his last execution – included not his name in the headline, but Lee's: 'Death of an Ex Hangman: The man who failed to hang John Lee'.

'The whole of the duties of an executioner are unpleasant,' Berry wrote of his two worst days on the job, 'but there are exceptional incidents occurring at times, which stand out upon the tablet of one's memory, and which can not be recalled without an involuntary shudder.'

In November 1884 Ms Emma Anne Whitehead Keyse was found brutally murdered at The Glen, the home she shared with her servants and cook. Her attacker had attempted to burn her body, after inflicting a fatal slash across her throat along with three other head wounds. Suspicions quickly turned to John Lee, a servant who had worked at the house since he left school. The evidence against Lee was largely circumstantial. Ms Keyse had been discovered in the dining room, surrounded by paper and covered in oil, in what was clearly an attempt to conceal the murder. A can of oil left in Lee's charge was empty when it should have been full. The proximity of his pantry to the room where she was murdered also went against him, as did the discovery of a bloodstained knife, blood and hair on his clothes and blood on the nightdress of one of the other servants – said to have been transferred to her clothing when Lee touched her.

The motive proffered was revenge. Ms Keyse had apparently lowered Lee's pay. On top of that, the prosecution alleged, Lee had already threatened to burn the house down if his elderly employer did not give him a reference. It was true that Ms Keyse had given Lee a nominal salary by the day's standards, but he received lodgings and board. Also, as one of the older servants told reporters in the aftermath of the murder, he was really only doing 'a boy's work', and it seemed Ms Keyse had only employed him as a favour, until he could get back on his feet.

In summing up, the prosecution said it was clear 'the prisoner was in Ms Keyse's employ at a nominal salary, and was merely for some reason waiting until she would give him a character,' reads a report in the *Jersey Independent and Daily Telegraph* at the time, adding that

> It was also clear that he was discontented and unsettled, and it was also clear that he had threatened, if Miss Keyse did not give him a character, he would lay the place in ashes. He also threatened for someone in the house, and had said that on a certain occasion if he had been near the cliff he would have thrown her over the cliff, and that he would have revenge.

Lee protested his innocence. The evidence against him, many thought, had been ably explained away. He had helped carry Ms Keyse's body after she was discovered, which would explain the blood. A cut on his arm he sustained on a broken window could also have easily left the stains on the maid's nightdress, though the prosecution would say he broke the window as a cover-up.

The defence argued that Lee had great affection for his employer, who had, in previous years, shown him kindness in rehiring him after he got into trouble with the law. They agreed that a murder had taken place, but pointed to the mystery lover who had impregnated Ms Harris – another servant employed by Ms Keyse and Lee's half-sister. How had she become pregnant? Who was to say the lover had not been fleeing through the open window when he encountered Miss Keyse?

But their arguments fell on deaf ears; the jury quickly found Lee guilty of murder, and he was sentenced to hang at 8 am on Monday 23 February 1885. In the weeks following his conviction on 7 February he maintained his story – he was, he swore, an innocent man.

Berry had followed the case keenly in the papers. He always did. Lee's unwavering commitment to professing his innocence would not have had much effect on Berry's resolve. A convict keeping up a story was nothing new. What did concern him, as his train left Bradford Station on 20 February 1885, was the scaffold at the gaol. He knew ahead of time that the apparatus had never been used in the configuration he would find it. It had been some time since the gaol last hosted a hanging, that of a woman named Annie Took, 'the wretched woman who murdered in horrible fashion the unhappy infant committed to her charge because its existence had become a drag and a burden to her'. The same scaffold had since been disassembled and re-erected in a different location at the prison grounds.

Berry's policy of avoiding train journeys at night saw him take the train only as far as Bristol, where he slept. The following morning, on 21 February, he boarded a train at Bristol Station and made for Exeter, his final destination.

Berry skipped the customary cab, as he often would, electing to walk the short distance to the county gaol. After signing in at midday, a warder showed him to Governor E. Cowtan's office, where he arranged to leave the prison to get something to eat before beginning his preparations for Monday. After finding a place for dinner, he returned again to the gaol just before 2 pm and was shown to an officer's room in a new hospital ward – his accommodation for the weekend. He then went to check the scaffold.

Berry had a feeling early on that something wasn't right. After he settled into his room, two warders accompanied him to the execution site. Since the execution of Mrs Took, the apparatus had been taken down and moved to a coach house, where the prison van was usually kept. Immediately, Berry knew the mechanism was much too frail for its purpose.

'In the coach-house I found a beam about four inches thick, and about a foot in depth, was placed across the top of the coach-house,' the hangman would write in a letter to the undersheriff, Henry M. James. 'Through this beam an iron bolt was fastened with an iron nut on the upper side, and to this bolt a wrought-iron rod was fixed, about three-quarters of a yard long with a hole at the lower end to which the rope was to be attached.' The pit was a simple construction with a stone-covered floor. It was about 11 feet deep, with the hatch about 2 yards by 1½ yards. That wasn't unusual, but Berry noticed the trapdoors were quite thin – about an inch thick. They should have been three or four, at least.

The doors weren't promising – even the ironwork seemed flimsy. Despite his reservations, he reached for the lever, which was placed near the top of the doors, and pulled. They fell just fine. He asked the two warders to raise the doors again, and again they opened easily with the pull of a lever. It was now that Berry turned around to meet the gaze of the governor, who was watching the executioner closely through the window of his office in the opposite building.

Berry left the two warders and made for the governor's office, where he explained his concerns. The frail metalwork and thin doors were one thing, but Berry had also noticed a lack of an essential spring to hold the doors in place once they fell, preventing them from bouncing off the walls of the pit and hitting the falling body on the way down. In reply, the governor simply said he 'would see to those matters in the future'. Berry went back to his room. He didn't move for the rest of the day, nor did he leave the gaol for the entirety of Sunday. It rained heavily over the two days and there was a familiar, nervous anticipation among the warders – one which always lingered in a prison when a hanging was approaching, especially if it was the first in a while. Berry whiled away the time in his quarters and went to sleep around 9.45 pm. At about 6.30 am on the morning of the execution, Berry rose. A warder came to get him an hour later and just after 7.30 am, he stood in the coach house, noticing everything was exactly as he left it. All was ready and everything well-tested.

Berry glanced at his pocket watch. Four minutes to eight. The governor appeared at the door of the coach house and escorted him to John Lee's cell.

'I proceeded at once to pinion him,' Berry recalled, 'which was done in the usual manner.' Lee declined to say anything to Berry, and with nothing else to prepare, the Yorkshire man gave the governor the signal he was ready. A crowd had assembled on a nearby hill to see the execution. This was commonplace, especially where a hanging was rare. But the crowd couldn't see much, save for a tall black pole that had been erected for the purpose of hoisting the flag once the sentence was passed. A group of spectators remained, however, including up to 10 members of the press, who watched the proceedings through the coach-house windows.

The death procession formed in the usual manner. The prisoner was pale, walking firmly with his head thrown back. 'The prisoner's bearing,' wrote a reporter in the *Exeter and Plymouth Gazette*, 'was quite in keeping with that which has characterised him all throughout his trial and incarceration, that of a man aware of the doom before him, and determined to meet it, if he must, without signs of wavering, and even with indifference.'

Berry walked behind Lee, followed by a group of warders. Lee was marched to the trapdoor and placed on the chalk mark. 'Just before the white cap was placed over the prisoner's face he gave one despairing gaze upwards – a look which was awfully sad in its utter hopelessness,' reads the *Gazette* report, 'yet, as he stood there all but face to face with death, he never flinched.' When Berry was fixing the rope, according to a number of witnesses, Lee turned his head and said something to him, though Berry would later say he kept quiet.

With the sound of the chaplain's burial service prayer ringing through the coach house, Berry dexterously and quickly did his preparations. He finished adjusting the rope under Lee's left ear and lowered the white cap. And then he pulled the lever.

Nothing happened.

A gasp rippled through the onlookers and Berry froze for a moment. Panic set in. The exacerbated executioner and two warders immediately began to stamp ferociously at the trapdoor to entice it to fall, each 'bang' causing Lee to wobble slightly, though he remained rigid. But the doors, as thin as they were, didn't budge. 'Again and again they stamped, but all to no purpose,' wrote another spectator, describing the 'terrible moments' as the group waited for the platform to fall.

Six minutes of stomping passed before Lee was taken off the platform. Reports differ as to where he was brought in the interim four minutes before he was returned to the scaffold – some said he stood at the front of the platform, white cap still donned. The accepted account is that Lee was led to an adjoining room with the chaplain, and the white cap and rope removed, revealing his ashen face to onlookers. One reporter noted the flutter of a white bird, which had begun flying in circles around the coach house.

When the black flag wasn't hoisted, those looking on from the hill began to whisper, and rumours spread. Was there a late reprieve? It isn't certain how news reached the crowd, but in the following minutes the truth somehow escaped the prison walls.

Back at the coach house, Lee stepped off the platform. Berry again tried the doors and they fell without any problem, giving off another loud, metallic 'thud'. Little consideration was given to Lee's experience at this point. The subject of Berry's most drawn-out hanging was in earshot of the tests; he surely also heard the second dry run, which passed off without a hitch. Lee was brought back and again Rev. John Pitkin took up reciting the burial service. Again the rope was adjusted, again the noose prepared, again the lever pulled – this time hard enough to bend it out of shape. And again, no drop.

The force caused the platform to jerk ever so slightly, enough to send a wince through the spectators and no doubt a shock through Lee, who surely thought the doors had given way this time. In his writings, Berry gives his recollection of the most famous mishap of his career, mostly in a bid to explain the failures technically and, understandably, to direct blame elsewhere. However, it seems his memory failed him amid the stress of Lee's hanging. Berry maintained he only made two attempts at hanging Lee, when all other accounts say the ordeal didn't stop there.

After the second attempt, Lee was again freed from the noose and walked back to the gaol. Members of the media said the spectacle had become sickening, and that at this point, Lee was barely able to stand. 'Awfully sad was the scene,' wrote one reporter at the scene. 'The wretched man's features were corpse-like, and he walked as he was guided, mechanically.'

At this point, some onlookers took nips from flasks of brandy, taken shakily from inside coat pockets. Berry examined the doors thoroughly and even descended into the death pit at one point, to check under the mechanism. 'It was suggested to me that the woodwork fitted too tightly in the centre of the doors, and one of the warders fetched an axe and another a plane. I again tried the lever but it did not act,' he wrote. Warders then took tools to the doors, hacking off a piece of wood from one, just about where the iron catches were. Using a crowbar, the catches were knocked off entirely, and the doors fell down, the loud 'bang' accompanied by rumbles of muffled, shocked commentary, which took up during these in-between moments. The governor and undersheriff, at this point, were losing their cool.

Once more, Lee was brought out. For the third time in about half an hour, the noose was adjusted, the white cap donned and the lever pulled as the chaplain again resumed his recital. For the third time, he remained alive, standing on the unopened trapdoor.

After 30 minutes and three attempts at hanging John Lee, Berry was asked to remove the rope for the final time. Lee broke his stoic silence as the Italian silk was removed from his neck: 'You should try those on yourself,' he said, turning to Berry as he walked off the scaffold. 'Then you'd know what they felt like.' This 30 minutes, by the standards of the day, was an excruciating amount of time to let a man wait to be hanged. This came at a time when Dr Kinkead, at Galway Gaol, considered the three minutes of walking from the cell to the last moment of the 'tragedy' to be too long. The warders resumed hacking at the doors, but the undersheriff ordered that the execution be postponed, until he could speak to the Home Secretary, and he left for London. Later, the verdict came through – John Lee's sentence was commuted to penal servitude for life, which was 20 years at the time.

The mystery malfunction threw up a number of theories. One blamed the heavy rain that fell between the time Berry tested the apparatus on Saturday and the moment he tried to pull the lever for the first time on Monday. The moisture, it was theorised, had caused the wood to swell, adding pressure to the doors. With the weight of Lee placed on top, the trapdoors were forced against each other and stuck tight; this explained why the door worked when Lee wasn't standing on the platform – though Berry didn't fully buy that.

Rumours spread that the failure was a product of sabotage, or just a joke, conceived by the inmates who had actually built the scaffold. Another story said a board in the platform, immediately in front of the trap, had warped, and that when the chaplain stood on it to read the burial rite, it had moved, and somehow blocked the trapdoors from falling. This would explain why the drop worked properly in Lee's absence; the chaplain accompanied him off the scaffold each time.

George Cuthbert, engineer to the prison department, examined the scaffold and said he believed the failure 'was entirely due to what I might call one of the long bars or long hinges being quite an eighth of an inch longer than it should have been'. He added that, although it was true that the wood had been too thin, if the trapdoor had been tested by the hangman with the appropriate weight the fault might have been located.

Berry was asked to write an official statement for the undersheriff, which he used to clarify any doubt about his own actions in the case. 'I am of opinion,' he wrote on 4 March,

> that the ironwork catches of the trap-doors were not strong enough for the purpose, that the woodwork of the doors should have been about three or four times as heavy, and with iron-work to correspond, so that when a man of Lee's weight was placed upon the doors the iron catches would not have become locked, as I feel sure they did on this occasion, but would respond readily.

'So far as I am concerned,' he continued, teeing up his own defence, 'everything was performed in a careful manner, and had the iron and woodwork been sufficiently strong, the execution would have been satisfactorily accomplished.'

The media were kind to Berry, all things considered. 'The Governor of the Gaol, and the undersheriff, who were present, were terribly upset about the failure of the attempted execution, and the prolonged and terrible suspense in which the prisoner was kept,' Berry recalled years later, with perhaps a more blasé attitude, given the benefit of time. 'They were almost frantic about it, but nothing could be done in the matter.'

Media reports, in the aftermath, often commented on Lee's steely nerves throughout the ordeal. Besides a ghastly, ghoulish pallor, reporters said an onlooker wouldn't know Lee was a man waiting, at painful length, for his

John Lee: 'The man they could not hang'.

death. This reflected observations made at his trial. The judge, on passing the death sentence, had commented on how calm Lee had been. 'I'm calm, because I'm innocent,' had been his reply.

On a cold Christmas night, a rumour struck up in Abbotskerswell, Devon. It rattled between the small cottages of the town, like the car that had brought an unknown man to the house of old Mrs Lee. Some said he was back. It had been 22 years since famed hangman James Berry failed to hang John Lee for cutting the throat of his allegedly thrifty employer. More than two decades later, Lee looked a deal different, but one thing didn't relent: his insistence he was innocent. On 25 December 1907, a Press Association reporter managed to source the truth: yes, the man they couldn't hang was out of prison.

Twenty years is a long time, but interest hadn't wavered. Many believed at the time of conviction, and still believed on release, that Lee, now aged 46, was innocent. The opinion among his neighbours, as the stream of reporters filing into the town would gather that Christmas, was akin to 'a sort of halo of romance' around him, one wrote. Divine intervention, perhaps, for a wrongly accused man?

Berry, in the years following his career, didn't think so. Lee's guilt in the murder of Miss Keyse, as far as Berry was concerned, was beyond question; John Lee was respited on the grounds of mercy, not of justice. Petitions for Lee's early release had materialised over the years, and various campaigns had sprung up. While the theory of Ms Harris's lover's escape gained legs, Berry was quick to put down the notion, even going as far as to confirm that, by some simple, non-specified gesture, he had actually received a confession from Lee in the company of the chaplain. The clergyman, naturally, declined to confirm or deny.

Lee, on his release, used his notoriety well, including embarking on lecture tours. This wasn't a huge surprise. Even as he sat in prison, the offers rolled in. One he received just under two years before his release was particularly interesting: £100 a week to appear on stage with James Berry, according to a short report in the *Edinburgh Evening News*. What a pitch – the expert of the long drop, and the only man who ever survived it.

Whatever the case may have been, Berry considered Lee's hanging one of two of his worst days on the job. The second taught the Bradford man a salient lesson in keeping the head. Quite literally.

Berry looked at Robert Goodale closely. Sizing up a man was essential, and even in his frightened, hunched state, he could see the murderer's girth. Of course he would have been weighed, but sight was the first tool of a hangman. At this point, more than a year and a half into his career, he could pull out more or less the correct length of rope at a glance. Fitness, outdoor activities and a basic pride in his appearance was ingrained in Berry. No surprise then, that a mild disgust filled him when he surveyed his next 'victim'. The heinous crime was enough, but Goodale was a heaving, physical wreck of a man.

Goodale was more than 20 years married to his wife when he brutally murdered her. It was the cold-blooded treatment of Bathsheba Goodale at the hands of her husband that would catch media attention and shock the sleepy Cambridgeshire town of Walsoken. The couple lived with their sons – aged 18 and 21 – and the family cultivated a market garden nearby for a living. They worked the fields all day – 8 am until 6 pm – but at home, the marriage was marked by turmoil and plenty of violence on Goodale's part – evidence was heard that he was once seen chasing her maniacally, brandishing a billhook, shouting that he would 'chop her down' if she didn't stop running.

On 15 September 1885, filled with a jealous rage at alleged infidelity, he took the billhook to Bathsheba's head, and threw her body into a nearby well. She was rendered senseless by the attack, but died by drowning in the darkness. When police came to arrest Goodale, they found his clothes covered in blood. Reporters throughout his trial remarked repeatedly on his apparent indifference towards the whole affair, and it took a jury just 15 minutes to convict him; he was sentenced to hang on 30 November 1885.

Having travelled to Norwich to carry out the honours, Berry felt apprehensive about Goodale's physical state: so heavy, but certainly not tall or muscular enough to accommodate the weight. Weak-necked, perhaps? While Berry didn't believe in omens, on this occasion, he felt uneasy; on his arrival to the prison, having signed in and found his quarters, a warder had taken

Berry aside, begging him not to go through with this one. Terrible dreams had plagued the man. Three times he saw Goodale's head come clean off his shoulders at the pull of the lever. Berry, who was usually unflinching – or at least, he presented so – was taken aback, more than he would have liked to admit. He went as far as to write out a statement of refusal, though quickly balled it up and disposed of it. As was his custom, moments of weakness were abruptly stopped, and stiff upper lips prevailed. He was quite good at shaking himself loose of the grip of anxiety.

Of course, it wasn't just the dreams of a man he'd never met that gave him pause for thought. The flayed remains of Moses Shrimpton were still on his mind. Shrimpton had been hanged by Berry about half a year beforehand. From start to finish, the assignment had made the Bradford man distinctly uncomfortable. As a prisoner, Shrimpton was a curiosity – certainly a jailbird, but he lacked that usual acceptance of fate that the run-of-the-mill career criminal had. It was a type of built-up resolve ingrained in the lower man by years of hard life, Berry thought. Of the typical career criminal, he wrote:

> As a rule, he pays but little heed to the ministrations of the chaplain, or the condolences of his friends. He is neither piously inclined, nor hysterically fearful, nor abusively rebellious – he simply waits his fate. A kind of hard stoicism seems to keep him quiet; he has played a desperate game with his eyes open, has played for high stakes – and lost.

Shrimpton was different. He was a favourite among the warders at Worcester, where he would captivate them with tales of his misadventures. Berry, for his part, considered him a man of 'strong character and much determination'. His crime was the murder of a policeman, who caught Shrimpton red-handed stealing chickens from a coop. His death sentence brought about a profound change in the man's personality, and he seemed genuinely repentant. Berry always had problems with this type of prisoner; respecting a jury's sentence was one thing, but being unable to pigeonhole a murderer as a 'bad man' made the job all the more difficult.

On the day of the execution, Shrimpton was the model condemned man. He even drew his feet together, to help Berry strap his legs. When Berry pulled the lever, there came a rare sound Berry never got used to. A wet sound. The sound of liquid hitting the brick floor and the walls of the specially dug pit into which the condemned disappeared. When he descended the ladder, his fears were confirmed: the drop had been too long, and Shrimpton's head had been almost entirely ripped off; it clung pathetically to his body by a strand of tissue. Blood covered the walls and the lower part of the prisoner's dangling remains. Certainly messy and certainly unfortunate, but Berry had insisted that the nine-foot drop could not have been any less, attributing Shrimpton's age and weakened neck tissue to the mishap.

Those same sounds played on Berry's mind six months later in Norwich, as he clocked Goodale's flabby jowls.

There was a nervousness about the prison. Berry had felt it since arriving. 'It's all in working order,' an apprehensive governor had told the hangman when the two met. 'Tested it myself.' Berry was slightly confused. His numbers were impeccable, but it seemed the (failed) hanging of Lee and the gruesome encounter with Shrimpton had gaols everywhere on edge. No wonder the warders were having nightmares. Still, Berry understood the value of preparedness. What he understood less, perhaps, was the second test of the scaffold the governor made him perform. And then another, in front of reporters and the undersheriff. When something went wrong with a hanging, it was every man for himself; this can be seen repeatedly in any inquest report of a lingering death or, indeed, a more gory slip-up. Berry was quick to blame a weak neck, a government rope or a meddling official – and he made sure to get his absolution in writing; hang 100 men or 10, you were only as good as your last newspaper write-up.

Taking the man's weight and appearance into consideration, he reduced the drop, from 7 foot 8 inches, to 5 foot 9 inches.

Goodale and Shrimpton had more than a weak-looking neck in common. Goodale's callous indifference had turned to an apparent religious revelation – not unlike Shrimpton's earlier that year. 'The conduct of the prisoner after his conviction was exemplary,' reported the *Eastern Evening News* at the time, adding that he had taken to professing the principles of the Baptist Church. In his enlightened, benevolent state, he had even confessed to the murder, saying 'he struck his wife in consequence of her saying that she liked other men better than him'.

Efforts were made to commute his sentence to life. Berry, at this point, would have taken the £5 plus expenses, and the governor's nerves would have been the better for it. But the letter came through on Sunday: Goodale had to hang.

The convicted man slept well on Sunday night, stirring at 3.30 am, and rising at 5 am. He asked for food and then resumed prayer with Rev. Wheeler at 6 am. A short time later officials and press representatives arrived, filing up the narrow spiral staircase that rose from the cells and out into one of the gaol yards. Berry was summoned, again, to test the ropes at 7.30 am. Again, the governor was happy. At 7.55 am, a procession marched from the condemned man's cell. Goodale was agitated, very pale, and spoke only in response to the methodical readings of the reverend.

At three minutes to 8 am, Goodale was handed over to Berry and pinioned. His newfound peace left him on the sight of the gallows, and he flailed and fought. 'Good Lord, receive my soul,' he said, muffled through the white bag over his head. He wouldn't move easily into place, so Berry pushed him into position – he was held there by warders.

Berry asked him if he had any last statements – 'No,' he shot back.

Berry pulled the lever and Goodale was swallowed by the trapdoor. One of the warders who had been holding him up slipped, and his foot plunged in after the convict. Luckily, he caught himself before tumbling into the pit.

But the hangman wasn't focused on the warder or his foot. The rope, which had gone from slack to taut, had, in the blink of an eye, become slack again, and jerked back up. *The rope has slipped from his neck*, Berry thought in an instant. A disastrous incompetence on his part. A worst-case scenario. Or, perhaps it broke? Impossible – he had hanged Williams with the same rope just a week beforehand.

As the rope rebounded upwards, Berry peered into the pit and saw two distinct masses: Goodale's body, limp, on one side of the floor, and – a few feet away – his head, still in the white cap. It had been severed, cleanly, from his body. The gasps on the scaffold were barely audible over the sobs of the governor, whose nerves had finally got the better of him – he broke down as the black flag was raised, slowly, over the right-hand entrance of the gaol. Berry gathered himself, and looked to the doctor. Descending into the pit to examine the result of the drop was their duty – usually a formality. Needless to say, there was blood. The head had been removed as though with a knife's edge. Berry was overcome, and had to be assisted out of the pit by sympathetic warders.

After a stiff drink – more than 18 months of hanging will do that to any teetotaler – he was able to face the inquest, 'a trying ordeal for all concerned'.

The mistake didn't make sense. Until that morning, he had used Marwood's table of drops to the letter. In this case, he had even reduced the rope length. Berry pointed to the case of a man named Lawson – a brute of 16 stone 8 lbs who had fallen 8 feet, without even a mark left on his neck. He need not have been so nervous. By the end, his reputation was intact. All of the evidence absolved him from any responsibility. The weakness of the neck, and not the strength of the drop or any of the equipment – it had been tested well enough, Berry thought – was to blame. The governor, just about recovered, was asked about the machinery, which he insisted, truthfully, he had checked thoroughly. Then, the governor was questioned about the executioner, and defended him well.

'What took place?' the governor was asked.

'The head left the body,' he began, before adding: 'it was completely severed from it.'

'Was Berry perfectly sober?'

'Yes.'

'We have heard of such things, so I ask the question ...'

The governor sensed the narrative, and moved to stamp it out: 'He was perfectly sober,' he insisted, 'as sober as I am. Berry seems to be a well conducted, steady man, and I believe that no one regrets what occurred more than he does.'

'I am bound to say, before you leave the room,' said the coroner, addressing Berry, 'that as far as the evidence has gone there seems to be nothing to throw any blame upon you, either from want of skill or being in an improper condition.'

'I took every precaution throughout,' Berry replied steadily. 'I am very sorry to think it occurred.'

The gaol surgeon agreed with the coroner. At least he died quickly, was his platitude, according to a report in the *Liverpool Mercury* the next morning. It was a clean cut – and a far cry better than a slow death, they could all agree? 'The sentence was that he should be hanged by neck until he was dead,' he said. 'He was hanged and he died ...'

The jury returned the normal verdict – Robert Goodale died by hanging, according to the judgment of the law. Nobody was to blame for what happened.

Some of the papers weren't as kind the next day. The *Nottingham Evening Post* was one:

> The sickening scene at the execution of Robert Goodale for the murder of his wife will probably have the effect of bringing the peculiar mode of execution brought into notice and practised by Marwood under the scrutiny of men who from their knowledge of anatomy, and mechanics also, are able to say decisively whether our present system of carrying out the sentence of the law in cases of murder is humane and certain in action. If we must hang, and 'the long drop' is the most merciful on the whole, could we not have an expert to at least advise with the executioner and make such an accident as that of yesterday impossible?

It was just such an undermining that would result in another gruesome mishap later on in his career, and leave Berry no choice but to hang up his ropes.

20

DOWNFALL

Bungled hangings didn't exactly inspire confidence in authority. Delighted news reporters writing about bloodied death pits, exasperated hangmen and trapdoors that wouldn't open, in fact, did quite the opposite. As newspapers took notice, top government officials were taking keen interest. In light of a litany of high-profile mess-ups, chief among them Berry's two clangers, a committee was established by the Home Secretary under Lord Aberdare to consider the technique of hanging, as well as the apparatus and appointment of executioners.

The report from the Aberdare Committee set out, plainly, the concerns of the government at the time. There was no structure. No quality-control. Much to the frustration of a proud technician like Berry, the committee heard extensive evidence from medical men, and less from the practitioners of the craft. The report lamented the heft of responsibility given to hangmen: 'There are no fixed rules for the use of the apparatus, for the size or make of the rope, for the method of pinioning, nor for the length of drop to be given to the culprit; and the whole of the details of the execution are practically in the hands of the executioner.'

Beyond investigating the process, the character of specific hangmen also came into focus – something Berry left out of his diaries. The disdain for the public executioner and disrespect of his abilities was thinly veiled in the final document, but the evidence of the doctors and prison officials as contained in the committee's minutes was, at times, unapologetically contemptuous. The meeting minutes from the committee hearings at No 8 Richmond Terrace, Whitehall make very clear why James Berry felt he had to publish his side of the story.

The first to face the committee was Samuel Haughton. Haughton presented himself as a man in pursuit of mathematical knowledge. He had worked for many years in Ireland, where he said the long drop was much more widely used, and much earlier than in England. His evidence shows us that, far from being an anomaly, decapitation wasn't uncommon, despite efforts at inquests to dampen the zeal of excited reporters. Accidental decapitation, it seems, was no stranger to Irish authorities.

Dr Haughton got his first chance to dissect a victim of hanging in Dublin in July 1865, after the execution of Patrick Kilkenny, another man mentioned in the writings of Kinkead. Kilkenny was convicted of the murder of a woman at Palmerstown and executed at Kilmainham before a crowd of more than 1,000 people – the last ever public hanging in Dublin. He was also nearly decapitated by the drop given to him by a much younger William Marwood, though you wouldn't know it from the reports at the time. The aftermath of the drop was remarkable enough for Haughton to admit that the post-mortem results scared him. 'We were greatly shocked to find, from the length of the drop and the position of the knot, that the man's head had nearly been cut off,' said Haughton. 'The knot was placed on the occiput and all the soft parts of the neck except the skin were completely divided.'

At the next execution in Dublin, held in July 1870, the convict wasn't as lucky. Andrew Carr, hanged for the murder of Margaret Murphy in Dublin, was entirely decapitated. Not withholding an ounce of the bloody detail, *The Nation* reported 'a spectacle most horrible' two days later: 'On the bar being pulled the drop fell and when the body of the convict strained the rope, his head was literally wrenched off, and the trunk rolled in the gravel in streams of blood.' For good measure, the reporter claimed the head was 'still giving evidence of life' when it 'dropped from the noose on the gore-stained shingle'.

Thus it emerged why Dr Haughton had insisted on addressing the committee before any witnesses were heard. In evidence, he revealed he had attended a somewhat secret meeting of gaol surgeons at the Royal College of Surgeons in Ireland on 10 December 1875, long before the time of James Berry. The resolutions were, firstly, to recommend that the knot be placed under the chin, as opposed to the back of the head – or, indeed, behind the left ear as per the Berry method. Under the chin, or submental, placement meant the force was applied to the rope at the back of the neck first, which immediately met the spine and caused a barrier for the rope, which would otherwise pose a risk of severing the front, softer, throat tissue and veins before meeting the resistance of bone. They also decided the drops were far too long; a maximum of 8 feet was enough for the average man.

The aim of the game was to evoke the internal damage to the neck to ensure a quick death, but stop short of destroying the skin. A 'successful' long drop would see every internal soft structure in the neck destroyed, including veins and muscles. Haughton calculated that about 1,280 lbs of force was good for a safe break – dislocation, without decaption. Marwood's 14-foot-plus drop was a guaranteed head-removal equation: 'Wherever you put the knot, the head would probably have come off with that drop.'

Haughton then inserted himself abruptly into the lineage of the long drop, when he claimed these discussions had actually formed the basis of Marwood's table of drops, which would eventually become Berry's. Though the recommendations weren't published in the main papers, they were given to the *Medical Press* of Dublin. 'I have reason to believe,' declared Haughton, 'Marwood must have read a copy of the discussion, for he adopted the result with success. That explains my connexion with this subject.'

The next person in front of the committee was Leonard Ward, who, as the chief warder of Newgate Prison in London, had seen his share of long drops. For his sins, he had been in operation at the tail end of William Calcraft's career – perhaps not the best introduction to the class of 'hangman'. 'I never saw one of his more than 3 feet,' he recalled. These short drops would leave men twitching for seven or eight minutes afterwards, with shoulders, arms and hands all writhing. That would drop off, but gradually, and it was evident the men had experienced some pain, though it was a topic of much debate as to exactly how long they suffered. The movement tended to shut down limb by limb, with the hands stiffening last.

These experiences inspired Ward to create his very own mathematical table, which he handed into evidence. His work, he said, aimed to calculate the striking force of falling bodies at different weights. What he handed in to the committee was identical to the scale that Berry worked with, and described at length in his book. In cases he had seen, the striking force of 25 cwt had got the job done.

Interference on his part, he said, had been essential a number of times recently, in reducing the rope and preventing a bloody catastrophe and fodder for the media. He described having to quibble with a hangman over a length of rope on one occasion, and that on his insistence, a shorter length was used. He doesn't name the executioner at that point, but in piecing the not-so-subtle clues together, we can deduce that Ward lays full claim to the table of drops and striking force chart that Berry said he cobbled together with the help of 'an engineer' at Newgate.

After detailing a number of instances in which he had tussled for power with a hangman, he was asked if the executioner was wont to ignore the chief warder's advice. 'Yes,' he replied. He continued:

> I may say that when I drew up this scale I copied it and sent a copy of it to him as a friend, I thought I was doing him a kindness, with a letter explaining it exactly; and he wrote back thanking me and telling me it was just the thing that he had wanted. Almost the next week he went to Norwich and pulled the man's head clean off.

This account, interestingly, means Berry had the information to reduce the length of the Goodale drop before he went to Norwich, rather than tinkering with the scale as a result of that drop.

Berry was a different animal, and a loose cannon at the scaffold, as far as Ward thought. Ward's own pursuit of dominance in the realm of hanging theory probably means his review requires a pinch of salt, but by his guess, Berry was eager to make sure the drops were as long as possible and rarely listened to any advice. This tallies somewhat with Berry, who did openly refute any suggestion that he wasn't in the best position to decide a rope length.

As for the character of hangmen, Ward said 'they are of course a very rough class of men'. Drinking, too, was a problem. Marwood had certainly over-imbibed, as had Binns. Berry, as a well-known teetotaller at the time he began his career, escaped this line of punishing inquisition, though the cracks were already showing by the time the committee formed: 'I believe he was a teetotaller at first for a year or so,' Ward said, tellingly, 'but I do not think he is now.'

After Ward it was the turn of John Rowland Gibson. Gibson's introduction to hanging had been a farce in itself. William Calcraft had been the man at the helm then, and he was up to his old tricks. In this case, Gibson witnessed a grim comedy of errors that would lead to the use of pinion straps on legs.

The year was 1856 and the convict was a man named Bousfield, a particularly erratic and difficult prisoner who had burnt himself in custody in protest at his not being granted a reprieve. They figured he wouldn't go down quietly. They were right. In order to ensure his drop, he was placed on a stool at the edge of the open platform and pushed into the hole. The short drop, in this case, would prove to be more hassle than Calcraft could imagine. Bousfield managed to get the tip of his toes to the far edge of the platform, just about holding his weight and saving him from death. Warders immediately pushed him off, and what that created was a sort of 'pendulous' movement; he reached the other platform and again propped himself up with his toes. He was pushed off again.

This impromptu table tennis match between warders (or swingball, if we're being technical) came to an end when Calcraft walked underneath the platform, grabbed his legs and held him down until the shaking stopped. Calcraft, understandably, lengthened his ropes a bit after that, but never more than three feet, the doctor said.

Part of the value of the Aberdare Committee minutes is their tendency to demystify the technical aspects of the aftermath of hanging, as clarified by medical practitioners. Newspaper reports, where they could, were quite descriptive, but they also had a tendency to use tropes like 'a good death', meaning a quick one, or that a culprit 'lingered' before dying. Gaol doctors, for their part, were starved of opportunities to examine the bodies; but with the committee, many were brought together, so the volume of case studies is instantly improved.

Gibson, without doubt, backed a longer drop. Though the neck could break with a three-foot drop, the majority of short-rope executions were hard to bear witness to. Gibson experienced a 'lingering' death at the execution of a man named Herbert for the murder of his sister-in-law at Finsbury Park:

'In the short rope there was a great effort at respiration; they used to bring all their muscle into play to breathe, their shoulders would be heaved up in a most violent manner, and frequently their arms would move; of course they were pinioned.' The feeling, he said, was like drowning.

Gibson's view of hangmen was simple: 'I think they are always a low class of men, and rather prone to taking supplements.'

Over his own three appearances before the committee, John de Zouche Marshall regaled members with useful medical tales, as well as a scathing review of the long-drop method, generally. It quickly emerged that he was trying to push an invention of his own: the chin trough – a device that kept the rope fixed to the centre of the front of the chin and caused the neck to break by leverage as opposed to force. 'Dislocations,' he posited, 'generally occur when your joints are in the wrong position.'

In painting a grim picture of the long drop, Marshall's recounting of his experience at the gallows was at times harrowing. He mentioned in particular the hangings of the 'Maamtrasna murderers' in Galway by Marwood (one of the three Connemara men executed in 1882, Myles Joyce, was pardoned in 2018 by President Michael D. Higgins); 'When one of the Maamtrasna murderers was hung, the executioner had allowed the rope to hang down behind, where it caught in his pinioned hands, so that the unfortunate wretch was thrown forward by it, and suspended horizontally, and the executioner had to kneel down and kick him off in the most brutal way.' Despite plaudits from the committee, the chin trough was politely declined.

After Marshall came James Barr – a name Berry would become uncomfortably familiar with by the end of his career. As if by prophecy, Dr Barr's testimony showed a man with a robust professional opinion on the topic. One which he would readily share.

From the outset, Barr seemed particular in his tastes. He was suspicious about whether James Berry ever actually used a government rope in his life. 'I am not aware where he got his rope from,' he said of the Bradford man. 'He now says that he gets them from the Home Office, but where he may have got some of them from I am not certain.' What seemed like a routine and informative medical deposition then turned personal, when he was asked about the intelligence and demeanour of executioners.

'Marwood was much the superior executioner,' he declared. 'He was much more intelligent, more active about his work, less clumsy and altogether more expeditious.' Berry, on the other hand, was 'an ignorant man'. A clumsiness pervaded Berry's work, he said. 'There is a certain amount of intelligence about him,' said Barr, 'but he is a man with no accurate conception as to what length of drop, or any thing of that sort should be given.'

Barr's summation was to the point regarding hangmen: they often miscalculated simple measurements of ropes and failed to accurately factor in prisoners' height and the circumference of the neck. These, he said, should be simple measurements to take. 'Berry,' he said, 'stated in the case of Ernest Ewerstaedt that he was going to give a 9 foot drop, whereas he only gave 7 feet. In the case of George Thomas, he stated that he was going to give a drop of 7 feet, whereas it was 7 feet 11 1/4 inches.'

Berry's table of drops, he said, was a shambles. 'It was a most absurd production,' he opined, 'and the Newgate official who drew it up must have been ignorant of the most rudimentary knowledge of physics.'

The doctor preferred risking asphyxia to decapitation, but obviously a clean break was the least painful experience – for the 'shocked spectators' and the prisoner. Barr finished his testimony with one more implicit shot across Berry's bow: scaffolds should be deeper, he said. Due to the frequent error in rope-length calculations, it would take just a four-inch mistake, in some cases, to land a prisoner on the ground.

And then it was time. The final act in the grand show of the Aberdare hearings was to welcome the man himself – James Berry. He hadn't been invited; rather, he applied to give evidence; it's not surprising, given the popularity of the stories surrounding him and his two most famous mishaps. He gave a short preamble about his getting the job, before issuing an impassioned plea for recognition.

'One thing that I wish to give evidence on is this,' he opened. 'That I should like to have a certain stipend from the Home Office, and to be under the regulations of the Home Office, so that I should not have to depend upon a criminal's neck for my livelihood.'

'You wish to be paid by a fixed salary?' asked the chairman, to which Berry replied in the affirmative. It seems at this point that the hangman didn't grasp the true tone of the testimony that had gone before him. 'We have only a certain number of things to inquire into, and that is hardly one,' said the chairman.

Proceedings moved swiftly then to queries about Berry's techniques. He explained thoroughly his method of taking the height and weight of a man and consulting his long-refined scale, the construction of which, he admitted, included consultation with the chief warder at Newgate. Regarding the headless elephant in the room, he insisted his drops were shorter since the unfortunate blunder at Norwich, at the behest of officials, and that in the 12 months and 25 hangings leading to the day of his evidence, 'death [had] been caused in every case instantaneously, not even the muscles moving after the body had fallen through the trapdoors'.

Berry handed a stack of papers to the committee for perusal then, a consignment of the testimonials amounting to the same endorsement. But the chairman didn't let it drop. What about Edward Hewitt at Gloucester? Did Berry remember that case? Was death instantaneous then? Hewitt was 34 years old, 5 foot 5, 10 stone 4 lbs, and received a six-foot drop.

Berry didn't need reminding. And yes, death was instantaneous. The chairman then read from Dr Marshall's account of events, which didn't seem to echo the humane briskness scrawled across the sheets of paper before the committee. 'I descended immediately into the pit where I found the pulse beating at the rate of 80 to the minute, the wretched man struggling desperately to (I presume) get his hands and arms free,' read the chairman to Berry, from Dr Marshall's recollection. The picture was an unflattering one:

I come to this conclusion from the intense muscular action in the arms, forearms, hands, contractions, not continuous but spasmodic, not repeated with regularity but renewed in different directions and with desperations. From these signs I did not anticipate a placid expression on the countenance, and I regret to say my fears were correct, for on removing the white cap (about a minute and a half after the fall) I found the eyes starting from the sockets and the tongue protruded; the face exhibiting unmistakable evidence of intense agony ...

The chairman trailed off, not needing to go any further. 'You see,' he said to Berry, who was perhaps now anticipating the flavour of the rest of the afternoon, 'that statement is not exactly in accordance with yours, that death was instantaneous and that there was no muscular action.'

Berry looked through his papers. 'The doctor of the prison gave it in that death was immediate, and not only that, but that the culprit had never even suffered anything at all.' The chairman didn't pause to consider Berry's response, but only asked him if Dr Clarke was the gaol surgeon at the time. Berry said he was.

The chairman said: 'Dr Marshall states that Dr Clarke and he examined the corpse, but failed to discover any signs of dislocation or fracture.'

Things looked bad for Berry, who offered his own interpretation: that the inner connective tissue of the neck was ripped and that resulted in more or less the same, instant, death. Berry was then asked, of the bundle of testimonials he handed in, if the execution of Hewitt was among them. Berry, defeated, responded, 'I believe I have not that one with me.'

Without so much as a breath, the chairman came at him again, diving straight into another case where Marshall said he had to intervene to stop a miscalculation. Berry had found in Marshall an opinionated hanging theorist, as is clear from Marshall's personality clashes on the gallows and the manner in which he spoke of hangmen generally. As a self-considered expert himself, it wasn't a surprise that the two didn't get along. He denied the doctor's various accounts, saying he was mistaken.

That led the chairman neatly into his next interrogation topic. Stories had been told of the forceful shove with which Berry tightened a noose – to the point, in some cases, that convicts couldn't speak. It was partly conscious, as Berry explained.

Do you now tighten it more than you used to? 'I have followed it up of late, tightening the noose, but at the same time I have worked to the scale of the weight of falling bodies at different distances.' *Can you tighten the noose to the extent to which you do it now without inflicting considerable pain upon the culprit?* 'Yes, because if you have noticed the report of my last execution at Manchester, I was only a minute and a half from going into the condemned's cell and placing the man on the scaffold, and he was dead. Both the doctors at Strangeways Prison said so.' *That does not answer my question as to whether this tightening of the noose is not most painful for the culprit.* 'No, I do not think it is.' *Dr Marshall said that you use most considerable strength in tightening the noose?* 'He made use of that remark at Newgate at the time, and Dr Morgan and Dr Gilbert told him that it was much better than it should be so. And not only that, but he wanted to say at first that the neck was not dislocated, after he had felt the muscles of the neck.'

The exchanges were tense, and followed the same pattern. An opinion from a medical practitioner on high was thrown to the Bradford man, who parried it reasonably well. On technical aspects, Berry had collated documents that spoke to his ability, but the crucial question was just around the corner. The chairman teased out the particulars of Berry's behaviour when he went to the gaols; he usually arrived the night before an execution and went straight to the gaol. From time to time, he and the warders would walk about the town.

'Do you ever go to a public house on those occasions?' he was asked, to which he replied, truthfully and with the reputation of having been a teetotaller for at least the opening part of his career: 'Very seldom.'

'I do not know that it has been said of you,' said the chairman, 'but it has been said of an executioner (I think of Marwood) that he was in the habit of exhibiting the ropes with which he had hanged various criminals and, in fact, of selling portions of those ropes to people who were curious about such things; have you ever done anything of that sort?'

'I gave one to a gentleman of high position in the city, but I have never sold any in my life,' Berry retorted. *I suppose people are very curious in talking to you about these things, are they not?* 'Yes, there are some very inquisitive people; but when they begin to talk about the subject of hanging I leave the company at once. I will not introduce it at all.'

The prospect of morbid curiosity arose, a public phenomenon the Home Office sought to suppress and which wasn't aided by taking men's heads off their shoulders. Berry said he found too many reporters inconvenient to cater for at the gallows, and that sometimes, some higher-ups in society could be admitted to view the proceedings to satisfy their curiosity, at the approval of the sheriffs. Berry insisted, on pressing from the committee, that the decision about who to admit lay with the sheriff, though he 'should very much rather that they were not there'. Somewhat contradictory to this was an execution at Carlisle, when Berry let a well-known baronet assist him in pinioning three men, at the influential man's request.

Berry was succinct about his expertise, stressing that it wasn't a job that a stand-in could accomplish without prior experience, such as the mentorship given to him by Marwood. He agreed that training up warders to be assistants was desirable, with a view to them being able to step in should the appointed executioner not be able to perform. On at least two occasions, he said, he was very ill when pulling the lever, and would greatly have appreciated a substitute. The chairman asked him then, plainly, if he was aware of any charges made against him regarding poor performance. 'No, never,' he told the committee. 'I always think it is this way, that when people get into loose company, that is when they get slang thrown out to them.' *You keep clear of all that sort of company?* 'Yes, I keep select to myself.'

Berry's rope of choice, and the vague mystery surrounding his compliance with the government-issue specifications, were next under the microscope. The same committee had heard medical practitioners comment on Berry's ropes – sometimes in a tone which reflected a disregard on Berry's part for the expertise of those who put together the recommended ropes.

As for how he came about his ropes, Berry said it was all above board:

I write to Newgate for a rope, and then they send a letter to the sheriff to say that I have ordered one, and then he writes back to me, and says he is very glad and thankful because I have done so, and then they forward the rope, not to me, but to the person who applies for it when the culprit is going to be hanged.

To be exact, the sheriff or undersheriff sometimes offered to do this, and Berry would offer himself. Should it be the case that the sheriff gave Berry the go-ahead to order a new rope, there was a quantity of trust involved to ensure that he'd actually done that. At this point, it becomes clear why so many people weren't sure how Berry actually came by his ropes.

The ropes varied in elasticity, said Berry, though he also said he could see little room for improvement, save for the brass eyelet hole they used. 'The brass eyelet hole was in my opinion the very reason that caused the decapitation in the case of the execution at Norwich,' he said, unprovoked,

> and that was the opinion of the doctor as well, and not only that, but, being a large eyelet hole, in cases where a man has a lot of loose skin around his throat, the elasticity of the rope in descending into the pit causes the loose skin to vibrate, and the rope coming through a big eyelet hole causes the blood to flow in some cases.

His recommendation was for a smaller eyelet hole, akin to the one he preferred for his own ropes.

The supposed varying of elasticity evidently troubled the committee, though Berry insisted it was impossible to ensure they were all the same diameter and elasticity through weight-testing – they return to their original shape, or close to it, like rubber. Berry had done the experiments, weighing down ropes in his home before use, etc., but that meant a lower familiarity with the fibres of the ropes. It was better, he said, to monitor the elasticity and stretch it through real-life use. 'I have one rope at home that I have executed 16 persons with,' Berry declared,

> and every time that I have executed a criminal with that rope I have taken very particular notice where the leather washer stopped compressing the neck, and how far the rope has given, and I have taken notice where it has not given, and at the end after I had executed a lot of people, I found that it did not give above 6 inches or 6½ inches, but at first when I started it gave 14 inches.

Then you do reduce the elasticity by constant use? 'Yes, by constant use, but it is a risk to do it.' If indeed it were possible to artificially stretch a rope until you could guarantee it gave – or stretched – 6.5 inches after hanging its first culprit, then that, in theory, could be beneficial.

The admission of owning a 16-use rope revealed a key behaviour of Berry's, which he readily admitted; he kept the ropes after he used them. If the sheriff offered to pay for a new one – a guinea a pop – which they only sometimes did, he was happy to go with that. 'Some sheriffs are not particular to a pound or two, and others are very particular. You will find they vary,' said Berry, recalling a time in Kilkenny when he had to get a solicitor involved to secure payment. He didn't know who came up with the price at Newgate – he could get it for a fraction at Woods' rope manufacturers in Lancashire. 'A guinea is a long price for a rope 12 feet long.'

Thus the money for the rope was often withheld, so he used an old one. He preferred them, anyway. *Supposing there was no question about payment, would you rather have a new rope for every execution or one that had been used before?* 'I would rather have one that had been used before.'

Berry then took the men through his typical testing and measurement procedure. In one of the more blatant attempts to trip the former shoemaker up, Sir Frederick Bramwell took up the questioning, which descended into something of a maths test.

Frederick Bramwell: 'Let me ask you this: suppose you had a culprit 6 feet high and you wished to give him a 6-feet drop, and the point at which you were going to tie the rope was 8 feet, how would you set about measuring your rope in order to give the man a 6-feet drop; what would you do?'

James Berry: 'I should tie my rope and leave 6 feet clear, so that his head would be where his feet were when I had done it. The top of his head would be where his feet would be with a clear 6-feet drop.'

FB: 'You mean that in that case he falls his own height?'

JB: 'Yes.'

FB: 'What length of rope would you give?'

JB: 'Eight feet.'

FB: 'Would that be the whole without the allowance that you spoke of for the neck?'

JB: 'No, I should not give any allowance in a case like that.'

FB: 'Supposing that a man were 5 feet high, and you wanted to give him a 6-feet drop, and also that the attachment again was 8 feet above you, and everything the same as before, except that the man was a foot shorter, what length of rope would you give then to give him a 6-feet drop?'

JB: 'I should give him 8 feet just the same.'

FB: 'Say that you are 8 feet above a man 6 feet high with a 6-feet drop, what length of rope would you give?'

JB: 'I should give him 9 feet of rope.'

FB: 'Now then, supposing the same thing, except that the man is 5 feet high, what are you going to give him then?'

JB: 'I should give him 9 feet.'

FB: 'Would you give him a 6-feet drop?'

JB: 'Yes.'

FB: 'It would be the same as you give a 6-feet man?'

JB: 'Yes, but that depends upon the weight; I should want to know his weight.'

The tedium went on for a few more minutes, until Dr Haughton interjected to ask Berry his ideal outcome, in terms of the physical result on the neck. Berry replied as any honest-working purveyor of the long drop would: dislocation, of course. The committee then briefly gave Berry a look at Dr Marshall's chin trough apparatus, but Berry wasn't interested – though he did try it on himself. He said he preferred the rope behind the left ear and, taking off the apparatus, merely said he had no observations to make on it.

The hearing drew to a close, but Berry had not yet had the chance to address the issue of Lee, the man he could not hang: 'I have carried out every execution excepting one to the satisfaction both of the governors and the different doctors in the different prisons ever since I commenced.' *Which was the one exception?*

The committee likely knew the answer to that before Berry replied to confirm it was John Lee to whom he referred – 'the case where the trap would not work'.

Surprisingly, they went easy on him. Bramwell asked: 'It is only reasonable to say, speaking as any other man would, that if the drop would operate by itself without any weight upon it, still more must it operate when there is weight upon it?', to which Berry, of course, replied 'Yes.' Bramwell supposed it was entirely unexpected that putting weight on the trapdoor would logically make it less likely to open. The topic was dropped.

The government had now weighed in and suggested, among other things, their own table of drops – a concept that may not have endured but for Berry, but which now superseded his own calculations. At least officially. They dictated rope specifications, which he wasn't comfortable with; government ropes were 'all right to hold a ship, but no good to hang a man,' as he eloquently put it.

GOVERNMENT RECOMMENDED DROPS				
Weight of Culprit		*Drop*		*Energy developed*
Stone	*Pounds*	*Feet*	*Inches*	*Feet Pounds*
7	98	11	5	1,119
8	112	10	0	1,120
9	126	9	6	1,197
10	140	9	0	1,260
11	154	8	2	1,258
12	168	7	6	1,260
13	182	6	11	1,259
14	196	6	5	1,258
15	210	6	0	1,260
16	224	5	7	1,250
17	238	5	3	1,250
18	252	5	0	1,260
19	266	4	8	1,241
20	280	4	5	1,260

Medical practitioners came firmly into the fray, and interference in his job grew apace. This perhaps came to a head at the hanging of John Conway. The interferer, in that case, was a familiar face to Berry.

21

THE LAST STRAW

John Conway troubled Berry. Broadly, the executioner had been able to categorise his criminals with the exception of a few already mentioned. The one born into poor circumstances, the passion killer, the out-and-out animal. But as he read over Conway's case in the paper, he had difficulty getting his head around it.

Conway had no criminal past, save for the odd spot of public drunkenness. His clear record made his decision to murder a 10-year-old boy named Nicholas Martin in Liverpool, apparently without motive or provocation, all the more confusing. He prayed feverishly in the days before Berry's arrival. Intensely superstitious, he espoused fast-held beliefs in witchcraft, omens and the supernatural. His own prayers, he thought, were useless – though he performed them anyway. His only salvation would be in the prayers of a good man, he thought. He refused the sacrament of his church, insisting he wasn't eligible for it, but attended the services, begging one of his fellow prisoners to pray for his salvation.

Salvation didn't arrive. But James Berry did, just in time for the execution on 20 August 1891. At this point in Berry's illustrious career, it was harder to hide on the carriages. And, truthfully, he cared a bit less. He had well surpassed 100 hangings, and somewhere around the one-year mark, the drinking started. Never on the job. But other times, a lot. A number of the more gruesome spectacles had crept into this dreams and wobbled him over the years, but he had always persevered. As the train rattled into Liverpool Berry was coming straight off the back of the hanging of Robert Bradshaw at Wandsworth. The reformed teetotaler took himself to the Sessions House Hotel and sat in solitude, nursing a brandy and soda.

Kirkdale Prison's medical officer was a man Berry knew quite well – Dr James Barr. Considering Barr's attitudes towards hangmen as evidenced in the last chapter, the fiery exchange that was yet to happen is hardly surprising.

After signing in and setting his things down, Berry met with the doctor to check the convict's measurements. Conway was 11 stone 2 lbs and about 5 foot 7. Berry suggested a drop of 4 foot 6 inches. His opinion met a brick wall in Dr Barr.

The drop, according to Dr Barr's 'official' scale, closer to the recommendations of the Aberdare Committee, was to be quite a bit longer, at 6 foot 9 inches. 'No,' Berry said plainly. The doctor had disregarded Berry's knowledge under official authority, and the whole ordeal had thoroughly annoyed the Bradford man. He took it as more than a bureaucratic tragedy – it was a personal insult. 'Excuse me?' Dr Barr, perhaps, wasn't used to such strong rebuttals.

'You're going to pull the man's head off altogether,' Berry replied, teeth clenched and mind racing with memories of Robert Goodale's head in a bloodied white bag, detached from his limp body. With tempers flaring and his pockets already lined with the fee from Robert Bradshaw, he was happy to issue an ultimatum. If it was 6 foot 9 inches Barr wanted, then he could get someone else to do it. Or, God forbid, the sheriff could perform his lawful duty for once. The governor of the gaol was a man Berry got on with quite well, but he was bound to support his medical officer. As a compromise, owing probably to the late hour of the disagreement, the doctor did eventually yield, reducing the drop by about 10 or 12 inches, according to Berry. With reluctance (but perhaps buoyed by a minor victory over the system), Berry agreed. He had won the argument, somewhat, but the drop was still much longer than he thought was necessary. Or, indeed, safe.

The hour approached, and the death parade marched in procession to the platform, where Berry pulled the cap over Conway's face. Suddenly, Conway became livid, jerking his head from side to side and crying out. 'Hold on! Hold on!' he pleaded, 'I want to say something!'

Berry was in no humour. 'You won't say anything now,' was his blunt reply. Scaffolds were not the place for confessions.

'I must, I want to say something,' Conway begged, frantically.

Father Bonte put a hand on Berry's broad shoulder. 'Let him speak,' urged the clergyman, perhaps anticipating a public declaration of the written confession Conway had slipped him in the small hours, during prayer.

'Get out of the way,' Berry shot back, 'and mind your own business.' This flash of disrespect would lead the priest to later accuse Berry of being in a great rush.

'There is no hurry,' reasoned the priest. 'It will make no difference if he lives two or three minutes longer.'

Defeated, Berry lifted the cap. One huge argument was quite enough for the day. He shot a quick warning to Conway: 'Then say what you have to say. Quick.' This was a pointless exercise. The priest had the confession in his pocket. The small crowd fell silent, probably also in anticipation of the revelation of a motive which, thus far, hadn't materialised. To their disappointment, Conway only thanked the prison officials and his Father Confessor, who had shown him much kindness. 'I wish all my prosecutors to be forgiven by me and by my God,' he concluded. As Berry returned the material of the bag over his staring face, eager reporters heard Conway issue muttered pleas for God to save his soul. The lever was pulled and he fell through the trap.

Father Bonte began to read the man's confession, which did little to clear the mystery for Berry. 'Drink has been my ruin, not lust,' it said. 'I was impelled to the crime while under the influence of drink, by a fit of murderous mania, and a morbid curiosity to observe the process of dying ...' But Berry wasn't listening. An obscene splashing noise in the pit had grabbed his attention, and that of the collected reporters, who peered alongside him into the dark hole. Conway's body hung grotesquely from a strand of muscle which still connected the base of his head to his neck, the blood vessels around the throat thoroughly ripped, unleashing the cascade of a body's worth of blood onto the brick floor. Berry pulled back as the hot crimson, in his words, 'spurted' all over the death pit with vigour.

'Out!' Berry shouted, prompting the warders into action. 'Get them out!'

The press were hurried out as Berry steadied himself. What if he had not bargained for the extra foot?

Though Berry had done quite a good job of clearing the room, the worst had been seen and recorded. A Press Association representative noted that as the sound of the priest's voice carried over the gasps, 'blood from Conway's body was heard streaming on to the floor, and it was then seen that the body was hanging merely by the muscles of the neck.'

Berry left the prison quickly. Dr Barr could clean up his own mess. In his diaries, he revealed he suspected the doctor was acting on someone else's orders. The doctor's testimony to the Aberdare Committee, on the other hand, lines up quite well with the confrontation.

By the time the inquest rolled around, Berry was long gone. A juryman asked why Berry was not present, and the coroner replied that the governor had simply said everything had gone off as usual. Pulling a veil over cases in this manner was common – after all, the letter of the law had been carried out, and the less attention drawn to penny dreadful gore, the better. Dr Barr, for his part, corroborated, and said there had been no hitch as far as the execution was concerned. Of course he did. The jury found a formal verdict that the judgement of death had been carried out effectively; naturally, reporters present asked to see the body. They were politely informed that the governor declined their request.

The mix-up, by and large, was not attributed to Berry. In his diaries, as with the statements absolving Dr Barr, he was sure that the order for adherence to the government scale came from elsewhere. He was sure of this, because in 1884, the very same doctor had commended his table of drops after a successful hanging at Kirkdale. The length Berry had suggested also tallied with a letter that Dr Barr had published in *The Times* some years before, containing his own table of drops. Berry retained a letter of praise from Dr Barr, which included the line: 'You gave a sufficient length of drop, considering the weight of the culprit, and completely dislocated the cervical vertebræ between the atlas and axis (first and second vertebræ).'

Berry had a mixed relationship with the press, but on this occasion in particular, their antics wore thin. No detail was left out. Even his trip to the bar made a rather spectacular appearance. What had been, he insisted, a few minutes on a barstool with a quiet drink became an all-night session in the eyes of those intrepid reporters, complete with hearty laughing, comedic songs and the type of free-flow imbibing not befitting a man on an official job. The ejected reporters, gathered outside and anticipating a doorstepping opportunity, fired questions at Berry, as he left the prison moments after the mishap. They were keen to report Berry looking a little less composed than usual. 'You messed this one up, Berry,' one shouted from the pack. That stopped him in his tracks. The gist of the statement he issued then was in defence of his actions. 'I'm not to blame for anything,' he shot back. 'It's all left to the doctors now. They might as well do the whole job themselves. This is the fruit of interfering with my decision,' he declared. Had he given him the doctor's original order, 'it would have decapitated the man entirely!'

The headlines the next morning were not flattering: 'SHOCKING SCENE ON THE SCAFFOLD', 'CONWAY ALMOST DECAPITATED', 'BERRY BLAMES THE DOCTOR'. Berry was unfortunate that alliteration tied his name to 'blame' in that context. But slightly worse, perhaps, were the large number of papers opting for 'bungled' instead. One such publication was the *Sheffield Evening Telegraph*, whose correspondent discovered Berry in a 'by no means amiable frame of mind'.

Berry was asked, first, about the rumours of his singing and drinking at the pub. 'Anyone who knows me at all knows I can't sing,' he quipped. As for the 'bungle', he told the reporter it had nothing to do with him. 'It will fall on the shoulders of Dr Barr.'

The disrespect for his expertise had rankled. A couple of days after returning home, and still raw from the Conway incident, Berry hanged a man named Edward Watts at Winchester. But the seed was already planted, and Berry wasn't long for the hanging game. Besides, a barber named James Billington, who had performed one or two executions during Berry's career, was becoming more active.

Hanging, due to its precarious semi-official status, couldn't really be 'resigned' from, as such. One would simply just stop applying for individual executions. But Berry was a man concerned with his image, and rumours began to circulate that he was sacked by the Home Office. This was equally impossible though, unbeknownst to Berry, the Home Office had already decided not to recommend him going forward. In March 1892, by way of making it official, and taking control of the narrative, he sent the following notice to Henry Mathews, the Home Secretary, at Whitehall, London.

Dear Sir,

I herewith tender my resignation as executioner of Great Britain. My reason is on account of Dr Barr interfering with my responsible duty at Kirkdale Gaol, Liverpool, on the last execution there. I shall therefore withdraw my name now as being executioner to England. Trusting this will be accepted by you on behalf of the Sheriffs of England.

I remain, dear sir,

Your obedient servant,

James Berry, late executioner of England

A formal acknowledgement of the letter reached James Berry at Bradford some time later. It bore no expression of thanks.

22

SETTLED DUST

I t was about 6 o'clock in the morning when they spotted her. A woman approached the gate of the Galway workhouse with a weary stagger, barely able to clutch the infant in her arms. A young boy, about nine years old, soldiered on beside her, 'in such a state of distress as to elicit the sympathy of those who saw him', according to one report. 'A fine, handsome, ruddy-faced little fellow,' according to another.

Mary Moylan had realised, six months after the execution of her alleged younger lover Michael Downey, the value of having friends. The widow had returned to her little farm in Clonboo to find the small community, appalled by her hand in her own husband's murder, quite unwilling to help her tend the land which she had fully inherited.

Mary was housed in a hotel in Galway for a year, until Downey's execution in January 1885, whereupon she was sent home, with police protection. The cost of the detail was beginning to add up; expenses claims in Mary's file show that £5 8s 6d was granted by Dublin Castle for the cause, for the period of October to November 1884. Two constables patrolled her property, and it was evidently needed; she was not a popular woman in Annaghdown. Nobody spoke to her. Family disowned her. She couldn't tend to the farm herself and farmers refused to sell her food, or buy anything from her. She may have escaped Berry's noose by turning witness for the Crown, but nothing could save her from the ire of her community.

'She was possessed of a nice farm,' read a report in the *Dublin Express*, 'but could get no person to till it. Thus she became, as it were, isolated from the rest the world, and lived a life of solitude in her wretched home, with no companion but a little boy, nine years old, and a little infant ...'

The 'little infant' was born after John Moylan's death. An *Irish Times* report on the poor woman's situation said the baby was about 10 months old, meaning, technically, either John or Michael could have been the father, as it was likely conceived in the narrow window between John's return and his murder at the hands of Downey.

'The Government she so faithfully served seemed to have forgotten her in her desolation, only that they still afforded her police protection. She was without money and without friends, deprived of the means of earning a livelihood, and growing nearer daily to utter want and certain destitution,' reads the *Express* report. She applied for outdoor relief, but was refused by the town guardians. It was Friday 12 June 1885 when Mary gave up, and turned to the workhouse for help, walking about nine miles with her young son and baby and accompanied by the two police officers assigned to protect her. Her other children, four boys, were staying with friends, according to the papers – surprising as it was that she had anybody left under that label.

On arrival at the workhouse she was admitted, and by the next day she was officially an inmate. But the case didn't stop there. The guardians of the poor law union instantly met opposition from the ratepayers of Annaghdown, outraged at indirectly funding Mary's upkeep. According to meeting minutes, the guardians felt compelled to write to the Local Government Board, wondering if they were obliged to give her refuge. On 17 June, they resolved to ask the board to inform them if they were 'legally justified in admitting Mary Moylan of Clonboo to this house as a pauper and making the heavily taxed ratepayers of Annaghdown electoral division liable for her maintenance, she and her children having a home and land valued at the yearly sum of £6-15-0'. The board replied on the 23rd, saying 'the only question the guardians have to consider in connexion with this case is whether the woman is or is not destitute', regardless of the land she had.

The guardians, dissatisfied, resolved that they

beg to represent to the Government Authorities the great desirability of their making some arrangement to relieve this workhouse of the expense of maintaining Mrs Moylan their late Crown witness by either sending her out of the county to some place where her antecedent will be unknown, or any other way they may deem fit to provide for her.

We may say she is a most obnoxious person to have in the workhouse and she is the cause of great exasperation to the ratepayers of the division to which she is chargeable to be compelled to pay for her maintenance, that a copy of this resolution be forwarded to the chief secretary of the Lord Lieutenant.

On 4 July, they received a reply to say it would receive attention.

August saw the intervention of the parish priest of Drumgriffin, who asked the board to suggest some means of managing 'the matter of the property left by the late husband of Mary Moylan, the Government having declined to investigate the matter at present'. Discarded by her community and unwanted by the workhouses, reports indicate the guardians were forced to assist in selling her land. The *Express* report concludes: 'The mother expects the guardians will take some steps towards disposing of her farm, and thus enable her to go to some foreign land, where her history will be unknown.'

Galway city continued to evolve. Its last hanging took place in April 1902, when Billington executed a painter named Thomas Keeley for murdering his housemate, an elderly woman, with a hammer. After the execution of Thomas Parry, Dr Kinkead went on to publish a well-known medical reference book, *A Guide for Irish Medical Practitioners*, in 1889. He died in office, aged 83, on 16 March 1928. Galway Gaol officially closed in 1939; Galway Cathedral now stands in its place.

Mack's Royal Hotel would remain a mainstay of Galway's hospitality scene for many years after the murder of Alice Burns. By 1901, a retired, 62-year-old George Mack was remarried to a younger Manchester woman named Minnie, and living in Newcastle, West Galway. He died on 16 May 1919, aged 82. In 1903, after George Mack had left, the hotel's new proprietress, Mrs Kerin, brought the building into the 20th century, and advertised its services in the *Irish Daily Independent* as a 'first-class family and commercial hotel; newly renovated, hot and cold baths, electric light, coffee and commercial rooms, special arrangements for fishing parties'.

The hotel changed through the hands of a number of proprietors, until it was bought by J.T. Costelloe. The Costelloes then sold it in 1952 for £32,500; within a short time, the building was levelled, and a Woolworth's built on its site. It has since, again, changed shape and is now Supermac's popular flagship store. The Imperial Hotel, from which Thomas Parry enacted his plot on that summer's morning in 1884, is still there.

As for James Berry, after eight years and more than 100 broken necks, he had a change of heart. The nightmares had started around the century mark, and his descent into guilt was accelerating. His total, according to most records, was 134, including five women. Berry, in an interview shortly following his resignation, also said it was 134, but that claim gradually grew to 183. Part of the reason he purged his house of his memorabilia around 1890, though he was not wont to admit it, was to lose sight of those many faces that had haunted him, and turned him, with some vigour, to drink. Where scripture and a firm belief in the letter of the law had seen him through the early tasks, increasingly difficult questions about the righteousness of his actions required a stronger medicine. By 1892, liquor had replaced the Bible – a stark change in behaviour from the man who wrote: 'The number of men who are driven to crime through drink is something terrible, and I should think that no temperance worker could read the real histories of the murderers who have come under my hands without redoubling his efforts to save men from the curse of drink.'

In the same month he tendered his resignation, he embarked on a new career: that of lecturer. On Monday 14 March crowds gathered to hear him speak at London's Royal Aquarium, with reporters marking the disappointment among some quarters of the crowd that the spectacle wasn't simply an extension of Madame Tussauds' chamber of horrors, with displays of bloodied pinions and famous lengths of rope. Attendees of 'morose and morbid turn' seeking to satisfy their taste instead found a sobering plea for the abolition of capital punishment in Britain.

Berry railed against capital punishment, and advocated instead for a system of floggings, which would have just the desired effect on potential re-offenders. Government interference in the system, too, came under fierce fire. The former hangman discussed the trouble of hanging the insane, as

James Berry in later life.

well as the type of characteristics a hangman had to have. The first meeting concluded with Berry seeking a sort of motion on the abolition of capital punishment and directing attendees to sign a petition at the back of the hall on the way out. The book lay open, but attracted little attention.

Around the same time, his book came out, devoid of his recently acquired condemnation, in principle, of capital punishment. The lecturing continued, as did Berry's taste for the 'sins' of beer and gambling. Eventually, his show came to incorporate slides, and he toured it countrywide. The interest eventually waned and he took to inn-keeping for a time, as well as other side projects, though he wasn't short of money for alcohol. Berry would later say it was a minor epiphany that led him to stop drinking. A bottle of beer was handed to him in a hotel in Bradford, and something clicked. He stood and left the place, swearing off his wicked company and vowing never to drink again. In the stead of drink, he placed studying, and later, it would seem, dwelling on his past.

On Tuesday 21 October 1913, James Berry died at 61, after suffering ill health and retiring to Walnut Tree Farm in Bradford. Long before he suffered the heart failure that took him in the end, he had time to answer one more calling. That of God.

At the centre of the blackness filling James Berry in the years after he stepped down from the gallows, he would tell crowds, was finding out that at least two of his victims had gone to eternity as innocent men. Coupled with the discomfort of considering those executed who had mental incapacities, it became too much to bear. At Christmas 1904, plagued with guilt and wondering how many of the people he had dropped into death pits across Britain had simply been drunks, he decided to end his life.

James Berry walked from his house to the station in Bradford, where he planned to catch a train to Leeds, and jump off at the tunnel. A near decade of travelling Britain's railways told him when the express train would be coming in the opposite direction. Weeping, he awaited his last train out of Bradford. It was then, sitting on the platform in a 'desperate state', that 'a still, small voice' reached his ears through his own distress.

'Fear not,' it said, 'for I am with you.' Not a divine intervention, but a word of comfort from a mission worker named Brother Thomson, who had spotted Berry in his depressed state as he, too, waited for the train. The men talked at length, read scripture, and Berry cried properly for the first time in decades; 'It was like tub of water, the tears I had shed.' Berry was invited to the Mission House in Bradford and from that day, vowed to bury the 'old Berry', and begin working for Jesus. And so he did.

'From Hangman to Evangelist', pronounces a headline in the *Edinburgh Evening News* on Saturday 28 April 1906, topping a report from James Berry's new public outing. He had been conducting smaller religious meetings for some time, and the audience he found on his new campaign of lectures replied to his word with cries of 'hallelujah', instead of the gasps and moans he'd become so accustomed to fielding. On the podium he confessed his sins, spoke of his past career and detailed his life of 'wickedness' without the Bible, which had brought him nothing but sadness.

For such terrible work, he told his new congregations, he was 'heartily sorry … and regretted that he had ever tarnished his life by undertaking such a low-lifed abusive calling'. For eight and a half years, his work corrupted his sleep. A sting in his conscience had kept him awake. A man should suffer for crime, he certainly believed that, 'but not by taking away his life'.

As he spoke, his good humour was resurrected. A light he'd long lost down a bloodied death pit shone again. Before he was converted, he told his first crowd in Edinburgh, he would have hanged anybody. But he no longer could. His 'heart of stone' had been taken away.

'The devil,' said Berry, 'lost a good pale when he lost me.'

AUTHOR'S NOTE

I first discovered the two main strands of this story in the archive of *The Irish Times*. The full facts constituting the basis of the story, as well as other background data, were ascertained through consultation of multiple editions of other newspaper titles - listed below - and with the help of the excellent staff at the National Archives in Dublin, the archives at Galway County Council and the James Hardiman Library at the National University of Ireland Galway. Archive material consulted in Dublin included various Crown Solicitor Office Registered Papers, General Prison Board reports, Census reports, Convict Reference Files and Prison Registers, among other records. At NUIG, papers of Dr James Murray pertaining to the history of the college's medical faculty informed the story, as did the minutes of the Galway Town Commissioners (LA2, June 2nd 1881–October 2nd 1890). At Galway County Council archives, the Poor Law Union Board of Guardians minutes for Galway in the decade the story takes place were consulted. Below is a list of selected sources.

Newspapers

Ballinrobe Chronicle (1866–1903)

Belfast Newsletter (1738–1938)

Dublin Daily Express (1851–1921)

Dublin Evening Mail (1823–1962)

Dundalk Democrat (1849–current)

Dundee Courier (1844–1926)

Dunfermline Press (1859–current)

Eastern Evening News (1882–1910)

Edinburgh Evening News (1873–1955)

Evening Herald (1891–current)

Exeter and Plymouth Gazette (1865–1950)

Freeman's Journal (1763–1924)

Galway Advertiser (1970–current)

Galway Express (1853–1920)

Huddersfield Chronicle (1850–1900)

Irish Daily Independent (1891–1904)

Irish Independent (1905–current)

Jersey Independent and Daily Telegraph (1855–1909)

Kerry Evening Post (1813–1917)

Kerry Sentinel (1878–1916)

Leigh Chronicle and Weekly District Advertiser (1856–1914)

Leinster Express (1831–current)

Liverpool Mercury (1811–1900)

Luton Times and Advertiser (1885–1916)

Mayport Advertiser (1853–1905)

Morning Post (1804–1909)

Nation (1842–1897)

Nationalist and Leinster Times (1883–current)

Nenagh Guardian (1831–current)

Nottingham Evening Post (1878–1950)

Peterhead Sentinel and General Advertiser for Buchan District (1858–1907)

Press Association (agency) (1868–current)

Reynolds's Newspaper (1850–1900)

Sheffield Evening Telegraph (1887–1939)

Sligo Champion (1879–current)

South Wales Daily News (1872–1909)

The Cornishman (1878–current)

The Evening News (1881–1980)

The Illustrated Police News (1867–1938)

The Irish Examiner (1841–current)

The Irish Times (1859– current)

The Scotsman (1817–1950)

The Times (1785–current)

Totnes Weekly Times (1869–1909)

Tuam Herald (1837–current)

Western Times (1827–1950)

Westmeath Examiner (1882–current)

Weston-super-Mare Gazette, and General Advertiser (1845–1910)

Yorkshire Post and Leeds Intelligencer (1866–1955)

Books

Atholl, J 1956, *The Reluctant Hangman: the story of James Berry, Executioner, 1884–1892*, Long John Limited, London.

Berry, J & Snowden Ward, H 1892, *My Experiences as an Executioner*, Percy Lund & Co, London.

Curtin, G 2001, *The Women of Galway Jail: Female Criminality in nineteenth-century Ireland*, Arlen House, Galway.

Finnegan, P 2014, *Loughrea: 'That Den of Infamy', The Land War in Co Galway, 1879–82*, Four Courts Press, Dublin.

Murray, J 1996, *Galway: A Medico-social history*, Kenny's Bookshop and Art Gallery, Galway.

Other

Capital Sentences Committee (1888) Report on the Execution of Capital Sentences and Minutes of Evidence, London: Her Majesty's Stationery Office.

Griffith's Valuation, 1848–1864.

Kinkead, R 1885, Death by Hanging, *Lancet*, 11th and 18th April.